Brecht and the Writer's Workshop

Bertolt Brecht was born in Augsburg on 10 February 1898 and died in Berlin on 14 August 1956. He grew to maturity as a playwright in the frenetic years of the 1920s and early 1930s, with such plays as *Man Equals Man, The Threepenny Opera* and *The Mother*. He left Germany when Hitler came to power in 1933, eventually reaching the United States in 1941, where he remained until 1947. It was during this period of exile that such masterpieces as *Life of Galileo, Mother Courage and her Children* and *The Caucasian Chalk Circle* were written. Shortly after his return to Europe in 1947, he founded the Berliner Ensemble, and from then until his death mainly directed and supervised productions of a wide variety of plays, including his own.

Also by Bertolt Brecht

PLAYS

Brecht Collected Plays: One
(Baal, Drums in the Night, In the Jungle of Cities, The Life of Edward II of England, A Respectable Wedding, The Beggar or the Dead Dog, Driving Out a Devil, Lux in Tenebris, The Catch)

Brecht Collected Plays: Two
(Man Equals Man, The Elephant Calf, The Threepenny Opera, The Rise and Fall of the City of Mahagonny, The Seven Deadly Sins)

Brecht Collected Plays: Three
(Lindbergh's Flight, The Baden-Baden Lesson on Consent, He Said Yes/He Said No, The Decision, The Mother, The Exception and the Rule, The Horations and the Curiatians, St Joan of the Stockyards)

Brecht Collected Plays: Four
(Round Heads and Pointed Heads, Fear and Misery of the Third Reich, Señora Carrar's Rifles, Dansen, How Much Is Your Iron?, The Trial of Lucullus)

Brecht Collected Plays: Five
(Life of Galileo, Mother Courage and Her Children)

Brecht Collected Plays: Six
(The Good Person of Szechwan, The Resistible Rise of Arturo Ui, Mr Puntila and His Man Matti)

Brecht Collected Plays: Seven
(The Visions of Simone Machard, Schweyk in the Second World War, The Caucasian Chalk Circle, The Duchess of Malfi)

Brecht Collected Plays: Eight
(The Days of the Commune, The Antigone of Sophocles, Turandot or the Whitewashers' Congress)

PROSE

Brecht on Theatre
Brecht on Art and Politics
Brecht on Film and Radio
Diaries 1920–1922
Journals 1934–1955
Brecht on Performance

Brecht and the Writer's Workshop

Fatzer and Other Dramatic Projects

Edited by
TOM KUHN AND CHARLOTTE RYLAND

methuen | drama
LONDON • NEW YORK • OXFORD • NEW DELHI • SYDNEY

METHUEN DRAMA
Bloomsbury Publishing Plc
50 Bedford Square, London, WC1B 3DP, UK
1385 Broadway, New York, NY 10018, USA

BLOOMSBURY, METHUEN DRAMA and the Methuen Drama logo are trademarks of
Bloomsbury Publishing Plc

First published in Great Britain 2019

Selection, general introduction, *Fatzer* translation, organization and editorial matter
copyright © Tom Kuhn, 2019
Fleischhacker translation, organization and editorial matter
copyright © Phoebe von Held and Matthias Rothe, 2019
The Bread Store translation copyright © Marc Silberman and Victoria Hill,
organization and editorial matter copyright © Marc Silberman, 2019
The Real Life of Jacob Trotalong translation, organization and editorial matter
copyright © Charlotte Ryland, 2019
The Judith of Shimoda translation and introduction copyright © Markus Wessendorf,
editorial reconstruction copyright © Hans Peter Neureuter, 2019
Garbe/Büsching translation, organization and editorial matter copyright © Marc Silberman, 2019

The translators and editors have asserted their moral rights to be identified as such.

Texts by Brecht originally published in
Bertolt Brecht, *Werke*, Große, kommentierte Berliner und Frankfurter Ausgabe
(vols 10.1 and 10.2)
copyright © Suhrkamp Verlag, Frankfurt am Main 1997, except
The Judith of Shimoda
Bertolt Brecht, *Die Judith von Shimoda*. Nach einem Stück von Yamamoto Yuzo in Zusammenarbeit
mit Hella Wuolijoki. Rekonstruktion einer Spielfassung von Hans Peter Neureuter copyright
© Suhrkamp Verlag, Frankfurt am Main 2006

Copyright © Bertolt-Brecht-Erben/Suhrkamp Verlag
All rights reserved

Fleischhacker was translated by Phoebe von Held and Matthias Rothe
in collaboration with a feedback group:
Laura Killeen, Jane Robinson, Naomi Segal, Robert Stock, Sam Williams.

Cover design: Louise Dugdale
Cover image courtesy of the Bertolt-Brecht-Archiv, Stiftung Akademie der Künste, Berlin

All rights reserved. No part of this publication may be reproduced or transmitted in any form or by any means, electronic or mechanical, including photocopying, recording, or any information storage or retrieval system, without prior permission in writing from the publishers.

All enquiries concerning rights for professional stage production throughout the world except USA should be addressed to Alan Brodie, 55 Charterhouse Street, London EC1M 6HA, and for amateur production to Samuel French, 24-32 Stephenson Way, London NW1 2HD. In the USA application should be made to Richard Garmise, 1776 Broadway Suite 1002, New York, NY 10019.

Bloomsbury Publishing Plc does not have any control over, or responsibility for, any third-party websites referred to or in this book. All internet addresses given in this book were correct at the time of going to press. The author and publisher regret any inconvenience caused if addresses have changed or sites have ceased to exist, but can accept no responsibility for any such changes.

A catalogue record for this book is available from the British Library.

A catalog record for this book is available from the Library of Congress.

ISBN: HB: 978-1-4742-7332-9
PB: 978-1-4742-7328-2
ePDF: 978-1-4742-7329-9
eBook: 978-1-4742-7330-5

Series: World Classics

Typeset by Deanta Global Publishing Services, Chennai, India

To find out more about our authors and books visit www.bloomsbury.com
and sign up for our newsletters.

Contents

List of Illustrations vi

General Introduction 1

Fleischhacker
1924–9
translated and edited by
Phoebe von Held and Matthias Rothe 11

Fatzer
1926–30
translated and edited by Tom Kuhn 69

The Bread Store
1929–30
translated by Marc Silberman and Victoria Hill,
edited by Marc Silberman 181

The Real Life of Jacob Trotalong
mid-to-late 1930s
translated and edited by Charlotte Ryland 241

The Judith of Shimoda
1940
translated by Markus Wessendorf,
edited by Hans Peter Neureuter 293

Garbe/Büsching
early 1950s
translated and edited by Marc Silberman 373

List of Illustrations

1. Plot-line [A9] written by Elisabeth Hauptmann illustrating the attempt to integrate *Fleischhacker* and *A Family from the Savannah* 65
2. A page from Brecht's typescript of a *Fatzer* scene 73
3. Caspar Neher's sketch of the chorus of unemployed workers, from *The Bread Store* 182
4. Decorated 'worker activist' Hans Garbe (right) with members of his Socialist Workers Brigade at the Siemens-Plania Factory, September 1950 374

The cover of this edition features a newspaper cutting from among Brecht's *Fatzer* materials.

Picture Credits

Figures 1 and 2 (both © Suhrkamp Verlag, Berlin) and the cover illustration: by courtesy of the Bertolt-Brecht-Archiv, Stiftung Akademie der Künste, Berlin. Figure 3 (© Erbengemeinschaft Stoll-Neher) by courtesy of the Deutsches Theatermuseum, Munich. Figure 4 (photo © Hans-Günter Quaschinsky) by permission of the Bundesarchiv, Digital Picture Archive.

General Introduction

Brecht was an altogether extraordinarily prolific author. Alone and in his various partnerships and teams he wrote (going by the standard German edition) nine fat volumes of plays; five volumes of poems; five volumes of novels, short stories, and prose of various sorts; six volumes of writings on theory, practice, politics, and culture; and a stream of correspondence and, especially in the later years, journals. It is an astonishing output, the more so since he did not even live that long (he died at the age of fifty-eight in 1956). In addition, the German edition (the *Große kommentierte Berliner und Frankfurter Ausgabe*, or the Berlin-Frankfurt Edition (*BFA*), which we, for the most part, take as our standard) gives us two further volumes (10.1 and 10.2), or 978 pages of text, described as 'play fragments and play projects', 48 fragmentary dramatic projects in all. The Bertolt Brecht Archive handlist goes even further and catalogues 156 unfinished plans and sketches to which titles can be ascribed. In what follows we have selected just six of these: in order to give an insight into Brecht's writerly 'workshop', and simply to make these important texts available to an English readership.[1]

We have chosen projects widely recognized by Brecht scholars and theatre practitioners for their own intrinsic importance, for their substantial place in Brecht's oeuvre and for the degree to which they engaged his creative energies in the years in question. They are spread through Brecht's life from the early 1920s through to the 1950s. A natural emphasis falls in the late 1920s, simply because this is a particularly rich period of invention and experimentation. Still, this is just a selection, and it would be misleading to suggest that these texts are crucially representative of anything in particular. It is a feature of Brecht's work that scarcely two plays look the same, and, if one did not know, one would never imagine, for example, that *Baal*, *The Decision*, and *Life of Galileo* were all by the same man. The same is true, if perhaps to a lesser extent, of these less well-known and unfinished dramatic projects.

The fact is that Brecht was constantly engaged in almost every manner of project, somehow managing a bubbling ferment of creativity out of which a huge variety of writing appeared: for publication, for performance, for the theatre, or opera, for setting to music, or for illustration, for the radio and other new technologies, for friends and private use, and then for further processes of revision, re-thinking, re-contextualization, re-combination, and recycling. In all of this, Brecht was gloriously happy to break off work on one thing and move on to the next, to interrupt, abandon, and then after all revisit. There are particular years, above all in the late 1920s, when it is positively dizzying to cast a look into this artist's studio. In 1927, for example, the book edition of *Man Equals Man* came out and the play was broadcast by several different radio stations; Brecht met and started working with the composer Kurt Weill, initially on settings of the *Mahagonny Songs*, which went into rehearsal in July, and would subsequently become the opera *Mahagonny*; he began work on a *Ruhr Epic*, which was never completed; he also worked with the great director–producer Erwin Piscator and is co-credited with at least one adaptation in that context; various of his plays were produced in Baden-Baden, Frankfurt, Darmstadt, and Berlin, generally with Brecht himself in attendance and working on the script in production; he reworked *In the Jungle of Cities* for its first publication; he adapted *Macbeth* for radio (a text which is lost); he worked intensively on *Fatzer*; meanwhile *Fleischhacker* had progressed far enough to be announced by Piscator, under the title *Wheat*, for the 1927/8 theatre season (both *Fatzer* and *Fleischhacker* feature in the present collection); at the same time he was still working on another project, called *Dan Drew*, which never came to fruition; he sketched a fragmentary radio play on the subject of the biblical Flood; he planned a play on *The Last Weeks of Rosa Luxemburg* and a revue which was possibly going to be called *The Neanderthals*; he published half a dozen short stories and a number of important essays; he judged a poetry competition and published his own first collection of verse, the *Domestic Breviary*; and he wrote or sketched out maybe another forty poems; oh, and as if that were not enough, he negotiated a divorce from his first wife, Marianne Zoff, and set up what was to be his lifelong conjugal partnership with Helene Weigel. That was quite a year. It is hard – no, let us be more honest – it is impossible to keep track.

Even as a schoolboy, Brecht developed a semi-improvisatory approach to literary composition, trying out songs and dialogue with friends and only later formalizing the work, if at all. By the mid-1920s he had already established something of a routine, when his commitments in the theatres and elsewhere permitted, of writing for himself in the mornings and then very often gathering a group of friends and collaborators in the afternoon, with whom he would discuss and develop certain of the current projects, experimenting with dialogue, debating the thrust and purpose of what had been written, and typing it all up. Later, someone (Elisabeth Hauptmann was the first) would be given the task of creating a formal typed record of the day's work, to which first Brecht himself, and then the team, would return the next day. The manuscript evidence we have of these processes, insofar as it is preserved in the archive in Berlin, is complex and confusing. There are the notebooks in which, for the most part, Brecht himself jotted down his first ideas, poems, scraps of dialogue; then there are some more extended handwritten pages, plans, and outlines; and then the typescripts – often several competing versions of the same chorus or scene, sometimes with no way of knowing if there is some hierarchy of drafts or order of composition, and often annotated in preparation for the next reworking. It is true, there are also individual works which Brecht wrote in a much more concentrated and coherent, even linear, fashion, starting at the beginning and ploughing on through (*Arturo Ui* is one example, more or less written from start to finish in three weeks in 1941), but most of the texts in this volume are very far indeed from that model, as will be clear in the individual introductions to each work, which discuss in more detail the texture of the material and the nature of the processes refracted there.

Several of the texts for these projects were developed concurrently in overlapping notebooks, and it is often hopeless to try to date the work precisely unless there is also evidence from elsewhere. Moreover, several of the projects are themselves interlinked. In the examples from 1927, the projects with an American thematic and setting, *Dan Drew*, *Fleischhacker*, and another probably largely earlier opera plan called *The Man from Manhattan*, rework each other's material. And even in *Fatzer*, which has a very different setting, a speech from *Fleischhacker* is recycled. In this instance Brecht simply quotes the opening lines of the speech and then writes 'usw.' ('etc.'), and we have no way of knowing how much of the subsequent speech he then intended to include. Some of the so-called 'fragments' are much more extensive than others. *Fatzer* runs to some 500 pages of manuscript and typescript, some with fully drafted scenes, and others on which just a phrase or a fragment of dialogue can be ascribed to the project. That makes 142 printed pages in the German edition (so more than enough for a single play, one would have thought). But the manuscripts are by no means continuous or coherent in their organization. In contrast, *The Last Weeks of Rosa Luxemburg* consists of just four snippets of dialogue or chorus, occupying only two printed pages.

In some cases there may also be a question of authorship. Brecht himself had a head full of voices and ideas, but he was also happy to have the process fuelled by the voices and ideas of others. He was definitely the centre of all the creative activity, but he was also adept at making use of the skills and inventions of his several committed collaborators. 'Co-workers' played a more or less crucial role in the work on all the projects presented in this volume: Elisabeth Hauptmann, the writer and translator who became Brecht's assistant and then his editor; Margarete Steffin, another writer who became his close collaborator and lover and followed him into exile; Hella Wuolijoki, a Finnish writer who was his host for the year of his exile spent in Finland, alongside several others. Manuscripts in other hands, other typewriters, marginal annotations, and corrections all feature among the archived documents. We have tried to credit key members of the team in our editorial introductions and at the head of each project, following Brecht's practice in his early publications in the *Versuche* (Experiments) series. In short, we are dealing here with texts of very different and often contested status, and it stands to reason that the selection, edition, and presentation of the material are a fraught and equally contested business.

In this context it is a mistake to think of the 'fragment' or the 'unfinished' in negative terms. Rather, we should try to conceive of an almost continuous and multi-stranded process of invention and development, which only came to any sort of rest or conclusion in particular completed 'works' when the opportunity happened to present itself. Brecht was always working on something, or several things; it was often only when a commission came through, or another collaborator gave him a spur, or an opportunity for a theatre production was glimpsed, or a publication, that a work was allowed to crystallize. That is perhaps a bit of an exaggeration, but it is more productive to see these unfinished works in relation to a continuing stream of creativity, rather than to describe them simply as works that Brecht discarded, or could not finish. The projects presented in this volume are certainly not just works that Brecht gave up on, and certainly not just because he could not see how to make anything of them. They were, on the contrary, simply set aside for the time being, overtaken by other concerns – and who was to say when they might not be resurrected? We have enough examples in Brecht's creative output of works that we now think of as finished, which in fact went through radical reworkings: his early *Baal* (originally 1918) was re-conceived around 1929–30 as a 'learning play' called *Evil Baal the Asocial*, although never fleshed out in that form; his adaptation of Shakespeare's *Measure for Measure* was allowed to morph into something completely different, namely his own play *Round Heads and Pointed Heads* (1932–4); *Life of Galileo* went through three very different versions, one of them in English (1938–9, 1944–7, and 1947–56). More pertinent still, an early plan entitled *Fanny Kress or The Whore's Only Friend*, of 1927–8 (again), was amalgamated with a c.1930 plot-line to which he had given the title *The Commodity Love* – a pun in German, where 'Ware' (= commodity, merchandise) sounds the same as 'wahre' (= true). Then in 1939 these plans formed the kernel for a whole new work: *The Good Person of Szechwan*. Who is to say if circumstances had been different, if, for example, he had not been forced to spend so much of his creative life in exile or, later, contending with the cultural orthodoxy of the German Democratic Republic (GDR), or if he had lived longer, which of these works that come down to us as fragments might not have had a more illustrious and productive future?

Besides, in some cases the 'fragment' may perhaps be a thing in itself, not just a piece broken off some imagined ideal 'whole'. This is an idea that has a long and elevated tradition, especially in German letters, where we think of the Romantics as the archetypal thinkers and theorists of an experience of life and art too tentative, or too fragile, or too tortured to find expression in complete and rounded works. Brecht could, it is true, hardly be further from the Romantic sensibility, but there are other models too. Georg Büchner's *Woyzeck* was left incomplete at his death in 1837; the play was published in a heavily reworked version in 1879, but not premiered until 1913 and then published again in 1921. It had a huge influence on successive generations of German writers – Naturalists, Expressionists, and Brecht himself – partly precisely because of its unfinished state, which allowed them to project onto it their own visions for a new German theatre. Around 1928 Brecht wrote of *Woyzeck* that it was 'technically almost perfect' and that it was an instructive error to suggest that it could have been made more complete (*BFA* 21, 255). And in 1951, at the other end of his creative life and in another unpublished essay-sketch (*BFA* 23, 148), he contrasted the relatively formless 'great plays' of the German tradition, Lenz's *The Tutor*, Schiller's *The Robbers* and Goethe's *Götz von Berlichingen*, with the perfectly formed fragments: *Woyzeck* and Goethe's *Faust* – the latter of course renowned simply as the greatest work in all of the German literary tradition. A couple of years later he added Kleist's *Robert Guiskard* to the list of perfectly formed dramatic fragments (*BFA* 24, 431). Brecht was very conscious of literary history, tradition, and his own place in it. When, in 1930, he chose to publish a short series of scenes and a chorus from *Fatzer* and spoke of it as a 'fragment', he was of course aware that Goethe had chosen the same genre description for his *Faust. Ein Fragment* in its first publication in 1790; at an earlier stage he referred to a version as the *Urfatzer*, again in self-conscious quotation of Goethe's *Urfaust* (letter to Weigel, September/October 1928). Writing about *Faust* in 1953, when the Berliner Ensemble produced the *Urfaust*, Brecht asked, 'Is the staging of the fragment justified?' and answered his own question with the argument that the work belonged to a particular genre of 'masterwork-fragment' that, although merely sketched and with gaps in the plot, nonetheless achieved a wonderful and rich consummation: 'The art of sculpture is not yet the complete mistress of the stone, and we catch her unawares on the very cusp of her victory' (*BFA* 24, 431–2).

In 1939 Brecht reviewed his recent outputs and concluded, perhaps surprisingly: '*Life of Galileo* is technically a great step backwards, like

Señora Carrar all too opportunistic. ... First the *Fatzer* fragment and the *Bread Store* fragment would have to be studied. These two fragments are of the highest technical standard' (*Journals*, 25 February 1939). Following these two arguments, the one about the stream of creative outputs, the other about the potential of a genre of the masterly fragment, it seems that we might try to think of the unfinished projects documented in this volume as works in their own right, from which Brecht could learn and progress, which might well be 'perfect' in their unfinished state, or out of which he might still fashion other works.

In fact the idea of the 'unfinished' is central to Brecht's whole aesthetic. Especially as his ideas about literature evolved through the 1920s, he came to think of contradiction, which by its nature could not be resolved, as the key to a productive engagement with the world. Neat conclusions, resolutions, denouements could only ever be ironic. It was crucial to leave the audience, or the reader, with work to do. The *Lehrstück* or *learning play* experiments of the later 1920s were the first radical experiments in realizing a model of theatre in which either the participants were at the same time the audience or else the wider audience's participation was absolutely integral to the experience. The 'completion' could happen only outside the theatre, in the wider social world. Theatre events of this degree of experimentalism were really only possible in the Berlin of these years, where there were theatre professionals and an audience schooled in the political avant-garde and very largely sympathetic to Brecht's aims. In 1929 he wrote a poem entitled 'On the making of longlasting works', which includes the lines:

> So too the plays that we invent
> Are unfinished, or so we hope
> And the tools that serve our playing
> What would they be without the indentations, the
> Result of many fingers, those signs, seemingly of damage
> Which beget the nobler form
> And the words too that
> With their users so often
> Changed their meanings. (*BFA* 14, 35)

In exile from 1933 Brecht had to temper his practice and reassess his options. Nonetheless, the two-pronged notion persisted that texts should remain suspended in a state of flux and that it was up to the audience to complete the arguments. The most obvious example is *The Good Person of Szechwan*, which ends with Shen Teh hopelessly torn in half, and an actor stepping out in front of the curtain to exhort the audience to find a decent ending (in John Willett's translation):

> Ladies and gentlemen, in you we trust:
> There must be happy endings, must, must, must. (*BFA* 6, 279)

One of Brecht's great statements of indeterminacy is another poem, this one from 1935 and exile in Denmark, which tells the legend of the suicide on Etna of the Greek philosopher Empedocles, who – we are told – cast aside his sandal before slipping unnoticed into the crater. Or, the poem goes on, perhaps it was not suicide after all; maybe he fell in. Alternatively, perhaps he had never been mortal in the first place. Or, if his death was, after all, human and willed, maybe it was not a modest gesture of one retiring from the world, but a wily effort to install himself as an immortal. There is nothing we can do to establish the 'true' ending to the story; rather, we are left with what scant evidence there is, and with our own lives to lead and our own problems to solve, as well as we may – as once also the philosopher's pupils were, who

> Suddenly grasped in their hands, troubled, that tangible shoe
> Worn, made of leather, earthly. (*BFA* 12, 32)

The poem is given added piquancy by the fact that, despite his reputation in the ancient world, nothing of the actual writings of Empedocles survives, except in the substantial fragments and gists quoted by other writers. It is only now, after the poem as it were, that Empedocles' followers embark on their most important lesson and begin to seek the solution themselves. Seen like this, 'fragments' are no longer the exception in Brecht's output; they are not the 'leftovers', but rather the central gesture. Coming at Brecht by way of the selection of incomplete projects in this volume, we may realize the extent to which his other works too, even the most apparently finished, may be appreciated as unfinished, as works in progress: the author himself can no longer work on them, but we most certainly can.

Of course the projects of this volume should not all be approached in one and the same way. They date from different stages of Brecht's creative life, and may have had very different status for him. It must not be the implication of a general introduction that there is a generally 'right way'. As editors and translators, we too have approached the texts in different ways: for example, the version of *Fleischhacker* presented here is a quite close and literal representation of the materials in the Archive, whereas our *Fatzer* is a much freer and more speculative reconstruction. The substantial introductions to each individual project will offer a more varied and nuanced counterpoint to these remarks.

We have chosen, in our selection, to pass over the various unfinished projects of the very early years, where Brecht worked intermittently on sketches with titles like *Galgei, Herr Makrok*, and *Green Garraga* – all of which, one might argue, with their exotic settings and identity struggles, found their way in some other form into the published plays *Baal, In the Jungle of Cities*, and *Man Equals Man*. To some extent, the outputs of these years are already represented in the documentation of the various versions of *Baal* and the one-act plays in *Collected Plays: One*. The scraps of ideas and scenarios for plays on the subject of the biblical David, Pope Joan, Hannibal, and Alexander (all exercises in debunking heroes), or the beginnings of a dramatization of Selma Lagerlöf's *Gösta Berlings Saga*, we judged too insubstantial to merit inclusion in the present volume – which is not to say they are without interest. And so we start with the dual project of *Jae Fleischhacker in Chicago* and *A Family from the Savannah*, for which the earliest plans and sketches date from 1924, when Brecht and Hauptmann were in their mid-twenties and he was on the point of moving from Munich (and the safety of a parental home in nearby Augsburg) to set up truly independently in Berlin. It is in Berlin then that we get these seven whirlwind years of such extreme and various creative productivity. *Fleischhacker* occupies him on and off for five years, and overlaps with many other projects, including *Fatzer*, our next text. *The Bread Store* in turn, the drafts of which all date from the end of the decade, overlaps with *Fatzer*. The late 1920s and early 1930s are the years of the operas with Weill and the *Lehrstücke* (with various composers and other collaborators), and these are again fully represented in *Collected Plays: Two* and *Three*. In 1933 Brecht and his family and associates went into exile, fleeing from the Nazis, and in due course they settled on the Danish island of Fyn. Here most probably (the evidence is scanty) Brecht and Steffin developed their plans for a fable of the faceless petty bourgeois at the time of the depression, *Jakob Gehherda*, whom we have called *Jacob Trotalong*. Play projects from these years are relatively few and far between (otherwise in *Collected Plays: Four*). A *Goliath* opera was abandoned, and a *Julius Caesar* play turned into a novel. Brecht was cut off from much meaningful work in and with an actual theatre, and could see few prospects for a production: all the more interesting, then, that he should use the time for the relative experimentalism of *Jacob Trotalong*. Most of the dramatic projects, otherwise, from the late 1930s and 1940s, made their way into the familiar full-blown plays: *Life of Galileo, Mother Courage, The Good Person of Szechwan, Arturo Ui, Mr Puntila, The Caucasian Chalk Circle*. In among these comes *The Judith of Shimoda*, an adaptation of a contemporary Japanese play, which, exceptional among the projects of this volume, is more or less entirely roughed out, and all written in 1940 when the Brecht entourage was living in Finland. In 1941 they eventually escaped from Europe altogether, and they lived for the next six years in

California. Alongside the play projects of the 1940s there are various sketches for revues and musicals/operas: *Pluto-Revue* (after Aristophanes), *The Journeys of the God of Good Fortune*, *The Chariot of Ares* and, back in Europe from late 1947, *Dante-Revue* and *The Salzburg Dance of Death*, some of which, insofar as they are dependent on songs, are represented in English language collections of Brecht's poems and songs. Otherwise we have just a few beginnings of adaptations of plays by other authors. So the last project in this volume is *Garbe/Büsching*, a short and fragmentary sketch, but of enormous interest in its documentation of Brecht's engagement with the social and cultural politics of the newly founded GDR. In the German edition (*BFA*) the only other projects documented in this last phase of his life are equally fragmentary plans, albeit fascinating for their subject matter: *Rosa Luxemburg* and *Life of Einstein*.

In the case of the projects we are presenting here, only for *The Judith of Shimoda* are we translating an existing German edition (and here it is not the *BFA* text that we have used). For every other project we have gone back to the archive in Berlin and made our own assessment of the materials, before deciding how to present them for an English readership. And in each case we have been guided not only by principles of philological exactitude, but also by the desire to offer a text which is, to some degree at least, readable and usable. In other words, we have tried to make sense of the material, a sense that Brecht might himself have been in the process of making, without falsifying the record and simply fabricating. It follows from the very different state in which these projects come down to us, in manuscript, typescript, and even some published fragments, that they have each to be edited in different ways, and ways that best reflect the particularities of each collection of papers. In our own presentations, we have used a form of marginal reference to the texts as they are edited in the *BFA*, so that the reader can see just how our editions are put together and so that scholars can easily find the German originals should they so wish. The editors of the *BFA* divide the material for each project into three categories (which are in fact nigh impossible to hold apart): plans and plot-lines (given the letter A), scenes and dialogue (B), and commentary (C); and then they organize the texts according to a supposed (often extremely speculative) chronology. For our purposes it is probably only important to hold onto the fact that each marginal number – A17, B32, and so on – represents a separate archived sheet, from a different notebook or other source, and that the higher numbers probably refer to later stages of composition. In addition, while the scholarship of the *BFA* has been our overarching guide, we have also consulted other editions, where these exist, as well as the often unpublished work of other scholars or indeed theatre practitioners.

To all of these, as to the staff of the Bertolt Brecht Archive (Akademie der Künste, Berlin) we are profoundly indebted.

This is a volume which has also been, although we are primarily textual scholars, inspired and informed by practical work in the theatre. Our version of *The Judith of Shimoda* was first created for a production at the University of Hawaii's Kennedy Theatre in Honolulu in 2010. Our *Fatzer* was originally translated and assembled for a production at the North Wall Theatre, Oxford, in 2016. In addition, we have been closely involved in the workshopping and preparation of a stage version of *Fleischhacker* (London, TBA 2018–9). These three and *The Bread Store* have been several times staged in Germany and elsewhere. In some cases we have been able to consult production scripts, and we have welcomed the opportunity, while thinking about how to present our material to an English readership, to observe how it can be made to work in the theatre. As Brecht himself remarked, 'no play can be made ready without being tried out in production' (*Journals*, 11 May 1942). We offer this view into the writer's workshop now in the conviction that these play fragments are not at all just of historical interest, or merely reading material for scholars and students of Brecht, but also living, breathing works that can still make their way in the theatre.

TOM KUHN

Note

1 Our main source for Brecht's own writings, throughout, is the *Große kommentierte Berliner und Frankfurter Ausgabe*, edited by Werner Hecht, Jan Knopf, Werner Mittenzwei, Klaus-Detlef Müller and others (Berlin, Weimar and Frankfurt am Main: Aufbau and Suhrkamp, 1988–2000), which we abbreviate as *BFA*. English translations are for the most part taken from the standard Methuen Drama volumes. Where other editions are used, full references are given.

Fleischhacker

With Elisabeth Hauptmann

**Translated and edited by
Phoebe von Held and Matthias Rothe**

The translation was completed in collaboration with a feedback group:
Laura Killeen, Jane Robinson, Naomi Segal, Robert Stock, Sam Williams

Introduction

The idea for a play entitled *Mortimer Fleischhacker* is first mentioned in Brecht's journal in 1924 as part of a host of other project plans. Erwin Piscator's theatre announced it for the 1927–8 season under the title of *Wheat*. The majority of the archival project leaves, however, are simply labelled *Fleischhacker*, a heading we have adopted as the main title for the fragment which in fact resulted from the amalgamation of two play projects: *Jae Fleischhacker in Chicago* and *A Family from the Savannah: A History in Eleven Tableaux*.

Brecht and Elisabeth Hauptmann worked on *Fleischhacker* between 1924 and 1929, most intensively in 1926. In February of that year they also decided to combine the two separate projects into one. Both borrow to different degrees from Frank Norris's unfinished trilogy *The Epic of Wheat*, a set of Naturalist novels. *Jae Fleischhacker in Chicago* is based on the trilogy's second part *The Pit: A Story of Chicago* (1903). It revolves around a cut-throat commodity trader at the Chicago Wheat Exchange, Jae Fleischhacker, who attempts to 'corner' the market, that is, to control the supply of wheat in order to manipulate its price. *A Family from the Savannah* is loosely inspired by the first part of Norris's trilogy, *The Octopus: A Story of California* (1901), and focuses on a destitute farming family who come to the city of Chicago to try their luck.

Fleischhacker is the first play in which Brecht gives full attention to an economic subject: futures commodity trading. Its claim to fame in Brecht scholarship springs from two statements. In 1935 Brecht remembered the difficulties encountered in his work on *Fleischhacker* as a starting point for reading Marx:

> For a particular play I needed Chicago's wheat exchange market as a background. I believed I could quickly gather the necessary knowledge. ... Things turned out differently. Nobody ... could explain to me the workings of the wheat exchange market. Instead, I began reading Marx, and it was only then that I read Marx. (*BFA* 22.1, 138–9)

Moreover, in a lecture from 1929, 'Latest Stage: Oedipus', around the time when Brecht was about to abandon the work on *Fleischhacker*, he proclaimed that contemporary society could no longer be represented within the classic form of drama. *Fleischhacker* supposedly signified a turning point in his dramatic writing and approach to theatre at large:

A play taking issue with the wheat exchange market can no longer be represented in the great form of drama. ... So what should be our great form? ... Epic. Reporting. Such form should not assume that it is possible to identify with our world. The materials are monstrous; our drama must consider this. (*Brecht on Theatre*, 44)

And yet, while Brecht scholarship often points to *Fleischhacker* as a crucial crossroads, it has had little to say about it. What are the reasons for the lack of interest? Is the caesura the play supposedly represents difficult to conceptualize, in particular the relation between artistic form and economic subject? Or is it simply the profoundly disjointed nature and heterogeneity of the archival material that has been a deterrent to closer scrutiny?

The three files in the Bertolt Brecht Archive comprise about 270 leaves: incomplete dialogues, monologue fragments, poetic narrations, lines of dramatic speech without assignment to a particular character, various plot-lines, aesthetic reflections, and a substantial collection of supporting material such as an excerpt of the speculation scheme in Norris's novel, notes on the technicality of futures trading, and articles from the business section of German and Austrian newspapers. The boundaries between text and meta-text cannot always be determined. The partly handwritten notes and the correction patterns show that Brecht and Elisabeth Hauptmann collaborated closely on the *Fleischhacker* project.

Historical context and genesis of *Fleischhacker*

When Brecht set out to investigate the topic of financial speculation, he had witnessed the hyperinflation that brought Weimar's economy to a standstill. Despite economic stabilization in 1924, unemployment rates remained high, causing unprecedented misery and starvation. The supply of grain was precarious, its price fluctuating drastically. The German press reported on the crisis in sensationalist tones, attributing it to the speculative manoeuvres of powerful financial groups in New York and Chicago. Their style was not unlike that of sports coverage: 'A million Dollars lost in speculation! Madness at the New York Stock Exchange', was the headline of the *National-Zeitung* on 4 March 1926, for example.

In this context, it is hardly surprising that Brecht turned towards the topic of financial speculation, and in particular to Chicago's Pit, the city's commodities trading floor. Chicago was familiar territory that had already served as a setting in short stories and *In the Jungle of Cities* (1921–4). American culture in general, the modernity of the American city, jazz, and American literature were in high demand in Weimar Germany. Brecht adored Chaplin and read Upton Sinclair, Sherwood Anderson, and Jack London, as well as books on the history of American capitalism such as Gustavus Myers's *History of the Great American Fortunes* (1907). Yet with *Fleischhacker* Brecht's treatment of America undergoes a significant shift. While fascination with the image of the ruthless American pioneer fuelled *In the Jungle of Cities*, he now created a more detached take on his protagonist, Jae Fleischhacker, attempting something like an anatomy of the trader. There are nevertheless still blind spots in Brecht's reception of American society in *Fleischhacker*: For example, his adaptation of a minstrel song, *At the Tombigbee River*, testifies to an uncritical absorption of the racism inherent in the original song, reiterating stereotypes of black men as instinct-driven and carefree (see B31, in the main text of the translation).

Norris's *Pit* also inspired David Wark Griffith's *A Corner in Wheat* (1909), the film that pioneered cinematographic montage. In foregrounding the economic aspect of human interaction, both Brecht and Griffith dissolve linear storytelling. Thus their engagement with Norris's treatment of economics exposes the limits of Naturalism, with its focus on individuals and their milieu. It was, among other influences, Brecht's experience in avant-garde theatre practice that provided him with the necessary aesthetic tools for such a turn towards detachment, anti-psychological analysis, and abstraction.

As was common with Brecht, he pursued several projects simultaneously while working on *Fleischhacker*, allowing each one to affect the others. Fleischhacker's original first name, Mortimer, was carried over from *Edward II*, Brecht's Marlowe adaptation. Like the ascender to royal power, Fleischhacker ascends to become the 'king of wheat'. And much like with *Edward II*, Brecht predominantly uses here iambic verse and evokes the feudal setting of Elizabethan drama: 'I want these heroes to speak in Shakespearean verse', he remarked to his friend Bernhard Reich, 'the enterprises of the traders and money-changers – determining the life and death of tens of thousands of people – carry as much weight as the battles of the army generals did.'[1]

Thematically related to *Fleischhacker* was Brecht's work on *Dan Drew* between late 1925 and early 1926, an adaptation of Bouck White's 1910 fake autobiography of the railway speculator Daniel Drew. The nearly completed play still featured a classically realist approach to the main protagonist. *Fleischhacker*'s genesis also coincided with Hauptmann and Brecht's extensive revisions of *Man Equals Man* (1924–6). As with *Fleischhacker*, one of the main difficulties here proved to be the plot-line, in particular how to strike a balance between the largely self-reliant episodes and the continuity of dramaturgical development. *Fatzer* (1926–30) was also written in parallel to *Fleischhacker*. Both fragments point to a reorientation in Brecht's work: Whereas *Fatzer* is a precursor of the *Lehrstück* (learning play), *Fleischhacker*, with its primary focus on economy, marks a departure from the existentialist theme of survival in the city and experiments with new representational strategies that Brecht in retrospect associated with the invention of epic drama.

The use value of Norris's *The Pit*: Reconfiguring and fragmenting

Norris, a representative of American Naturalism, tells in linear fashion and with lavish detail the story of Curtis Jadwin's rise and fall in the world of financial speculation. Jadwin's growing obsession with the 'speculation game' endangers his mental health and most importantly his love and marriage. Speculation manoeuvres in the trading pit are described vividly. The location itself, with its balconies, the trading bell, and the excitement of the traders, conjures up a theatricality that Norris exploits to full effect. The public and male-dominated scenery of the wheat exchange is juxtaposed with the feminine privacy of domestic life and love. The story closes with a happy, sentimental ending: Love wins over money.

All these features of Naturalism are absent in *Jae Fleischhacker in Chicago*. Above all the 'heart' of the novel has disappeared: The trading floor scenes that give the reader a heightened sense of presence no longer exist. What was it that interested Brecht and Hauptmann in *The Pit* – what was its 'use value'? *The Pit* served them as an abstract model of financial speculation. Through the lens of *The Pit* they explored the speculator's rise and fall, the alliances and adversities among different groups of speculators ('bulls' and 'bears'), the dependence of speculation on public opinion and the press, and the interrelation between business and domestic life (marriage). Simultaneously, and against the thrust of Norris's story, Brecht and Hauptmann emphasize that a world dependent on speculation is a world in which human beings surrender to factors beyond their control. Whereas Jadwin's moves on the market follow his ingenious intuitions, Fleischhacker is driven by something unpredictable: the weather. The representation of trading is infused with an extensive weather dramaturgy. Moreover, Brecht and Hauptmann's rewriting of the relationship between business and love constitutes a direct negation of Norris's account. Jadwin's obsession with speculation leads him to squander his wife Laura's fortune, yet she forgives him. *Fleischhacker* destroys such sentiment. Nothing is exempt from economic logic. Jae's wife Annabel abandons her husband, once his downfall is clear, so that she can save her fortune.

What stands out in Brecht and Hauptmann's reconfiguration is the absence of any sense of narrative direction or coherence. The libidinous flow that propels Jadwin's infatuation with financial gambling, which also absorbs the reader into the story, has disintegrated into a multitude of scenic splinters. *Jae Fleischhacker in Chicago* thus presents itself as a collection of snapshots, each potentially self-sufficient. Brecht and Hauptmann seem to have embarked on a journey of fragmentation, microscopically accessing selected components of Norris's story, enlarging them, pushing their underlying logic to the fore, re-accentuating them if necessary, as if the truth behind the speculation process could be found in that condensed, single moment. They apply this strategy against plot construction most radically in the representation of cornering the wheat market, which is never dramatized, but only mentioned in the form of sparse summaries and newspaper reports.

The overall collection of scene sketches still adds up to the portrait of a trader, but this is a refracted image that allows no empathetic complicity; it no longer invites the viewer to identify with his motivations or to sympathize with him on his journey towards downfall. The logic can perhaps best be described as cinematographic, producing close-ups, jump cuts, and freeze frames. When Brecht turns to the achievements of film in the *Threepenny Trial* (1932), he observes that the medium of film focuses on *Haltungen* (stances) in situations, making us see the protagonists from the outside (*Brecht on Film and Radio*, 162), a description that captures well what had become of *The Pit*.

While the most dramatic core of the novel – the cornering of the wheat market – remains undramatized in *Fleischhacker*, many scenes are set at the beginning or end of the corner scheme, once its failure has become obvious. A sense of downfall and catastrophe permeates most of them – the spectator looks back at the events from the perspective of their ending, either through Fleischhacker's own melancholic reflections or prompted by an unidentified narrator: 'When you read in the records of your annals / About J. Fleischhacker's instructive downfall / Know this, a bit of late rain was the reason' (B30). In 1929, Brecht would define this technique as historicizing. By shifting current events into a historical context, the former are made to appear anachronistic and open to question: A sense of distance is introduced.

Such a detached stance is supported linguistically, for instance through a reporting or biblical style of narrative: 'But when they came to the threshold of his house and called: come out, Jae, come out, Jae came out and asked them: what is it you want? They said: return our money, for you have deceived us' (A17). However, the majority of the dramatic scenes are composed in a jagged-sounding, broken iambic verse that pivots around a classic Shakespearean iambic pentameter but then consistently breaks the rhythm's regularity. The effect is that of a jazz version of classical blank verse. In sum, the stylistic experiments that Brecht and Hauptmann conducted in the course of *Fleischhacker* eventually came to be subsumed under the heading of epic drama.

A Family from the Savannah: Completion through combining?

The relentless pursuit of fragmentation must have raised some concern: How could the disparate pieces be assembled into a finished play? In a 1926 diary note Hauptmann writes with relief: 'Idea: put together *Fleischhacker* and hurricane piece!!! Seems to be the solution'; and a few days later, 'lucky idea: Joe is the brother in the city whom the family is looking for ... because of Calvin and Joe the family is ruined' (*BFA* 10.1, 1071). By 'hurricane piece' she meant *A Family from the Savannah*, a separate play they had been developing which borrowed from Norris's *Octopus* the motifs of the farming family's move to the city, starvation, and prostitution of the daughter.

How did *Savannah* present a potential solution to the endless fraying of *Fleischhacker*? Both plays are set in Chicago, offering the same diagnosis: misguided appetites, entrepreneurial ambition, and a trajectory leading to downfall and catastrophe. Moreover, *Savannah* may have offered to the shambles of *Fleischhacker* a clearer episodic sequence in which the latter could be embedded. By combining the two, Brecht must have hoped to turn *Fleischhacker* into a 'real story' of family drama, with the theme of the lost son and brotherly rivalry providing proper dramatic conflict and structure.

However, the combination plan went no further than two plot-lines and a few scene sketches. These indicate how Brecht and Hauptmann tried to combine the two projects. The first outline suggests a classical five-act drama, each act divided into three scenes. The two narratives are causally interwoven (A9, A11). The second outline (A12) removes these causal links and replaces them with a loosely configured montage of eleven tableaux alternating between *Fleischhacker* and *Savannah*. Yet *Fleischhacker*'s temporal logic, which mainly explores beginnings and endings, resisted *Savannah*'s linear structure, which proceeded step by step. Moreover, *Savannah*, with its many direct addresses and choral pieces, is audience-conscious and confrontational, while *Fleischhacker*, with its emphasis on epic retrospection, provides no such direct points of contact. Finally, *Fleischhacker*'s focus on the wheat economy diverged from *Savannah*'s main interest in the city as battlefield.

In comparison, one can see why Griffith's pioneering use of montage in his cinematographic adaptation of Norris was so successful. *A Corner in Wheat* juxtaposes farming, bakery, and speculation scenes with no causal links. The economic correlation between production, speculation, and consumption holds all the strands together.

Fleischhacker and Marxism

'I got the impression that these processes [futures trading] were simply inexplicable, that is, they were beyond the grasp of reason, that is, they simply were irrational ... I began reading Marx, and it was only then that I read Marx', Brecht stated in 1935 with reference to *Fleischhacker*. What exactly was 'inexplicable' and how could Marx have offered a remedy?

Futures trading is not difficult to comprehend, and Brecht evidently had the capacity to do so. Traders agree to buy or sell a commodity, such as grain, at a particular price at a particular time in the future, and seek to gain through price fluctuation. In other words, they 'bet' on the price a commodity might achieve at a set date in the future, taking into account all available information on the factors that influence price development: harvest prospects, export-import taxes, political conflicts, and so on. That information can, of course, be subject to manipulation: For example, strategic purchases or sales can influence a commodity's price; or a commodity can be secretly hoarded in order to control supply and price. These fundamental elements of the process of futures trading are not, therefore, 'inexplicable'; rather, it is the very fact that grain is distributed through speculation that is 'beyond the grasp of reason'.

Futures trading in wheat, as Brecht and Hauptmann phrase it in *Fleischhacker*, institutionalizes 'human scheming against the bread of humanity' (B45). The 'irrational' element in trading is that it becomes an abstract ritual divorced from the human, existential need for nourishment. Thus, explaining how speculation works by simply telling its story says nothing about its raison d'être; on the contrary, it naturalizes its practice. In fact, as Brecht declared in 1926 with critical reference to Thomas Mann's model of the realist novel, *not* understanding might be our only chance (*BFA* 21, 167). It is, then, society's irrational rationality that Brecht and Hauptmann aimed to expose through their reconfiguration of Norris's novel, persistently undermining its Naturalist thrust, moving away from a form of literary critique that promises insight through a naive, mimetic realism.

Yet such intentions encountered an inevitable obstacle: Brecht and Hauptmann's perspective remained limited by Norris's angle on financial speculation. Even though they disrupt the narrative's flow, the majority of scenes in *Fleischhacker* are still conceived from the speculator's point of view and buy into Norris's sensationalism: The dramatic event of a corner does not represent the normal workings of the market. Corners are exceptions and their effects short-lived. Finally, the focus on futures trading alone could not provide an adequate account of capitalism as it should be considered in relation to the spheres of production, consumption, and distribution.

It seems Brecht and Hauptmann were aware of these constraints in their source material. Their decision to combine *Jae Fleischhacker in Chicago* with *A Family from the Savannah* may have been not only an attempt to contain fragmentation, but also to situate the trader within a more complex interplay of social forces. It allowed them to juxtapose the entrepreneurial speculator with the enterprising farming family, the thirst for money driving them all. However, although this decision helped to overcome the one-dimensional perspective of the speculator, it reinforced the idea that money and finance are the cause of society's misery. As Herwig Seliger points out, Brecht and Hauptmann's combination of the two plots sacrifices any distinction between social classes: Money ruins everyone.[2] Their burgeoning critique of capitalism thus comes to share with their American literary sources a general distrust of finance, money, and the 'abstract'.

After reading Marx, Brecht did indeed attempt a fresh start on the topic. Marx equipped him with an understanding of the different socio-economic spheres and their interaction. *Saint Joan of the Stockyards* (1932) attempted to stage capitalist economy in its entirety as it moves through various cycles of crisis. Futures trading is contextualized in relation to production, distribution, and consumption. Investors, factory owners, merchants, and workers represent the different economic spheres. However, this new Marxist dramaturgy was not entirely unproblematic either. It risked, as Adorno saw very clearly, compromising the constitutive openness of art in favour of politics:[3] Brecht on the one hand aimed at a faithful depiction of the workings of capitalism, but on the other wanted to refrain from forcing a political message on the viewer.

Fleischhacker: A failed experiment?

No play entitled *Fleischhacker* was ever completed. In late 1929, comparing *In the Jungle of Cities* to *Fleischhacker*, Brecht concluded that the former had represented an excess of intellectual freedom vis-à-vis reality, whereas in the latter 'the irreconcilable dualism between idea + reality ... led to the utter destruction of the project'.[4] His remark alludes to Marx's dialectic of consciousness and being: the reciprocal effects between the thinking self and material reality. *In the Jungle of Cities* was still unconcerned with that dialectic. The thinking subject and its desire to shape reality drive the play, dictating a more obvious dramatic structure. With *Fleischhacker* Brecht and Hauptmann aimed at making individual action contingent on material conditions. But as shown earlier, the perspective adopted from Norris proved insufficient.

Another obstacle to the completion of *Fleischhacker* might have been a dramaturgical one, relating to their method of fragmentation. Hauptmann and Brecht found themselves in the same position as the epic actor. Their challenge was to create a sequence of events from a collection of snapshots, 'despite, or better, by means of jumps and ruptures' (*BFA* 24, 49). They had to create such a plot anew, after purposefully having dismantled Norris's narrative. Here a conflict arises between, on the one hand, aesthetic modes of production striving for fragmentation, and, on the other, a respect for classical dramatic conventions. In other words, their working methodology was perhaps more radical than their expectation as to what represented a producible play.

Certainly, other reasons can be found for the project's state of incompletion, but it may be more useful to interrogate the notion of failure itself. Perhaps there was no failure, but only ongoing production. The *Fleischhacker* experimentation led to the 1926 poem 'This Babylonian confusion of the words':

> Recently I wished
> To intrigue you with the story
> Of a wheat dealer in the city
> Of Chicago, in the midst of my speech
> My voice fled me
>
> (*BFA* 13, 356–7)

In 1935 *Fleischhacker* provides the material for another poem:

> When years ago studying the workings of the Chicago wheat market
> I suddenly understood how they manage the world's cereal there
> And at the same time did not understand it and laid the book down
> I knew immediately: you have got yourself into
> An evil business.
>
> (*BFA* 14, 296)[5]

Moreover, Brecht rewrites the *Fleischhacker* material into no less than three film treatments: 'The Story of Two Brothers' (1929), 'The Hamlet of the Wheat Exchange' (1940) and together with Ferdinand Reyher 'The Bread-King' (1941).

Both *The Resistible Rise of Arturo Ui* (1941) and the famous subway scene in the film *Kuhle Wampe* (1932) revolve around the topic of commodity speculation (cauliflower and coffee beans respectively), and *Saint Joan of the Stockyards* extensively reuses *Fleischhacker*'s material. The *Fleischhacker* fragment also embodies a transitional moment in the rebalancing of the topics of economy and city. The subsequent plays *Rise and Fall of the City of Mahagonny* (1930) and *Saint Joan of the Stockyards* achieve in this respect a reconciliation that Brecht searched for but never accomplished in *Fleischhacker*.

Ultimately, we have to ask if *Fleischhacker* could have triggered such wide-ranging productivity if it had been completed. Brecht himself was well aware of this and pointed to the project as a thematic complex in which he was exploring a new dramaturgy that simultaneously staged and critiqued capitalism. By stalling completion, *Fleischhacker* opened up a field of experimentation from which emerged – for better or worse – a new Marxist Brecht along with the conception of epic drama.

Structure of this *Fleischhacker* version

While the *Berliner und Frankfurter Ausgabe* (*BFA*) has organized the individual texts according to a chronology of three different work phases, thus interweaving *Jae Fleischhacker in Chicago* and *A Family from the Savannah*, we separated the plays into two main sections, with a third, shorter section containing the pieces that clearly demonstrate a combination plan. Within each complex, we have attempted to trace a rudimentary dramaturgical structure that brings out thematic connections through which we hope to make the fragmented material more accessible. *Jae Fleischhacker in Chicago* is organized in a two-part layout, taking into account that the majority of scenes focus on either beginnings or endings. *A Family from the Savannah* is structured in a more linear fashion, following in loose clusters the family's journey from their arrival in Chicago to their ruin.

As we have shown, *Fleischhacker* is characterized by a high level of fragmentation. We have therefore been cautious not to give the false impression that the textual material constitutes a finished play that could be performed without further intervention. Rather, our version aims to provide an insight into *Fleischhacker*'s work-in-progress character, tracing Brecht's ongoing search for formal solutions. The characteristics of the fragment are for example present in the lack of assigned characters as well as finalized names or titles. Fleischhacker's first name 'Jae' is a case in point. Brecht derives it from *The Pit*'s main protagonist's nickname 'J.', the first letter of his surname 'Jadwin'. Brecht transposes the English pronunciation into German: 'Jay' becomes 'Jae' (phonetically 'jæ'). But this version exists in parallel to 'Joe'. Furthermore, Brecht and Hauptmann often did not allocate a named character to the dramatic speeches they wrote. Only where these 'anonymous' speeches can clearly be assigned to Fleischhacker have we inserted his name in square brackets, but there are many other scenes where speakers are left open in accordance with the manuscripts.

In order to prevent the misleading sense of a finished play, other style conventions normally applied in drama have been avoided. For example, we did not provide a list of characters at the very beginning, as this would require a worked-out plot supported by those characters. Finally, we have not cut or reinvented wordings in the translation where the German original is difficult to understand, allowing glimpses into the rich experimentalism that marked Brecht's work on *Fleischhacker*.

PHOEBE VON HELD AND
MATTHIAS ROTHE

Notes

1 Bernhard Reich, *Im Wettlauf mit der Zeit: Erinnerungen aus fünf Jahrzehnten deutscher Theatergeschichte* (Berlin: Henschelverlag, 1970), 287.
2 Helfried W. Seliger, *Das Amerikabild Bertolt Brechts* (Bonn: Bouvier, 1974), 124.
3 Theodor W. Adorno, 'On Commitment', *Performing Arts Journal* 3.2 (1978), 9.
4 Bertolt Brecht, *Notizbücher 24 und 25*, 1927–30, ed. Peter Villwock (Frankfurt am Main: Suhrkamp, 2010), 260.
5 These two poems are quoted according to the new versions in Bertolt Brecht, *Collected Poems*, translated and edited by Tom Kuhn and David Constantine (New York and London: Liveright/W. W. Norton, 2018).

Part One: *Jae Fleischhacker in Chicago*

[A17]

On Fleischhacker and other histories

1)
First present all the material like in the bible
(But when they came to the threshold of his house and called: come out, Jae, come out, Jae came out and asked them: what is it you want? They said: return our money, for you have deceived us. Etc.)

2)
Then as a newspaper report

3)
Table with technical terms
Expensive
Cheap

[B32]

The one whose name escapes me now tell me of him

    Chicago he calls jungle, tigers us, and himself
    Master of the Tigers

So from this day watch every card
He does not play

The sickness in my body, now
For seventeen years, is keeping me away from business

[A5]

Nathanael Fisk, the cork. Bloated, unhealthy, liver disease, shining blue eyes. Always dressed in white. Stock market expertise. Engineer. Took part in five corners, but never a corner himself

Exits when Joe enters. Reappears after the tiger has scoffed his first breakfast and proved himself to be a genius. Joe tries to get Fisk's opinion out of him. Fisk has his liver to deal with, dies. Death notice at stock exchange. Fisk shares fall through the floor. Joe goes for it again. But Fisk has secured himself right and left. The corpse pockets everything

Fisk leaves Joe the woman, whom he had brought to Fisk in her prime. Woman leaves Joe before crash

Joe   Even if you have to open his mouth with a crowbar

Clerk   His mouth is wide open, yet nothing comes out but foul breath from a sick liver and bloated body

[A18]

Prologue to Jae Fleischhacker

Money
Money is something very important. This is widely acknowledged, yet very few people are actually comfortable with this. Even though money brings great honour to the person who owns it, almost all who honour him because he owns it are ashamed. It is not seen as honourable to make much of it. It is seen as best to receive it for efforts held in very low esteem such as those of industriousness or connections or amusing smartness, and it is not even seen as particularly wrong to obtain it without any service in return. For example, many assign little value to women, yet to give a woman away for money is seen as shameful: only women themselves are permitted to do this. It is honourable to lie for your fatherland and it is honourable to own money but it is not honourable to lie for money. That is why all things which revolve around money are little known, and for many things what is unknown about them because it relates to money is much more significant than everything that is known about them. Because of this a wrong impression emerges. Such a wrong impression almost always emerges, for example, in the case of wars.

[A13 end]

Purpose of the wheat exchange

Mitigation of risk. Allocation of world wheat. A fixed price eventually takes its hold on the wheat. The price stands, between the harvests.

In excess of youthfulness
Committing follies
Later, seeing people for what they really are
Morons and rogues
For in the face of growing impoverishment
Life to him seemed dearer by the day

1
Standing around him and praising him.

[B18]

John Table What I appreciate about you is your sense of humour

Fleischhacker They are like children and need someone to take care of them.

2
Fleischhacker and four bears, amongst them John Table and Archie Brown

Fleischhacker
For now Chicago's milk glass face
Is turned to us, Jae Fleischhacker

4
MEETING WITH THE BIG BEAR
The four are forever asking questions, he is always saying 'no', has trouble keeping them on board

[B16 middle]

Milk
We fished the penny, you and I
Out of the gutter
You're sending me away, me who
Drank with you for one long year
From one cup and ate from
One hand
For I washed myself *after* you
In the same bowl.

[Fleischhacker]
When you are sorrow-stricken
Do not let your hair hang
In the bowl from which we eat with gentlemen
Eat together

[B26]

2
Wheat Exchange

Jae Fleischhacker *and four bulls*: **Table, Brown, Shaw** *and* **Beket**; *standing apart* **Mathew Milk.**

Jae
For now the milk glass face of this Chicago
Is turned to me, Jae Fleischhacker
I shall obey the wish of the immense Chicago
At such a height to change
To gain in virtue and
Before rising any further, to test myself, how
Good my health is and thus
(*Approaches* **Milk**.)
I will now hack you, my right hand
Though useful still today, once indispensable
My dirty hand from troubled times, today I'll hack you off

Shaw
It's more than we expect, Jae

Brown
It's good

Table
It's dangerously good

Jae
It's dangerous to rise. Leave Milk. Your hand
Though in my service rough for seven years
It bears the stench from far below. Along with you
I shrug off the slaughterhouse's brutal blow and go on fighting
WITH MY HEAD

Milk
Fight well, fight desperately well, and do not fall
Asleep at night, don't eat, don't drink, don't scream
For, from this day you have just marked
Chicago's milk glass face will never look
Away, but it will count

28 Brecht and the Writer's Workshop

The beat of your heart, the flush and pallor of your cheek and will
Not turn away, before it hears your scream
In the tongue that truly is your own, the language of your spleen
In which you'll cry out for your mother

Jae *laughs and pushes him away:*
Now go away. Don't let yourself be
Caught when we cast our nets
(*Exit* **Milk**.)
For
Now the best of times commences. The Wheat

[B15]

Mortimer Fleischhacker

A fair few part company with him, the bad ones stay

She   For not as many as came here with you will leave with you from here.

He
The city grows
Time trickling away. Good that the days no longer need nourishing

[B16 beginning]

1
[Fleischhacker]
In this humanated piece of land
Here human stench rises
Twenty floors high and every foot of it
Has a human face.
(*To* **Mile:**)
Just go and buy some lads
Who put it in the papers
That there is no rain, the wheat
Will die of thirst!

Oil is heavier than water and floats!

Take a chair with you to the dollars! You'll stay there!

2
The Dinner

> Have a cigar, Jim!
> Have some wine

Beket   As long as there is any!

Fleischhacker   As long as this little town is standing!

Dexter, Flowers and Glancer

First Glancer and Dexter: they come to an agreement.
Then, unexpectedly, the bulls.

Fleischhacker 'acts' like a bear. Glancer laughs – it's raining.

> You do it! It's a real fiddle to undo your trousers with a fencing glove.

[B16 end]

He now does a calculation:
> And yet it's difficult to count such assets
> The brain provides no guarantee

Fleischhacker to Archie Brown:

Fleischhacker
You sold meat in Cincinnati? Good!
I know something about meat!
One calves make two calf! Isn't it so?
You eat it from a tinny thing in which
Anything in there unfailingly
Resembles calf!

Brown
I do not understand. My trade
Was honest. What I sold was good

Fleischhacker
What I meant was: what you ate! I do like
Making fun!

Almost like my brother
In London? To whom we send
Money.
           What for?
So he can tell us if the sun is shining
In London!

        [B29]
[Fleischhacker]   Nobody knows how much grain there is in the world. Yet just like the poker player, who doesn't look at his cards, but lays them face-down on the table in front of him, only contemplating the faces of his fellow players, I now want to buy as much as possible of the wheat that exists in the world. Not contemplating whether it is possible, I am now going to, whether possible or not, simply do as good a trade in that grain as I am a good man.

        [A4]
First Jae's *baisse* speculation. He has sold wheat and needs to get his hands on wheat.

He has advised the four others to buy, so he can sell to them at their high price.

When the rain sets in, promising a good harvest, he cancels the purchases by the four bulls (he makes a gain by speculating on thin air), accepts their wheat at a low price. The price drops. He continues to sell.

The rain persists and there will be little wheat. He needs to buy to cover his sales, and that's why the price goes up.

He needs to get 1000 bushels for each of which he receives 5 Marks. By the time he has his 1000 bushels (panic buying), they have already cost him 8000 Marks, he has an actual loss of 3000 Marks. In order to make up for it, he has to change sides. He needs to continue buying.

He buys another 1000 bushels for the price of 8 Marks, assuming the price would go up to 11 Marks. Then he would break even. Yet because he doesn't just want to break even, but to make a gain, he buys another 5000 bushels. At least to protect himself to some extent, in case the price might ultimately fall, and especially because it has stopped raining and there is talk again of a good harvest, *he buys actual wheat.*

Suppose: the entire harvest will be 7000 bushels. He owns 5000 bushels. He buys the remaining wheat as standing crop, then those who need to supply him with the 5000 will have to purchase from him the wheat that he actually owns for the price of 20 Marks in order to sell it to him for 8 Marks per bushel. He will be able to release them from their obligation if they pay him 12 Marks per bushel.

But he did not factor in everything, they do not need to buy from him, suddenly wheat is flooding the market.

Realizing a gain by betraying people, he goes bankrupt.

[B40]

1 Jae says to the four bulls: you have to buy grain. We had four good years; this year will be a bad one. As you know there is drought all over the world. Grain will be very precious. You have to buy grain. And it will fetch a high price.

Jae says to his broker: fools will come; they'll want to have grain and they won't look out for either rain or sun, but they'll only listen to what someone tells them, and they'll pay a good price. So you should sell them grain. And sell the grain for me too, as much of it as possible.

2 After some time the drought ends and it rains. The four bulls to Jae: now it is raining. Everybody says there will be a lot of grain. We'll be able to get as much grain as we want, and it will fetch a low price. And on your advice we bought grain. There was also someone driving the price up, so we only got the grain at a high price.

Jae says to the four bulls: try again. If you buy lots of wheat, wheat will become scarce and you will get a good price. My advice is: tomorrow go and buy a whole heap of grain in one go.

And to his broker Jae says: tomorrow wheat will become very expensive. So sell a big heap of it tomorrow at the price it's at tomorrow, and say you will get the wheat at that price in three months' time, because by then there will be plenty of wheat and you will get it cheap then and they will have to pay you a high price for it.

3 Rain is good for the grain, but then it doesn't stop and now it'll be bad for the grain.

[A6]

The god who sends rain, he also makes the sun shine

The rain is for him

He advises his friends to speculate on *baisse* (good harvest), while he speculates on *hausse* (war rumours etc.), and on top of that it rains.

Somewhere there is an acre

[B20 beginning]

Fleischhacker/Chicago

You have come at a bad time
Yellow hurricane cloudlet

Price increase between 11 and midday
Every stalk is worth a hat

You dogs, why didn't you buy just now
When it was cheap and lots, but now it's getting expensive
It's eleven o'clock and at midday
There'll be an increase, then every stalk
Will be worth a hat
You fools, this evening
You could stuff the harvest of this continent in a hat
We will eat nothing
For dinner tonight

Joe's KO

[A7]

H. Cliffe tries to get in on the corner, is rejected. Rents silos and, as the controller of the silos, confronts Fleischhacker in the 4th act. Finally, he is allowed on board the sinking ship.

To pull off the corner is very difficult
 1. To get warehouses
 2. To get the money
 3. To get the transport

4. To pay the rent
5. To pay the interest
6. To thwart the machinations of the railway
7. To bribe the interfering press

[B19]

Fleischhacker   Send seven lads to Mike Gross to the top of Lincoln Square, lads with elbows, whose chins run like knives through Melbury Viaduct's knots of people.
(*Exit one of them.*)

One of them   Can't you speak to him?

Fleischhacker   The phone networks have been jammed for the last two minutes. It's the Red River Corn Sell-Out, but three of them are clinging to their tin cans for us like drowning men.

The one (*back*)   It's almost eleven. The street strands of the viaduct are so laden with people, they are getting longer. The viaduct's concrete gorge is clogged up with herds of cars, all tangled up. Melbury Viaduct itself is swamped with people so that its cement jaws are stretching like elastic.

Fleischhacker   What sort of people did you send?

The one   Seven steam saws.

Fleischhacker   Then wait and switch yourselves off like ships' engines so that these minutes won't exhaust us, for, regular and unrushed, the grey general stream carries our business affairs along.
(*They stand still.*)

Messenger   Message from Mike Gross. Talks about rumours of the acquisition of the granaries on the Lower Huron by a secret bull.

Fleischhacker   At this very moment, everyone will know. If Mike Gross doesn't get in there right now, we are sunk.

[B23 end]

Jae
It's in the papers that
A great mind has made its mark
On the wheat business; the
Front page knows my face, the lads
Put it underneath their plate with ground

Meat at lunch, covering themselves with
It, the boys wrap themselves up in the garages of
XX, contemplating what's going on
In that Wheat-Jae's head at night!
The city is waiting for its rabbit punch!

[B39]

Buy, people. (*Exit people.*)

[Fleischhacker]
In them
We have people
Who are easily confused.
If a shadow falls on the sun, they shout
The Flood is coming. And when they
Gape at the faces that happen to be around them
When they eat their steak
They forget the size of the globe
On which, everywhere, at top and bottom,
Wheat grows, under sun and rain
Taking turns, because the year is long.
That's why we want to write down now
What our opinion is, how the year will go.
After a brief, calm look
Over the markets of the world
Ere we dive into the bustling tangle
Of traders. Now, here is our opinion:
Good weather on the whole, lots of wheat.
Sell, John.

[B27]

Fleischhacker
My word is
Freshly printed news smelling at midday
Of printer's ink and stretched wide
By greedy arms in the subway
Between work and eating
At once being read from two sides.

[B20 middle]

[Fleischhacker]
Come, I'll show you

How to start up a business from nothing
Have you got a penny
It doesn't matter without a penny it's hard but
Not impossible, for take a look at the city
There are big houses with many holes and later
There will be yet another city, New York, not too far away
And there
Will be even bigger houses and I hear
They've got a market for cotton there
When we are bigger let's go and take a look.

[B48 beginning]

5/1
Pale Ale Bar near the stockyards

Fleischhacker goes fishing for a man of youthful years.

Fleischhacker
I think you are a decade younger than
You look. The city takes its tithe but
You look very young. Your face is
One of those with promise on the market, resembling shells
Of crabfish. For people like yourself
The street's a pool to fish in for ten years, at least. You will still learn
From knock-out punches, won't you? Good, good. You like your food
The shops on Wall Street offer lots of things
Made just for you. Five department stores you could consume
All by yourself. Good. Sitting in a room with you
Is nice. Confidence sits freshly
At the table by your side. Good, good. You still look
Shameless, just a little. Not too alarmed. The thing you lack
Is money. Well, here is money. A handful will suffice. More
Will come later by itself. You need this handful but you cannot
Raise it. For, there are many like you, yet dollars are scarce
All 'round each one cuts off their pound of flesh
And yet a possibility for you I do not see
Maybe you're meant for money and for clout and
For the hustle of the market, all of this
But a possibility for you I do not see
For, it's just a handful of such money
And you understand the language of the market

As only people of the market do, and that way you'll never learn
But that's what you don't have and never will
And so
A possibility for you I do not see

(*Takes his money back and sits down at another table.*)

[B37]

[Fleischhacker]
Welcome Chat, it stinks of downfall here
From Frisco to New York there's nothing quite as
Foul as J. Fleischhacker's business. I see
There's many here who bet their last penny on me
And some who fear I'd do the most atrocious things
Yet I know nothing.

Chat
Ha, that is great fun

Fleischhacker
You think I should buy today

Chat
Yes definitely buy

Fleischhacker
Or hold back

Chat
No, buy

Fleischhacker
Do they love me on the market

Chat
They buy what you buy

Fleischhacker

[B21]

Storm on the grain market

10.3.
Experts have enlightened this newspaper about the causes of the American wheat *baisse* and its effects on the world market as follows: For some days now the American Grain Exchanges have reported panic-stricken slumps in the wheat price. The wheat price dropped by 80 cents in the space of two days. The price is still falling. The situation on the Chicago Pit is being described as out of control. If the price slump persists over a longer period of time, there is no way of knowing, given the extent of this speculation and speculation it is indeed, what the governments of the United States and the other countries concerned will do to counter the rapid and dangerous fall in grain and bread prices.

10.3.
Bread prices lowered in Budapest

10.3.
Canadian farmers request an increase in grain tariffs in the House of Commons

11.3.
Panic on the international grain market – a manoeuvre by the Chicago Baisse Group? A new corner?

The massive wheat *baisse* of the last few days can be traced back to the machinations of Joe Fleischhacker. As we have learned, this *baisse* is the result of the collapse of a gigantic corner, unlike any other recorded this century. We have received the following information:

Until Spring 19… Joe Fleischhacker was a member of the Barnes Baisse Group, which had ruled the Chicago wheat market for three years. Unexpectedly, Fleischhacker then switched to the opposite camp, which turned out to be immensely profitable, as he was soon considered the strongest of the bulls. The entire Pit had been unaware that Fleischhacker was planning a corner. In the autumn, however, enormous purchases were made by an unknown bull, whom many, even at the time, identified as Joe Fleischhacker. Fleischhacker had, alas, miscalculated his corner. At the very moment that Fleischhacker probably believed he had seized the entire wheat supply down to the last grain and was certain of his victory, an enormous sale's offer suddenly appeared, which immediately put pressure on prices. This offer has proved so significant as to cause the current panic on the international wheat market. One may hope that Fleischhacker will get away with just a black eye.

14.3.
War between X and Y? Diplomats to be recalled?

14.3.
Our Chicago correspondent reports as follows with regard to the rumours of war during the last few days: yesterday, the stock exchange experienced something sensational and hitherto unheard-of. Overnight, Joe Fleischhacker's doomed wheat supply, which soon would have completely drowned him, was transformed by the rumours of war into a gold mine that even he had not expected. The consequences for the world market are unforeseeable.

[A16]

First half: dramatic actions objective and dry, as striking as possible in their arrangement. The whole thing *bafflingly* concise, arid and childlike the unfolding of the wheat battles. In the manner of a Japanese woodcut.

Second half: dramatic actions as ballast for an aspiring inwardness.

[B41]

[Fleischhacker]
And thus I see: I can
Destroy them all but
Not choose who I destroy.
Crush them all underfoot but spare no one.
This net does not choose its fish.

[B13]

Times are good, change is sharp
Disaster by the day
For famished stomachs poisonous fare
Most bloody disaster on the railway tracks
Which we travelled on with others an hour ago
The greed of mouths pressed up against window panes
Behind which we dine adds spice to a hurried meal
With little sleep in beds under arches, or else nothing but sleep
Too much to eat or nothing to eat
This one at this hour has Dakota

In his hand and in the next he does
Not even have the hand

The drought on the prairies of Dakota or
Torrential rains in India, the cold wind of Siberia
Too hot a wind in Argentina

We sweat in the drought of Dakota's
Prairies and drip with the rains
Of distant India, by night we shiver
From too cold a wind on the Black Sea
Yet at the same time Argentina's
Wind is too hot for us

[B23 beginning]

Clerk – a walking scar!

Josua and Dexter in Jae's empty flat.
Now that the days of your spring are gone
I bring you here to the man
Jae Fleischhacker for whom
You are not too high, just within reach
And still good enough, ere
In the swamp of your skin a horse drowns
So I hope you will depart from here
Not with me! Yet I advise you
Be quick! Ere such a house is in-
habitable, its landlord's
Time will be over! Yes, these walls
Don't dry as fast as such
Men's best time evaporates!

[B47]

Monologue of a woman

There is nothing I fear more than if he
Were to eat a lot, surely I'd feel nauseated
If I saw him eat. Even a few weeks ago –
For my time is running out now by the day
Bringing changes by the day to my body –
I slept with no one who did not

Eat a lot. Today I fear
A man's appetite, wishing only for
The one who sits there day by day
In a corner behind smoke, whose voice
Day by day emerges from its hiding-place
And talks to me about
My things. On entering
He does not raise his hat and yet I
Hear him putting down his walking cane and know:
He's there. If this Fleischhacker
Is not of that kind I'm afraid he will find
Nothing in me that is of use to him

[*BBA* 818/35]

Dry women. Watery
Flesh and the cold contemplation of
Smoke – all this I dislike.
Profoundly.
Certainly, it won't last much longer, certainly
It will soon end.

[B31 beginning]

Ever since this copper-riveted face
Turned up on the market at the spot where the call
For more came from

Again he puts a breakfast
Together of flesh from over-gorged bulls and
Tear-soaked dollars

'Tis quite a lot in the offing: for two days
He's eaten nothing but raw flesh

On me, the child, they made a strong impression
Those whisky stores that lured with iron ovens
More than they did with whisky, putting salty oysters on display in open
    tanks
In close reach of everyone
Free for the poor at any time, but
Followed by a ghastly thirst for whisky
For thirst costs more than hunger and the urge for warmth

At the Tombigbee River love for Negroes today is
With a panting Jula between grey knees
In a gum tree canoe, on their head
A banjo, above them moon, between toes
The rudder, this is how we fare with wheat
You

[B11]

But if such a person can find someone
Who got to know his hand through punches
And his eye by its cold look
And knows his face which because it's human
Is depraved, and yet raises his hand for him
He may go unhindered and in honour and you
Have seen a man who has achieved the highest
That can occur in human life

Of someone lonely
        He ate alone
   Or
        He slept beside someone and ate alone
Of a woman
        She has many pasts and no future

[B28]

[Fleischhacker]
Write well for me, I belong to you
Since I was but three weeks, that's almost all I've known
Almost the only thing
For swaddled up was I in sheets of newsprint
And laid before a door and thus
My mother – see –
Has lumbered you with me and you must
Write well about her son.

[A14]

Jae Fleischhacker in Chicago

THE GREAT WHEAT CRISIS AT THE CHICAGO WHEAT
EXCHANGE IN THE YEAR 1908

Two months
Twice the same in almost the same order. Stroke, counter-stroke

That hacking machine that we have made

To do what is possible. Not to avoid
What is unavoidable and perpetually
As long as there is blood in your veins to love with vigour
Change of ownership, change of loss
Oh joy of buying and selling

[B38]

1
I did like your scarred face, Jae
This month
You will certainly devour an ox
The people of Chicago wish to pay for it
With a man like you
I don't ask what he does with his penny, for
If you cheat me, I'll bury you under the asphalt
And who wants that?

2
See, I am not attached
To that money, think of it as inherited, but don't forget
You promised me to double it, for
I have always been determined to
Sleep and not worry; that kind of person remains
Dangerous. Nobody gladly takes
His money that is lying in the street
I trust you

3

Fleischhacker
Why don't you ever change your coat any more?

John Table
It was
Worn by a contaminated person. Once you're
Slain, I'll take it off and burn it

4
Here I bring you the money
Of my begetter. Let him sleep in the mud
For having made me out of indifference
For such a world, take it and
Squander it, for in any case you'll go down
To the dogs who, so as to devour you
Have been fasting for a month

[B46]

4
[Fleischhacker]
I think that he to whom this dangerous Chicago
Which rains knives low at flank height, same
Direction as the ground, which has electric chairs
For tired people, is nothing but a fishpond on a lazy day
He is frightened by his own hand's trembling more than anything
Else. I say it as it is: it's almost worried me
For quite some time, not long, but quite some time
That I am no longer unconcerned
I feel the easy ways are gone, I hope
With them the easy times are not gone too
For I am no longer unconcerned
As I once was

5
To a broker:
How old
  Round about forty
How many employees
  Three employees
How many years of business
  Thirty years of business
How often do you eat meat during the week
  Five times, every so often
Good sleep
  Rarely
It's good business, better than
Some. Chicago has
Room to sleep millions. There are countless names
Almost every morning
The figures change anew

[B45]

In this hour, the people of Chicago
Eight persons wide and silent
Unarmed take to Chicago's streets to profess
That human scheming against the bread of humanity
Is inhuman
Just by carrying their faces
Destroyed by sorrow
Through the city of their birth which has been laid to waste
Just by showing silently the mass
Of those rejecting inhumanity

Joe
It seems I've been too much hung up
On just one thing. It would be good to have
Some foreign inflow and
Far away am I from my place of birth, cut off
From images of the past, my mother

[B36]

In my good days
When I was changeable like weather, had
Hardly plan or purpose but simply changed direction
With wind and weather, lacking my own
Face, I was great and made
My gains from any weather, slept where I stood
Stood where I ate, ate where there was food
And was feared

[B34]

Before Fleischhacker's downfall:

Fleischhacker, John Table and **Archie Brown** *at the table:*

John Table   I will keep my coat on!

Archie Brown   Are you in good health?

John Table   I fear this will be your last cigar.

Fleischhacker   His chatter irks me.

Josua Clerk, the scar

Call Dexter

[B35]

But let us
Attack swiftly, so we shall not fall at brother's hand
But by bread-eaters, our like, in times
Of price increase

They understand as much of it as herrings understand of a tin

Bearing in mind his evil days
In this new heaven he could not behave
Otherwise than
On holiday

[B43]

[Fleischhacker]
If only I had known what that feeling was
When I saw her first and suddenly
Was it great fun which made my heart
Sing suddenly, or only
Feeble possibility? How hard it is
To recall a feeling!
It would be so important, but I let her
Go. How was I to know
What sort of people they might be! But can anyone
So rational have feelings?
Also, I don't know what will become of me
Right now, for inside me....

[B44]

Fleischhacker
For inside me is the fear
I can no longer earn
My living
Not fleeting fear, appearing quickly
And passing quickly too, no no
For years and a day, like water in a stream

There's fear inside me that I'll starve
Not having cheap bread instead of expensive meat
But *no* bread.

X
If you don't know, I do: this was inside you
When two moons ago you stood here laughing
– Never.

Fleischhacker
Be this as it may
It's late and these nights now
Are meant to be slept through
And yesterday is long ago
Also
As they say, we know it, now is now. And
We are not starving yet, are not dissatisfied, leave, we are
Joe Fleischhacker, Wheat-Joe, for tonight
You know it well

[B33]

[Fleischhacker]
Stand at the front, so in this savage crowd
Which has already formed, I see a face before my eyes
That I can recognize.

So what I'd really like is *your* hand
I would forget that its intent is
Not friendly and remember that
I loved it once.

Yet that such a man as I
Could disappear like water in the ground, that
Is quite unthinkable.
    Curtain

[B48 end]

5/2
Hall in the Complex of the Wheat Exchange

Fleischhacker receives his wife's visit.

Annabel Fleischhacker
On the street they know, it's in the papers
Too, today you're facing slaughter like there's never been before
Since Wall Street's birth; that you're very much involved
Utterly wrapped up, ensnared with all that money
In one single matter that's hanging by a hair
And no one knows how it will end, that's why I've come
To ask you how you are

Fleischhacker
It's true, I'm hoping for a change of fortune
Have knife and rabbit punch prepared for that
And am in danger, just hope for luck in battle
And so I thank you that you've come to back me up

Annabel
If this is true indeed, then I would ask you
Not without asking for forgiveness too
For troubling you perhaps with something weighing little
That you put it into writing, legally attested
That all that you have given me – not little
Belongs to me

Fleischhacker
That's so indeed, much more belongs to you
Whatever else I own – will own one day

Annabel
Forgive me, that's not what I ask, but just
That you shall put in writing what belongs to me
And that it does not belong to you

Fleischhacker
That's what you want now

Annabel
Right now. There is still time. Just think
It's weakness and faintheartedness. Don't dwell
On it but write it down for me

Fleischhacker
You know that then we will be separated
From bed and board before midday and that right soon

Annabel
I know

Fleischhacker
And you, who think a lot, don't think
The day will pass, whether good or bad, will pass
And money will be gone and a man
Can't give protection 'gainst cold, hunger, age
Yet even less his money

Annabel
You may mean well and trust me it is irksome
To be so blunt and act with so much haste
Yet your opinion only strengthens me
And
I'll say it as it is: you make me worry
With that view of yours

Fleischhacker
You aren't lured by the prospect of much more: the game and battle?

Annabel
Not anymore. Don't think of me
As stronger than yourself, I beg you
I would not ask for a final account did I not know
I don't have much accounting still to come

Fleischhacker
Here have it. Leave. Make haste and don't look round
And ask not how it ended, tomorrow. Leave

[B20 end]

[Fleischhacker]
I've had
The wheat of America and I wanted
To have the wheat of the earth
I've had
Money to buy this city and I wanted to have
More money
Twice, two harvests, I was the greatest man
And I wanted
To be greater than I was myself
Great fun

[BBA 524/58]

Joe Fleischhacker's rise

J FL 5

Stop switch off the machine stop I cannot bear it
THE TOOTING STARTS UP AGAIN

                        (in 3. already like that – for him)
I'd sooner die than hear it

On entering he faints
                        (at the end???)

[B30]

Ere the wheel turns back

When you read in the records of your annals
About J. Fleischhacker's instructive downfall
Know this: a bit of late rain was the reason
In faraway blood-soaked India, or better
Because his hat was grey instead of black
On a day
Of this bloody month October or because it rained
Cobblestones, unexpectedly water ran from earth
To sky, not in reverse, the more we rushed our meals
The more meat there was on the table, eternal stone
Crumbled ere eternal was over, for on this day
Of this bloody October eternal was shorter
Than usual
Know not too much if this you know

Part Two: *A Family from the Savannah.*
A History in Eleven Tableaux

Peculiarity of money catastrophes [A13 beginning]

The hurricane which the Mitchel family come to face must be as sober and cold as possible. Without romanticism. Blows of fate from rubber truncheons, their downfall plays out through words as flat and worn and unpoetic as coins. Most of all, catastrophes caused by money must not resemble those occasioned by passions of war or love. The way these catastrophes play out is much thinner, drier and without atmosphere. What needs showing is exactly that thin, invisible, destructive power of money, which is so horrifying. Lack of information. Poor suitability. Too little or too much adaptability instead of devastating emotions. Impossibility of communication. Perpetual changeability from several sides, making orientation difficult. The horrendous insecurity of the giant cities. This is the battlefield.

[A2]
1. They are being betrayed and they are betraying others
2. The pigeon above them shows the way, their chance lies below them
3. Calvin puts the light on, he said at 11 o'clock
4. Some families are doing badly here
5. Not a needle gets lost in Chicago. In Chicago no one kicks the bucket. The city feeds its people. Some better, some worse, but everyone gets by
6. One is just like the other, see 2
7. The tramway and the people / ever-changing viewpoints
8. Father's curse and Niobe's pain
9. The Mother: Our children are better children. That's why there's hope
10. It's a real good thing this city, anything rotten just drops off, whatever people might say
11. Always one step after the other

[A3]

Hurricanes

8 Here at least there is no wind
   If only Bess were here

9 Salvation Army. Tinny music. It's snowing. Posters: Oh come to Lord Jesus. What are you waiting for??? Why are you resisting??? Bess is preaching

10 Downfall of the family
   Anybody in charge here???

   Suddenly it all goes quiet

[A1]

1) Francis, the son, goes on ahead to find lodging

2) He earns

3) The family, waiting for him, lose all they have in five minutes. The milkman takes them under his wing

The milkman is a poor devil who takes nothing from them but what he needs for food. He rips them off from top to bottom. In exchange he guides them and sells every piece of advice

Francis, the son, a radiant tough guy, runs like a knife through Frisco, eats his share of meat, ruins his share of women and crash-lands on the electric chair

One daughter leaves at once. The other, of a mysteriously indolent disposition, wants to do nothing and is sold by her family

The boy leaves the last three who have recently been mowing each other down with knives. He leaves in the night from Saturday to Sunday, which preceded the end of the November strike of the power station workers. He wanders all through the icy night and does not turn back in the morning to see how they are, as they'd surely have frozen to death
– I can't look at it, it must be horrible, also it won't do them any good now.

Allan, the boy
I haven't had a meal for seven days
And not a penny in my pocket left
The streets of Frisco are as long as pipes
And like such pennies seem to me the faces
Of all the people hereabouts. Beneath the cars
Is where I'll sleep tonight
In the house of seven floors
There's no room for the likes of us, but the policeman
Has a rubber truncheon which he feeds us

[*BBA* 524/18]

Father	52
Mother	44
Calvin	25
Daughter 1	18
"	17
Boy	12

Calvin Mitchel
The innate passion of these cities
Is enormous. These cities' people remained
Confused about what sprouted helplessly, continued growing
And every day served less and less the growing need
And shrunk to such extent
That it grew feverishly and overnight a heart had
Which beat inhumanly and disavows
And all of its own accord

[B2]

1
A farming family: father, mother, son, two daughters, a boy. With a car and belongings on the street.

John Mitchel, the father
Hello
On account of crop failure, cattle plague in the wheat district
Caused by flood, rain, drought
Three full years and after two failed lawsuits
Against the Northsouthern
We set out fourteen days ago

From Lake Michigan and are coming
Six souls high
With a car and our belongings and seven thousand dollars
Hard cash
To the big cities of the eastern continent
To this here Chicago first
To try our luck

The Family
To bet a penny and cut off
Our pound of flesh
And show them how we make money at home
This Chicago should be on its guard
So people of our ilk won't gut it like a cow
Ere evening falls
And hang out its skin to dry

John Mitchel
The big cities they say are dangerous
But favourable to enterprising people

Family
That's who we are

John Mitchel
Together we are old: a hundred and seventy years
Yet no one older than fifty-two, no one younger than twelve

Family
That's the right age

John Mitchel
I, the father, designed the battle plan
And considered it carefully too

Family
For father sleeps badly

Bagaglia Mitchel
I am the mother

Family
Tent and roof over our heads against rain and hurricanes

Bagaglia Mitchel
I prepare the food

Calvin Mitchel
Enough chatter

John Mitchel
This is Calvin, our first-born son
Never content

Calvin Mitchel
Let's go

Bagaglia Mitchel
Not bad nor unfruitful
But truly restless

John Mitchel
What was it you said once when in Ohio's wheat basket we
Had bread enough and
An abundance of jazz

Calvin Mitchel
For bullfrogs

Bagaglia Mitchel
And yet our clothes were clean

Calvin Mitchel
Clothes are good and yet bad

Kate *and* **Bess Mitchel**
He is always against everything
And he knows nothing else

Calvin Mitchel
Yes I, Calvin, am your blank page
Unwritten

[B2, Notes]

Calvin
Yes, I, Calvin, am your unwritten page
Not fond of a tightly tethered home

Daughter
But one which the wind blows away

[Calvin]
Yes, which it blows away. Don't think much of wheat farming, dislike your motorized ploughs and highly pathetic threshing-machines and all that work

Loathed by Calvin Mitchel
Yes, I loathe it

Mother
You, our smartest son

Father
So you, too, go ahead to the city of Chicago
To set up lodging the way we need it, on Thursday
When the clock strikes eleven, we'll be at the red town hall which that
Man from Chicago, who stayed with us, told us about

Daughter
By that traffic tower with the floodlights

Calvin
Yes, just come and bring everything with you

Mother
Watch out for the flood of people, carriages, horses
With a cool eye, so you won't suffer harm to life and limb

Father
The wind is rising, there will be rain before nightfall, pull the tarpaulin
Over the truck, get down girls, you who are weaker

Boy
I am twelve years old

[B3]

2
Calvin *and a* **Man**

Man Did it not occur to you that November falls rather late in the year

Calvin In Ohio, when we left, it was still summer

Man Have you not heard it's never been as bad as this since time immemorial

Calvin It's always been that way

[B5 beginning]
Kate Mitchel reveals to her parents her base desires

Kate Mitchel
It is not without anguish, not out of recklessness
That I've decided to open my
Mouth and to you
My parents, even after years and years, to renounce
Silence
Know that since we have been thrown into these cities, seduction
Has parched us so, that we now thirst for more than
One man. Don't give me
Bible verse and sponge of vinegar. Time
Has moved on. Another moon in these thin houses
With the noise of crap and copulation
(Even a thin trickle down the waste pipe makes us shudder)
And we stand for nothing
Nor do I find ugly, as drummed into me
Since childhood, what I now do wish for and
I'm dizzied by the scope of my desires
Oh to be soaked right through by a man
Thrown onto the chair, into the body's midst
Drilled to be left lying by one's brother
All used up at once, that
Could perhaps still satisfy us and so
I fear I am running out of time, and so I want to
Make myself up, so that
Someone will take me for sure

[B5 end]
Kate Mitchel announces to her family there is turmoil on the way

Kate Mitchel
I know that here it is the law to smile
Etched into, painted on to us since ancient times
Alas, our buyers prefer us with eyes closed
Though little time remains for us
To see you world. Yet once we are used up
You wish to tease out innocence from each one of your honeycombs
Your own faces'
Smile's already carved into your bones. Your faces
Are like those of animals for fear
Our lips could open, and thus I tell you:
Wait no more. Hope not they will be
Sealed until this year comes to an end
Rather know:
Each night we rub off from our face your smile

[*BBA* 524/81–82]

The daughter
I know that here it is the law to smile
Your faces are like those of animals for fear
The word we know could arise, wait
No longer, do not hope it will remain
Unspoken. Keep on smiling but
Be on your guard.

Let's get
Made up so that someone will take us
No man's
But many men's mouths'

Turning flesh to rotten meat

[B7]
The young man and the young woman have married

The Man
It makes me angry that I wasn't man enough
To take the fruit the way it

Sates me, and that I didn't sense or know that
The wife who sleeps with me is like green wood that does not burn
And lies with open eye in bed while
Before my lid the world is swimming, and asks
In a dry voice about my lust and dries
My sweat off, playing along, evading
And is not hungry, is not full and in the morning lies
With stupid head, utterly astounded
And even more annoying, pities me, and the world
Makes sense to her no more. And so my
Years dry up and my eyes
Are dull by day and no longer do I
Know my enemy, and not knowing my arm's length
I no longer reach the things of this world as others do.

[B6]

Kate Mitchel gives an account of her wedding night

3
My mother says: it's against nature
That to me this lust was nothing more than eating
Not changing me, just in me speaking
So long I didn't have the member of a man
Inside me, then with no aftertaste, not even a bitter one
After such brutish
Cold, detached mating that proves nothing. I
Am ill at ease. This numbness
That I've nothing left but a little wetness in my shirt
Whose source I could no more recall
Proves
I shan't live much longer nor shall my sex

[B4]

1
Calvin
Hey man, it's my sister, I'll calculate the
Share of usage
And pay the price

Man
    I heard that you and your family
Are up to your neck.
Etc.

Calvin
1000 dollars if there is no threat of injury
Other than the loss of quite some virginity

Man
Here's 2000

Calvin
So I'll take out 1000
On my account, Calvin Mitchel
And put it through the books as
An amount to be
Paid or carried over

2

3
Result: devastation!!!

4
Calvin
I'm a little sad
It's the rain that's so up-
Setting me as well as this unnatural
Echoing between the buildings

Man
Of the wind? You call that un-
nat

[B8]

Calvin Mitchel
As if I saw with a fish's eye
Black trees in the asphalt
Casting off what disquiets me
As if aging easily and all too quickly
Seven years were lost to me between a question and its answer

On the electric chair:

Man
Your age, Calvin Mitchel

Calvin Mitchel
When you began the question, forty years
But after the word Mitchel
Already forty-four
Now at least fifty
And still I hope for quiet time ahead
Up to those eighty years I'm destined to

[B9]

Calvin in the electric chair on the entry of humankind into the great cities at the beginning of the third millennium

Calvin
Many say the time is old
Yet I have always thought (known), it is a new time
I'm telling you, it's not from thin air
That for twenty years houses have risen like mountain ranges
Many move to the cities each year as if they were expecting something
And on the laughing continents
Word gets round that the vast ocean that is feared
Is a small water

I will die today, but I do believe
That the great cities are now awaiting the third millennium
It is starting; it can't be stopped. Even today
All it needs is one citizen and one single man
Or one woman will be enough

True, many will die in these upheavals
But what does it matter if someone is crushed by a table
When the cities pull together
This new time may only last four years
It is the highest granted to humankind
On every continent you see people who are alien
The unhappy are no longer tolerated, then
To be human is a great thing
LIFE WILL SEEM TOO SHORT

[B10]

Tonight and tomorrow and
Also in the coming years still
Many will go to waste.
They have to come to terms with it
I am asking them to hurry
You only need to tell them that
It is a new time, now when they
Are gone; that will comfort them
The cities are better than them
That may give them courage

We, scum that we are, will
Cease
I am the first to die

[B14]

Song of a family from the Savannah

1
We had a farm in the Savannah
Horses, a car and fields of wheat
This is bad, said Billy
But in Frisco it will be better
  And we had our bread in the Savannah
  A cool wind and the moon on Saturday night
AND STILL IT WAS BAD FOR US IN THE SAVANNAH

2
We had a house in San Francisco
An engine shop and new clothes
And: this is bad, said Billy
But in Massachusetts it will be better
  And we had our food in San Francisco
  Pretty clothes and jazz on Saturday night
AND STILL IT WAS BAD FOR US IN SAN FRANCISCO

3
We had a tent in Massachusetts
An oilfield and a drilling machine
Yet: this is bad, said Billy
But in Chicago it will be better

>   And we had our roof in Massachusetts
>   A stove and the bible on Saturday night
> AND STILL IT WAS BAD FOR US IN MASSACHUSETTS

4
> We don't have a room in Chicago
> No dollar, no prospect, my God
> This is bad, says Billy now
> But nowhere will it be better
>   And we once had money and prospects
>   Work during the week, free on Saturday night
> AND STILL IT WAS BAD FOR US EVERYWHERE

[B12]

John Mitchel (*to* **William**)   The great flood came after it had not rained for half a year and I think in the beginning it was a little drizzle in the morning. It's raining, people said, at last it's raining. Come out for a stroll. The rain will make you grow. You saw many families pottering about in the rain. But it stopped again quickly. And everywhere people said: there is no more rain. Years ago there were rainy seasons that lasted five weeks. And this is when the Flood came.

When did that start to stop raining so hard?

Yes, the grown-ups say: started slowly, son.

And then it poured down?

No, the entire time throughout the Flood, it never poured. It was only stringy rain, like threads.

How do you actually know this?

Well, you see, this is how John Mitchel imagines the good Lord to be.

Part Three: Pieces combining *Jae Fleischhacker in Chicago* and *A Family from the Savannah*

[A15]

Grey, colourless
Things
Fleischhacker flat as a pebble
At the back photography of Chicago
All dramatic figures recommended for severe judgement
Each word unassailable as a coin
A physical story about money, in between
A sentimental family story from a penny dreadful
Somewhat bulky, the outline not too composed
Spreading good humour
Cheap
With a lot inside, flat
Bible

[A8]

Fleischhacker
John Table
Archie Brown
Jimmie Shaw   leader of the bulls

Beket
Glancer   leader of several banks
L. Mile   Jae's broker
Josua Clerk   leader of the bears

Mitchel
Bagaglia
Calvin
Kate
Benjamin
Milk
3 Frasers

[A9]

I
1 Arrival in Chicago
2 J persuades the four bears
3 Ruin of the family

II
4 Rain
  Glancer

5 Family. Decline and disintegration
  Siege
  Whore's room cancelled

6 Betrayal. An unknown bull causes a stir

III
7 Corner

8 Calvin's strike

9 Calvin's downfall determined by J

IV
10 Calvin's arrest
   Death of the Mitchel family

11 Chicago goes back to work

12 Calvin's death and speech

V
13 Wheat battle

[A10]
1 The Mitchel family on their way to Chicago

2 In Chicago Fleischhacker causes a stir with a speculation on wheat, which pushes the city to the brink of disaster

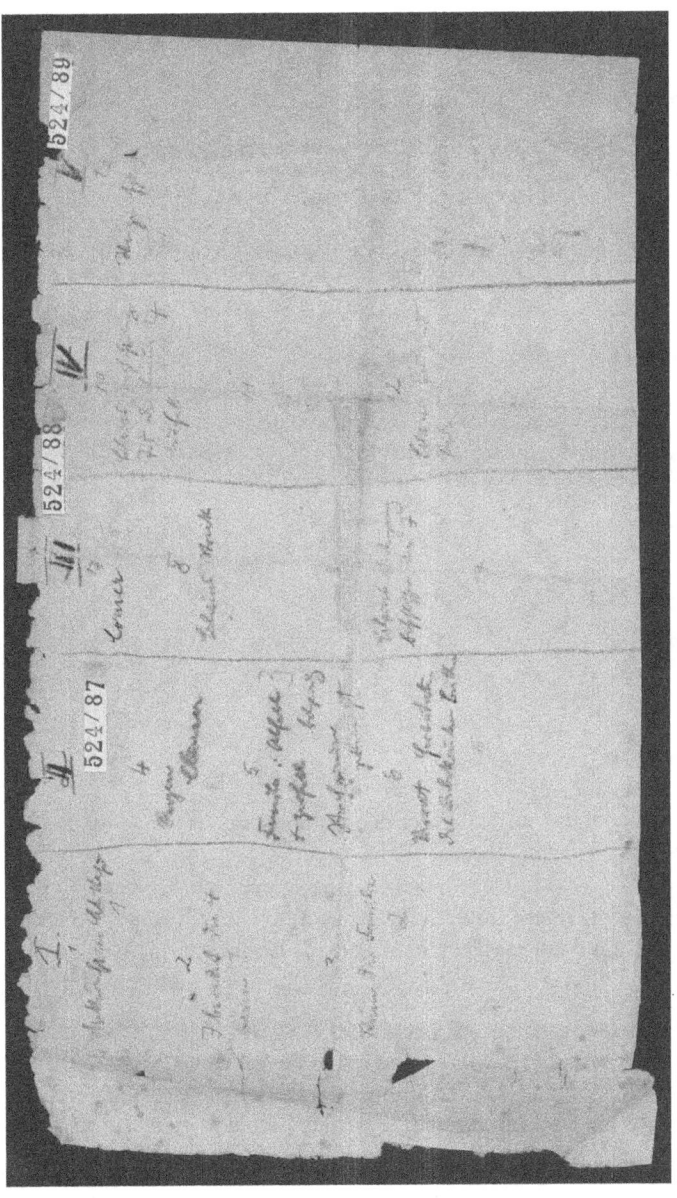

1 Plot-line [A9] written by Elisabeth Hauptmann illustrating the attempt to integrate *Fleischhacker* and *A Family from the Savannah*.

[A12]

1. Entry of the Mitchel family into the great city of Chicago
2. Where J Fleischhacker causes a stir at the market with a group of bulls who buy up the grain
3. Robbing of the Mitchels on the first day
4. Fleischhacker's betrayal helped along by the rain
5. Disintegration of the Mitchel family upon invasion
6. Continuous rain and ignorant fear confuse Fleischhacker. He secretly becomes a bull and gets caught up in a corner
Radio. Strike
7. Death of the Mitchel family
8. Fleischhacker's great corner
9. Calvin Mitchel's speech and death
10. The wheat battle
11. End

[A11]

The Hurricane

They read about the hurricane in Cuba while the floods are going on. They are very frightened.

1. The boarding house. Tables laid. We fear no one will come. We are pleased: a full house. (People take bread and butter away with them. They don't pay. One writes a note saying he owes them something).
2. Flour is getting expensive. People are grumbling in the shops. In the nearby streets, they are thrown out onto the pavement. Buy flour or pay the rent? Flour will be coming / they're no longer baking bread. (Fleischhacker's 3 minutes)
3. The mother comes back: the rooms have been cleared out. They are thrown out onto the street. There's a strike. They take the flour with them in sacks. Then they die.
4. The fight over the best spots in the railway stations.

[B22]

His father makes enquiries at the wheat exchange; he learns how powerful
Jae is; he says: no, this man cannot be our son; seven houses on the
Hudson! Josua Clerk does not raise his hat to our son.

[B24]

Today I went
To the meat grinding district
There was, years ago, a man by the name of
Joe Mitchel
But they said he had sold his meat grinder
And lived on the south side
But once I got to the south side
Where the grain sheds are
The man had left said place.

Alas, more easily than your son in such a city
Will you find a drop of water in the ocean!

[B25]

Through this city rush so many folk
Who resemble your brother in hair and eye

It's only days that separate us
From seeing our son

Why get an apartment if we are meeting
Joe, our son, who has
Many apartments

Fatzer

**Translated and edited by
Tom Kuhn**

Introduction

Four men, in the third year of the First World War, walk away from their tank and desert. But what next? They find their way back to one of their hometowns, a strange and fictitious Mülheim, which Brecht sometimes refers to as 'on-the-Ruhr' and sometimes as on the front – perhaps he was thinking as much of Mulhouse in Alsace (Mülhausen in German) as he was of the real industrial Mülheim in the north. Wherever it is, they now hunker down in a basement room where, before the war, one of them lived with his wife. They are hungry and frustrated, but, in danger from their own authorities now, they hardly dare go out. In this explosive claustrophobia they begin to imagine, and to debate: a future, a new world for themselves, social change for all. Their charismatic, visionary leader seems at times their only chance, but he, it becomes increasingly clear, is a wild egomaniac. The others painfully reconstruct themselves: A complaisant entourage becomes a criminal gang, then a collective very much with a mind of its own – but will they hold together, and will that mind be a revolutionary one, or simply murderous?

In 1926 Brecht was twenty-nine years old, when he conceived of a figure with the name 'Fatzer', and sketched the first scenes of a drama that would become a project which occupied him, on and off, for some four further years. Not uneventful years. This was right after his first formulations of an 'epic theatre', after the productions of *Life Story of the Man Baal* (Berlin), *Man Equals Man* (Düsseldorf), and *Mahagonny* (Baden-Baden) – years punctuated by the beginnings of the great collaborations with Elisabeth Hauptmann, George Grosz, Kurt Weill, and Hanns Eisler – years full of experiment and of concurrent projects, within and against the contemporary theatre, some triumphantly realized, but just as many discarded along the way. *Fatzer* is the greatest of the ruined torsos of the 1920s, with *Fleischhacker*, *Dan Drew*, and others – ultimately all eclipsed by the operas and by the learning plays. Here is a man with a keen sense that the world must surely be on the cusp of change: 'Soon now / A new beast will emerge / Born to unleash humanity'. But who is this Fatzer? What is the 'new'? Will we catch a glimpse of his vision, and then, of what sort of future? German literature after both the First and Second World Wars is studded with the dramas and traumas of returning soldiers, but none so bleak and claustrophobic and brutal as this. As one of the characters says, casting his eye over the soldiers and citizenry of Mülheim, 'The more you look, the less / A human being seems human'. Brecht's *Fatzer* appears like a great work that could have been. And it has attained almost legendary status in Brecht's own oeuvre. Everyone knows it is there, and Brecht himself hinted how important it was for his own development, but few have come to grips with it, fewer still outside the German-speaking world. There have been other versions for the theatre, notably *Fatzer. Ein Fragment* by Brecht's great successor-dramatist, Heiner Müller; and there are several German editions; but the truth is it is still hard to know what to do with this seminal work.

The material constitutes less a 'fragment' or an unfinished play, and more ... an unholy chaos. There are only three or four more or less worked-out scenes, and otherwise over 500 archived sheets – some typed, some scribbled – which we can ascribe, more or less confidently, to the project: Scraps of dialogue, speeches, even isolated lines and phrases, many of them not attributed to any speaker; bits of choruses, bits that look like choruses, or poems, or commentary, or something else entirely; plans, new plans, outlines that contradict other outlines; expressions of dismay at the intractability of the material – and all of this spread over nine separate notebooks and half a dozen other archive folders (with notes on loose sheets or even paper napkins), all the time rubbing shoulders with drafts of poems, and notes towards other plays and plans (*The Threepenny Opera, Fleischhacker*, a play on the life of Rosa Luxemburg, *Keuner* stories, learning play fragments, etc.). There are some passages where the deciphering of Brecht's ugly handwriting is itself disputed. Much of the notebook material is written in pencil, and time has not made it any the clearer.

The editors of the German edition (the *Berliner und Frankfurter Ausgabe*, or *BFA*) divide the work into five 'work phases', but, since these run one into the next, this does not actually tell us very much more than that there are contributions to the project from almost every part of every year from 1926 to early in 1930. A speculative chronology can only be deduced from developments in the elaboration of a plot, or changes in the names of the characters, or, finally, the context of the notebooks in which successive drafts are written. But there are all sorts of overlap, simultaneity, blurred distinctions, and distractions, so that nothing approaching clarity can emerge. *Fatzer* is very seldom mentioned in Brecht's correspondence with others. Nonetheless, even if the *BFA* editors' speculative chronology of the material and their relatively neat phases pretend to a precision which we can never really hope to attain, we can still distinguish tantalizing moments in the process of composition. At one point Brecht cuts out pages from a notebook and glues them onto larger sheets so that he can surround them with additions and annotations (*BBA* 109). Then sometime around 1927 or 1928 the project starts, hesitantly, to migrate from notebooks to typescript. The materials also include a couple of Brecht's own diagrams, and images cut from newspapers which were somehow clearly significant in his conception of the figures and their situation. (We have included a typescript page with a face stuck on it among our illustrations, and the cover image for this volume also comes from the *Fatzer* folders.)

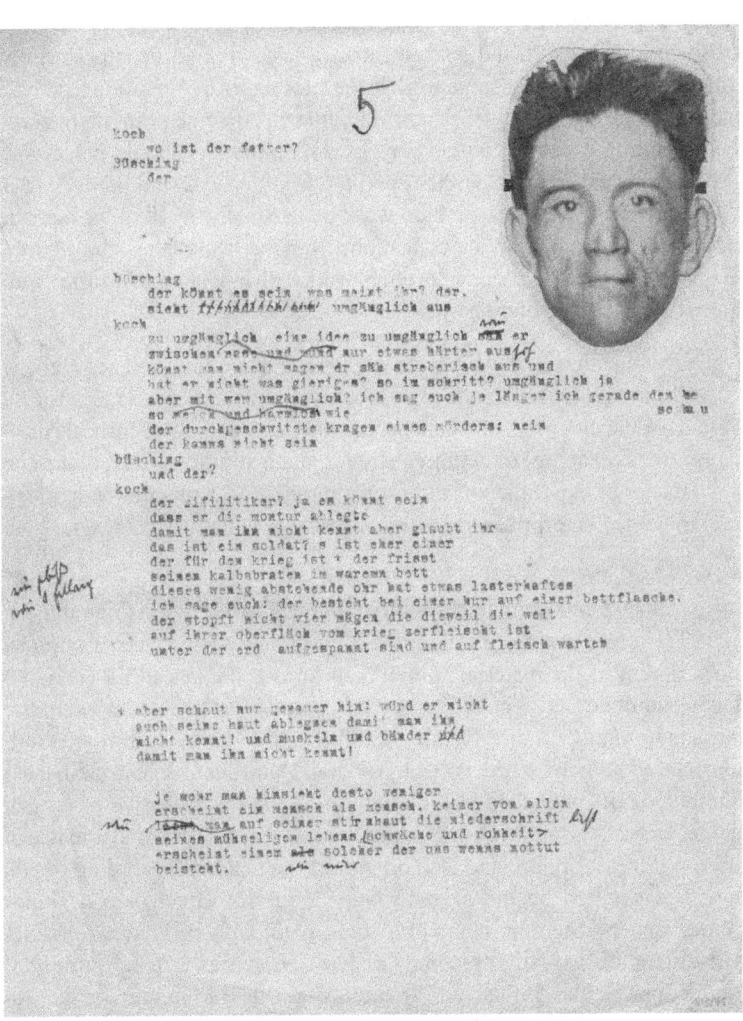

2 A page from Brecht's typescript of a *Fatzer* scene.

Around the turn of 1927–8, Brecht also starts to use the heading 'Fatzer document', implying that he is beginning to think about a further level of commentary which will, eventually, mark *Fatzer* out as an important step on the way to the *Lehrstück* or learning play. Interestingly, and in contrast with several of the other projects in this volume, nearly everything appears to be in Brecht's own hand, and written more or less without the support of his collaborators, except for some work in the later stages by Hermann Borchardt and some corrections by Elisabeth Hauptmann. At some point there comes the despairing cry: 'The whole play, *as it's impossible*, should be smashed to pieces for experiment, without reality! For *"self-understanding"'* (*BBA* 109/56). But he still does not stop work on it. Finally, in 1930, he launches his series of pamphlet-style publications from the 'workshop', the *Versuche* (Experiments), with, alongside other works, two scenes of *Fatzer* and a chorus. In a Preface there he writes:

> The publication of the *Versuche* takes place at a time when certain works are no longer intended so much as individual experiences (or to have the character of 'works'), but instead are directed towards the use (the reshaping) of certain institutes and institutions (having the character of experiments) and for the purpose of explaining individually fragmented enterprises in continual dialogue with their contexts.

As well as the *BFA*, we also have the painstaking work of a succession of other scholars and dramaturgs, although much of it remains unpublished. In 1972 Reiner Steinweg attempted a chronology and made a complete transcription of the material, which then formed the basis of a version by the Schaubühne Berlin in 1976 (the world premiere, presented in exemplary extracts in *Theater heute* 17, no. 4 (1976)). Then, in 1978, Heiner Müller constructed a new stage version for the Deutsches Schauspielhaus in Hamburg (now published by Suhrkamp). In 1984 a collective of scholars at the University of Münster made a renewed attempt and created an improved transcription, and also organized the material according to what they perceived to be the argumentative thrust of Brecht's play. Rainer Lenze, one of their number, prepared an unpublished critical edition, with an eighty-two-page 'reading version'. There was a rush of important productions in the 1980s, in Paris, Vienna, the Berliner Ensemble (the GDR premiere in 1987), Augsburg, Bonn, and Cologne. There is variety in the titles of these versions too. We have gone simply for *Fatzer*, the title under which Brecht himself published those 1930 scenes, as a taster of the work in progress, but he also referred to it as *Downfall of the Egoist Johann Fatzer*, and just as *Johann Fatzer*. Since the 1990s the *Fatzer* texts have become something of a favourite with experimental theatre groups. In

2000 a Viennese 'theatercombinat' produced a thirty-six-hour event which combined bits of *Fatzer* material with texts from Aeschylus' *Agamemnon*.

To make any sort of theatre and, even more so, any sort of drama out of this stuff necessarily entails some violent intervention, speculative organization, even completion of ideas that Brecht may, or may not, have had. It seems clear that, when he started, Brecht had a reasonably conventional play in mind, as conventional at least as his previous experiments in the 'epic theatre' that he was developing. Not a few critics are determined to categorize *Fatzer* as a learning play, but Brecht only began to develop the whole pedagogy-through-practice theory that characterizes the *Lehrstück* at the beginning of 1929, so quite near the end of the period when he was working on *Fatzer*. At this point he undoubtedly started to rethink the material as something from which he, the practitioner-writer, could learn, and then by which other theatre-makers might also learn. It is also very plausible that the experience of labouring on *Fatzer* was one of the elements that fed into and informed the whole experimental theatre-world of the *Lehrstücke*. But it is a very particular choice to approach the project as a whole in this spirit. In contrast, we have tried to rethink it as a sketch which marks out the path, precisely, from an epic drama in the style of, say, *In the Jungle of the Cities*, to a *Lehrstück*. What that means for the reader, or indeed the theatre practitioner, remains a problem to puzzle over. In the person of Fatzer himself we have one of those overbearing solipsists, still somewhat in the mould of Brecht's first dramatic hero, Baal; but this time his life and world and selfhood come to grief in a way that invites us to reflect more critically on social being in the world. The conundrum for any more worked-out 'realization' of the experiment is that Brecht never quite fathomed the origin of this disaster. Is Fatzer a representative of the 'new', or does he founder on some quite different new order? Is it the world, or society, or is it the promise of a communist revolution, sketchily represented by the character of Koch? If Fatzer's energies are misdirected, where is the positive energy; or is there none? The work is not unfinished because Brecht never got around to finishing the 'story', or because he failed to find a motivation for his characters, but rather because he could not complete the argument (he would have said, the *Fabel*). Fatzer comes to a fall in a shocking confrontation of ideologies, interests, and appetites: The old, already under threat from the war, is swept aside but, in the battle between Fatzer's self-interest and Koch's nascent revolutionary socialism, the sides and the advantage are far from clear. Different choices from among the archived materials, different orderings of the scenes, will imply different interpretations. In this sense, what we have is indeed *Fatzer-Material* (quoting an essay by Heiner Müller) and not *Fatzer: A Play*.

Readers should not underestimate the degree of intervention that was necessary in order to create the version that follows. The first editorial principle has been to include as much as possible of the extant dialogue and choruses, insofar as they are not evidently repetitious or successive drafts of the same. Much of the rest of the material consists of outlines, scene, plot, and argument sketches, and a great deal of this becomes effectively redundant when we have a realized script. As for the structure, it is absolutely clear that the play was to begin with the tank scene and to end in bloody disaster, but little else is certain. A recent production at the Deutsches Theater Berlin (*The Downfall of the Egoist Johann Fatzer*, directed by Jürgen Kuttner and Tom Kühnel, premiere 12 November 2016) slapped some scenes together but gave up altogether on organizing them, instead inviting the audience to draw lots to determine the order in which they would be played each evening. Although one can appreciate the reasoning, this is an exaggeration. There is a very clear beginning, over-elaborated and in several iterations, and an ending, roughly curtailed: what looks like a final scene ends simply: 'I am Fatzer! / Etc.'. And although there seems also to be far too much middle for just one play, there are several plans and plot outlines to guide us through the jungle of the drafts. An outline does emerge. Nonetheless, we have taken liberties here too.

For example, we restructured the opening of the play in response to the experience of preparing a production at Oxford's North Wall Theatre in 2016 (under the seasoned direction of Di Trevis and the dramaturgical nous of Thomas Bailey). We broke up Brecht's long opening scenes, consigning some of what may have been his Scene One to a Prologue, along with material for the Chorus. Then we took up the rest of the scene again in Chapter One (where we also included some choice bits from alternative drafts). We also inter-cut the tank scene and the conclusion of the desertion from the front (our Scenes One and Three) with the scenes of the women back home (Two and Four). None of these were Brecht's own strategies. But as he was fond of saying, 'Without the stage, no play can be finished – the proof of the pudding'. The references in square brackets in the right-hand margin give some inkling of how much organization and reorganization has been undertaken. Each number refers to a separate archived sketch; only continuous scenes have a single reference. The A, B, and C references are to the *BFA* edition, where the editors divide the material, sometimes dubiously, into outlines and plans (A), dialogue, speeches, choruses, worked-out scenes (B), and commentary (C). In addition, there are a couple of references to elsewhere in the *BFA* or to the Heiner Müller edition (HM). There is no spoken text in our version which is not by Brecht.

We have also undertaken some rationalization. The names of characters, for instance, are not constant from draft to draft. Fatzer is always Fatzer, but in the last sketches Koch, to pick out a possibly significant example, becomes Keuner. Keuner is also the name given to the lightly and ironically autobiographical 'thinking hero' of a number of prose sketches and stories, which Brecht also started writing around 1929–30, *The Stories of Herr Keuner*. In addition, some speeches have been reattributed, some shortened and lightly reorganized. The division into scenes and chapters is our own, although the structured division into chapters is anticipated in Brecht's notes (he uses the word *Kapitel*). We have taken out the descriptive titles that Brecht gave to only a handful of his scenes, and we have introduced some very light stage directions, and some punctuation (much of Brecht's unpublished drafts are punctuation-free). The selection and positioning of the Choruses is not Brecht's, but he does appear to have had at least three sorts of Chorus in mind: as commentary, speaking to the audience; as an intervening player in the action, speaking to the characters; and as the antiphonal Chorus/Anti-Chorus, presenting an argument. Some sections which exist only in narrative in the drafts are ascribed in our version to a Chorus, whereas it is unclear in fact how far Brecht might have intended to realize these in dialogue.

It may be helpful to run through just a couple more specific examples. The 'pivot', our Chapter Four, is at one and the same time both the obvious crux and, presumably for that very reason, the most chaotic part of the play in the sketches that survive. It is clear that the 'sex scene' (Scene Thirteen) was envisaged throughout as having some narrative element, rather than being fully acted out. Our version realizes a playable script from a couple of prose fragments by ascribing dialogue to Fatzer and Therese, and sketching in the rest with narrative that is here given to the Chorus. But one can equally well imagine versions with even less, or no, spoken dialogue. Then the whole order of the seduction and the 'binding' is unclear; Brecht appears to have contemplated two completely different motivations and sequences. At the end of the scene we have inserted a piece which Brecht calls 'Reading of the Manifesto' (B73), but he gives no detail, and we have chosen a suitable passage from *The Communist Manifesto* (set in square brackets to mark it off as not by Brecht). At other points in the material there are direct and indirect quotations from the writings of Marx, Engels, and Lenin, which Brecht appears to have been reading at the time. What happens to Koch after this scene and at the end of the play is unclear – has he joined the revolution (or launched a failed one-man revolt)? In any case he does not speak or apparently appear at all in the final scene. In short, there have been many editorial decisions, and a director would have to make many more – simply to make sense and give direction to the material. It is, after all, only Chapter Two that was published in Brecht's lifetime – and of course that too is no guarantee that he would not have gone back to it and made major changes.

Finally, the rendering of Brecht's language itself has enjoined some decisions and interventions of the sort that a translator might not normally wish to make. Brecht set some store by what he called the 'Fatzer-line', and later reckoned he should write more like this. However, the verse form is often far from clear. Most of the play is in uneven and disjointed short lines, of lightly rhetorically elevated, free verse. It is a striking form that seems to emphasize the uncomfortable and fragmentary nature not just of the work, but of the characters and their thoughts as well. There are very few rhetorically expansive moments. The form, moreover, while it in some ways allows Brecht to imitate the broken ductus of everyday conversation, also permits him to cast emphasis (at the ends and beginnings of lines) in non-naturalistic ways. The scenes in which the form is most worked out are our Scenes Five, Six, and Eight, in other words the parts of *Fatzer* that were published in Brecht's own lifetime in the *Versuche*. In the UK, actors in training are taught to 'walk the verse' of Shakespeare's iambic pentameters, to find in their gestures as well as in their inflections the rhythm and the poise that go with blank verse; it is perhaps no accident that it is in walking around this Mülheim that Fatzer and Brecht most characteristically achieve the verse form of their new, modernist age: broken, jerky, nervous, and anything but poised. But, as well as this Fatzer-verse, there are also passages of blank verse among the sketches, and moments of other forms. Some of what the standard German edition (*BFA*) represents as verse seems in fact to be an editorially confused imitation of the very short lines of prose enforced by Brecht's narrow notebook paper. The chorus at the end of our Scene One, for example, is, in manuscript, not evidently divided into verse lines, likewise the end of Scene Fourteen. Then Scenes Seven and Eleven are in longer, predominantly trochaic lines, as if Brecht were contemplating a more classical form, but the form is only very fragmentarily and loosely realized. We have decided to approximate the verse form throughout to the style that dominates the rest of the play. To translate a text and create an English verse form, where no one can adequately characterize the original, is a curious enterprise, by turns hobbling and strangely liberating. In general, in this as in other aspects, we have imposed some degree of loose coherence which may be absent from, indeed which may to some degree falsify, Brecht's own fragments.

Fatzer is a hugely significant project, possibly a crucial key to Brecht's development. By the late 1920s Brecht is often taken to be an already well-formed if unorthodox Marxist (he was never a card-carrying communist), but this work reveals all sorts of ideologies in horrible conflict, mortal combat even. It is as if the author of *In the Jungle of the Cities* had taken a hefty dose of politics, but had not yet reached any sort of stable position of his own. Instead of any consistently promoted line, we have a kind of enquiry into human motivation. The starting point is perhaps a conflict of leadership in an extreme situation, but before long all sorts of material, even biological imperatives – hunger, sexual appetite – find themselves contending with both the psychological and the social; the body wrangles with the intellect, the individual with the collective. There is so much in this ambitious project, it can be no surprise that quotations, figures, and motifs all resurface, as they are taken up and developed in Brecht's later work, *The Threepenny Opera*, the *Lehrstücke*, *The Mother*. And the strain of the argument on the dramatic form, alongside the gradually emerging inclination to teach and learn and demonstrate a method (the first steps towards a dialectical method), lead Brecht to a rethinking of structure and form which will prove both revolutionary and extraordinarily productive in the years that follow.

Brecht was aware of the project's potential importance. At one point he writes to Helene Weigel (September/October 1928) that he hopes soon to have ready an *Urfatzer*, and by that choice of title he makes reference to the greatest and altogether most famous work of German literature, *Faust* (also published in fragmentary form as *Urfaust*), which occupied Goethe on and off for sixty years, more or less throughout his writerly life. That was some model to contemplate! Over a decade later, in his journal on 25 February 1939, Brecht is still invoking *Fatzer* as a model, in contrast with what he describes as the 'overly opportunistic' work of *Life of Galileo*. And in the very last phase of his creative life, in the summer of 1951, when he is working on *Garbe/Büsching*, he contemplates reviving the verse form of *Fatzer* and takes *Versuche* 1 on holiday with him to the Baltic (*Journals*, 10 July 1951). What might he have achieved if he had come back to the wreck of *Fatzer* itself? Or perhaps, instead, he was content to register a fragment as the form which could most closely engage with such large and important issues of contemporary history. The rest of the argument was, and is, left to the reader, the theatre, the audience: 'But when all was done, there was / Confusion. And a room / Completely wrecked, and in it / Four dead men and / One name': FATZER.

TOM KUHN

Principal sources

Fatzer occupies pages 387–529, and notes 1114–50 in volume 10 of the *BFA*.

Previous publications

Versuche, Heft 1 (*Versuche 1–3*) (Berlin: Kiepenheuer, 1930).
Bertolt Brecht, *Gesammelte Werke* (Frankfurt am Main: Suhrkamp, 1967), 7.

Bertolt Brecht, *Der Untergang des Egoisten Johann Fatzer*. Bühnenfassung von Heiner Müller (Frankfurt am Main: Suhrkamp, 1994, originally 1978).

Bertolt Brecht, *Untergang des Egoisten Johann Fatzer*. Spielfassung Manfred Karge, Hermann Wündrich (Berliner Ensemble Programmheft Nr.158, 2014, originally 1987).

Other versions and transcriptions are at the Bertolt Brecht-Archiv of the Akademie der Künste, Berlin.

Bertolt Brecht, *Notizbücher*, especially volume 7 (1927–30), edited by Peter Villwock (Berlin: Suhrkamp, 2010); and the electronic edition at: http://www.brecht-notizbuecher.de/.

Documentation of productions at easydb.archive: https://archiv.adk.de/.

Judith Wilke, *Fatzer*, in: *Brecht-Handbuch*, ed. Jan Knopf, 1 (*Stücke*) (Stuttgart, Weimar: Metzler, 2001), 167–77.

Characters

Chorus/Anti-Chorus

The four deserters:
Johann Fatzer, *mechanic*
Karl Büsching, *cold-blooded materialist, passive but treacherous*
                   [*in some drafts called* **Schmitt** *or* **Frühhaupt**]
Koch, *cattle dealer, fair-minded*
                   [*in some drafts called* **Nauke** *or* **Keuner**]
Gottfried Kaumann, *boiler-maker, taciturn, fat-bellied pessimist*
                   [*in some drafts called* **Mellermann** *or* **Leeb**]

Therese Kaumann, *his wife*
                   [*in some drafts called* **Rosa**]
Woman/Girl
Soldiers, butchers, men, women, townsfolk

[C7]
As well as the deeds of man that were,
there are those that could have been.

Prologue

[B63]

Chorus
This you know
In the second decade of this century
There was a war of all the nations
And they dug themselves in.
From one ocean to the next
They scuppered and sank
Their unsinkable ships
And for four years they dwelt under the ground
In concrete holes.
With ten thousand tons of metal they bombarded one another
Ate grass and the flesh of their horses
On tin machines of latest contrivance they flew through the air
Against one another, and rolled in steel wagons
Against one another. Which war endured full four years and
In our own times already
Was condemned a crime.
And it threw up a breed
Scabbed and leprous
That lasted a brief while and
In its descent tore down
The world grown old.

[B30]

Koch
Ach Fatzer, I cannot
Any longer go on with war.

While the instruments of war are paraded on screens, such as warships, aeroplanes, big guns, and so on, the three soldiers bewail their fate.

Koch
Who amongst you will be a friend and dig me
Down into the earth? So that nothing more can
Touch me. Oh, but there's no place I can
Crawl to now they are shelling
Even ten metres under the ground.

Büsching
Everything that is must be
Done away with, where there's a city, it must be
Wiped away and no stone shall stand, and
Where it once was shall be a hole, and
There will be shelling and shooting, even into the sea.

Koch
Let's not be shooting any more. A body can't
Even swim on the surface of the waters
But the swimmer will be strafed by
Their battleships. A man can't
Fly through the air, or else he
Takes death up alongside him. Where can we go to hide?
Everywhere
There is man!

Büsching
Man is the enemy and must be done away with.

Koch
Our refuge is a tank out of which we
Hail bullets, but if it falls in a hole
No one will ask after us, for we are
The lost. We are
The done for. They'll get us before long. Why
Were we born at this hour when
The air is full of metal?

All four
Warships, aeroplanes and cannon
Are ranged against us
Shells and mustard gas
Combine to annihilate us
To exterminate and drive us from the earth's surface
Everything is against us, and conspires and
Never pauses
Our mother is a tank but she
Cannot protect us
We will be
Smashed to pieces.

War conference

[B64]

Chorus
That is the reason why
So that we may withstand this third year of the war
Which persists rather longer than foreseen
We must divide the land anew and distribute
And with new measures, stricter, sterner, stretch
Provisions, so that
They will last, and reduce the ration
To one quarter pound of meat per person per day
And likewise flour, shoes and clothing, so that
We
With every last atom of our strength
Withstand the world's greatest war
Of one nation against thirty
And in the bitter end
Raise up our nation above all nations.

For this reason we must discover
What the attitude of the lowest folk is, the general mass
Towards the war.

Tough and patient still
No man yields in the trenches, but this
Will only last until – one man *does* yield.

Our country, populated only by women
But at its borders ringed by
Men in trenches.
By their number doubling
The mouths to be fed
In the enemy's country.

Cold, and sickness engendered by cold
Hunger, more biting for the cold in
Their sick bodies.

They will last it out.

Chapter One: The repudiation of war

Scene One

[B9]

Night, towards daybreak, in a war-ravaged landscape. Out of a bomb crater a tank emerges. From it a voice.

Voice
Hey, hello!
(*A soldier climbs out.*)
Anybody there?
It's like after the flood.

Voice (*from within*)
What is there out there?

Fatzer
Not a thing, come on out.

Voice (*from within*)
What's he say?

Fatzer
There's nothing here.
(*Three soldiers climb out of the tank.*)
Come on out, there's
No one here.

Kaumann
Not a thing.
Like after the flood.

Koch
No crossfire? No lead in the air? We have taken
A wrong turning. Hallelujah, we've come
To a wrong place.

Büsching
Let's get back in.

Koch
Why?

Büsching
They're sure to start shooting again soon.

Fatzer
Those who were here
Are all done, they won't be shooting
Any time soon. We've arrived too late
For guns. This is a good place
To sit ourselves down.
(*He sits down under a half tree.*)
Look here, I'll cast lots
With this pale and this dark stone
Whether I'll ever get out of this hell
If it's white I'll get out
If black, then never more.
(*He throws.*)

Kaumann
Black.
(*All but* **Fatzer** *laugh loudly.*)

Fatzer
So now I know I am to die soon
I want to know if you lot will live
You throw too.

Büsching
Not I Fatzer, a throw of the dice
Is worse than any machine gunfire.

Fatzer
Cowards.

Kaumann
All right, I'll throw.
(*He throws.*)
Black.
(**Fatzer** *laughs.*)

Kaumann (*to* **Koch**)
What are you waiting for?
(**Koch** *throws.*)

Kaumann
Black.
(*to* **Büsching**)
Don't stare at me with your cold eyes, it may be
You're immortal.

Fatzer
Throw, you dog.

Büsching (*throws, but holds his fist closed for a long time*)
Before
When you threw, Kaumann
I breathed secretly into the hollow of my hand
And smelt my breath, and it
Smelt foul, so
I said to myself: I'm to die soon.
(*He shows the stone to the others, without looking himself.*)

Fatzer (*laughs loudly*)
Black
All black, now we can be
Friends again. Give me
Kaumann, your tobacco. I'll smoke it
Though it's your last, since we're
Friends again, for now
It's decided: we'll soon
Smoke no more nor see
Even half a tree such as this.

[B10]

Büsching
Get back in, and let's drive on!
When the sergeant wakes up from his stupor
And looks out on the world
And doesn't see you! He'll tear you to pieces
He'll truss you
To a stake, Fatzer! Come on in.
(*to* **Kaumann**)
How can you sit there stuffing your face, Kaumann? You pile of dung.
Where there's a tree standing, even half a tree!

Everything must be razed
Till the whole place is an empty wasteland.

Fatzer
If you don't shut your mouth Karl
Then the spot where you're standing now will be
The empty wasteland.

[B30]

Fatzer
And now under this half tree I'll smoke
Our tobacco
I
Won't wage war any longer
It is good that I
Came here, to a
Place in the world where I
Could just think for three minutes
Now
We can walk away.

Büsching
You'll be shot. The sergeant
He'll shoot you.

Fatzer
I don't believe
In Sergeant Schmitt.
(*sings*) [*BFA* 13, 391]
> Jonny Schmitt, what was he thinking?
> As good a man as you are, but
> Now his coffin's nailed shut
> And his flesh has started stinking.

[B9]

I'll wage
No more war. I'm going home
Right now, I shit
On the order of the world. I am
Lost.

Kaumann (*gestures towards the tank*)   [B15]
And what's with this
Tin can here?

Fatzer
That can stay there and rust till
Kingdom come and the
Next shelling, and then tell them all
As they pass by: in me
They emptied their bowels! And
So let it be written.
(*He scrawls on the tank:*)
Scheiße!
And now forwards, march!

Koch   [B10/15]
But where to Fatzer?
To the right it's all red
Behind us it's all in flames
And in front it's silent
And that's the worst.

Fatzer
Left! You arseholes!
And if we meet anyone
We strike him down.

Koch
Left, that's where it's quietest.

Büsching (*gesturing to the tank*)
That was our Mama, that
Iron lady there, and we're
Her whelps.
Born again.

Fatzer
Forwards – march!

[B9]

Büsching
Now the guns are starting up again
And louder.
They go off slowly.

[B20]

Chorus
And so, now that at some
Point on the earth's surface
An idea has bodied forth, even the best men
Desert their stations and there's nothing
Can hold them back. Time shivers
Into the old and the new, they'll do
Nothing old now.
But time keeps rolling on.

Scene Two

[B67]

Frau Kaumann *and two other* **Women**, *at* **Frau Kaumann**'s *home.*

Therese Kaumann (*shouts*)
Where are they?
Three years
Are too many years!
Why won't he come home
And lay himself down on me?
As of today I've had it, I must satisfy
My flesh.
My nakedness
All withered, surely
My days are already numbered!
The cows in the fields and the bitches in the streets
Get satisfaction when it's their time
And I too demand, I
Shall have satisfaction!
Let me not always be grieving
For my womb, which yawns empty
But live, like you do!

The two Women
You can shout as much as you like!
When you're done yelling
It's all
Just the same as it was before.

Therese Kaumann
I ask you
Why did he go?
I need him!
Why doesn't he come back?
Here, where he is so missed!

The Women
Because they took him, he's gone
And because they're holding him
He can't come back.

Therese Kaumann
What is it to me
What they're doing with him.

[B15]

First Woman
Any woman
Needs
More than just gruel and
All that stuff and love
That's just for the la-di-das, but
In the night she needs someone
Everyone says it, even
The doctors!

Therese Kaumann
I've got a man, I've got a man already, it says so on the
Door, with his name.

Second Woman
And that name is on the list
The tally of the missing.
You can't go to bed
With a name

[B67]

First Woman
We can't bring him back for you
But I have a brother
He has no work
And he doesn't have anywhere
To sleep.
Should I send him?

Therese Kaumann
Yes, send him!
He can spend the nights here, since there's
A roof here
I'll give him meals
Whatever he needs
Since there's a plate
And there's a suit of clothes here too!
But tell him
It's not that I need him
And I don't want to need him.
Let him come.
But me, I'm full of work
And at night
Like a stone.
Besides, it's not the
Arms around you.
But to have someone sitting there
In the evening and in the morning
Washing himself next to me, for that
I am grown used to, like you.

Women
So be it.
Have no fear
And be not ashamed
For what is human, that must be allowed.

Both exit.

Scene Three

[B15]

Dawn. **Fatzer** *supporting* **Koch**, *sets him down.* **Koch** *falls over.*

Büsching
His legs are done for.
Get up now, Koch.

Fatzer
Why not leave him
Lying in the mud?

Büsching
Let him have some air, he's
A man, not a dog, stand
Up, Koch, you dog!

Fatzer
Give him the schnapps.

Büsching
That's against the rules, it's
Iron rations.

Fatzer
Give it him!
(*Silence.*)
What day is it today?

Koch
Wednesday.

Fatzer
So, then it's on a Wednesday that
We've had it up to here.

Büsching
For my part, I'd had it on Monday, long since
Enough of all the crap we've had
Round here.

Fatzer
But it wasn't till Wednesday that we
Buggered off, Büsching; on
Wednesday. Now take your
Thick skull in your hands and pay
Attention: on this Wednesday, I
Fatzer, and you Büsching, Koch and
Kaumann, we're going to walk away from this war
That's no longer our concern
Not going back, but
Forwards, so those in the rear
Can see our filthy backsides
Up in front – and there ahead
Is a gap, I can see.

Büsching
You can't get through there!
That's the enemy.

Fatzer
The enemy is up in front and
Back behind us too. That's what this
Wednesday tells me.

[B56]

Two long years lying
In the mud of gun emplacements and trenches, dodging
The shells, always seeking
Cover – and thinking
For two years about my situation and employ, I find myself searching
For a way to show myself where I'm at:
And as of yesterday I keep remembering
A little drawing I
Once saw in a book
I'll sketch you something like it.
That point, that dot is
Fatzer.

Büsching, Koch, Kaumann
We don't want to learn.

Fatzer
Who does?
You don't want to learn, you say, but I say
It's someone else entirely who doesn't want you
To learn.

[B52]

For this war
Is being waged against ourselves, our own hands
Do battle against us, and
The sides
Are all wrong
The wrong armies take up
Battle stations
Friend and foe in the one army
And in the other likewise friend and foe.
And so they fight
All accustomed to following some plan
They can't understand. To be
Selected for any task is satisfaction enough, just as
For a woman, to be fucked; the men who
Work the meat grinders want nothing more
Than just to turn a handle.
And so the serried
Mass of humanity marches out
For the wrong purpose
And so
The new art, the modern delight that is
Synchronicity is horribly abused.

[B57]

That point, that dot is
Fatzer
That's me and here ranged against me
An unending line, those are
Soldiers like me, but they are my enemy
But here all at once
I see another line
That's drawn behind me, and it too
Is against me. What is it? This is
The people who send us out here, that is the
Boer-sh-wazee.

[B53]

This isn't
Our business that's
So bloodily transacted here.
At last after all these years
I recognize the enemy –
See, behind you!

[B43]

Fire and water do battle on the one side
On the other fire and water too
If they would just cast a backward glance from out their
Bloody embrace, they'd see
Each one, standing behind them
The enemy, just as I
After three years of blind raging war
Suddenly looked round and saw
It all. Namely
In front of me, the man I was fighting: my brother
But behind me, and behind him too: our real enemy.

[B55]

Chorus (*rejoices*)
Now they see – or one at least
Sees the truth: and now
The rule of war and of ignorance
Is over and done with.
March on, Fatzer!

[B66]

The Chorus invokes the power of capitalism.

Chorus
Ranged against you:
A thousand ships
Tanks, aeroplanes and
Deadly gas.
Against you:
Books, schools and newspapers
Prisons and cathedrals alike!
So think better of it and knuckle under!

Anti-Chorus
Ranged against us: ships, but
Who steers them?
Tanks and aeroplanes
But who sits inside them?
That precisely is
What we must discover.
If the Fatzers are dead, then
Your ships will sink
Down into the ocean
Your tanks will be scrap metal
And
Your cathedrals will stand empty.

Chapter Two: Homecoming

Scene Four

Frau Kaumann's *flat*.

[B15(2)]

Calls from outside the door.

Therese Kaumann
Who's there, I shan't
Open up!

Kaumann
Open up, it's me!

Therese Kaumann
How did you get here?

[HM 48-9]

Fatzer
The way we always come
Just take it from me: from
The backyard of hell! And
However we come to be together
We're here now, though that was never the plan.

[B15(2)]

Kaumann
These are my friends.

Fatzer
And you'd better treat them well
With a proper meal, and whatever else you've got
Bring it on now!

Kaumann
Yes, what have you got to eat?

Therese Kaumann
Are you on home leave that you
Turn up so suddenly?

Fatzer
You can call it leave.
But ask too much and you'll learn
Too much.

Koch
There's not a lot of room here!

Büsching
If you don't like it, go
One house along. In the barracks
They've been butchering a feast for you
Koch!

Fatzer
You must have a couple of blankets
Everyone's got that.

Büsching
Yes, lay them out on the floor.
That curtain there, there's no
Need of that.

Therese Kaumann
So are you all staying here?

Fatzer
Yes. All of us.

Therese Kaumann
Shall I tell your friends
You're here? They'll
Want to see you!

Fatzer
No, he has no friends
Who want to see him, only us.

Büsching
That's a chair. A man can
Sit on that.
He rocks back and forth.

Therese Kaumann
Here's bread and the soup
From midday. Have some
Potatoes, Gottfried, are
You still so hungry?

They eat.

Fatzer
When I walked through the railway carriage
I saw
How dissatisfied everyone is
I like that.

Koch
Yes, it'll kick off soon.
We only have to wait.

Büsching
And stay firm.

Laughter.

Fatzer
When it kicks off, we have to
Stick together.

Koch
If they take us one by one
We've had it. We
Mustn't go any further, here at
The border
They're the most dissatisfied and
In the factories!

Fatzer
Yes, here. So let's

Resolve
We'll stay together
And you can't go to Passau
Koch.

Büsching
Nor me to Liegnitz.

Therese Kaumann
Tomorrow I'll find you
A place to stay.

Fatzer
No need for that.
There'll be nothing doing yet tomorrow.
We're staying with
You, just swallow that and
Don't try anything on! It won't
Be any use! So what season is it
Now? Spring! It may take
A while yet. But I've got my
Eyes open and I've seen
The dawning of a new era.
With these people
There's something new afoot
You see people walking round such as
You've not seen before, it's
On account of
Everything that's down below
Is rising up
Where once
There was one person and then another one person
Now there's the masses
The masses-man
And everyone and everything clings
Together
And they won't go nicely back into their houses
And they'll have food enough for you
Kaumann, and for you it'll work out
Fine, Koch, you've got this
Passion that it's all got to
Come together.

And it's not
Because there's a god – there is
No god – but
Because mankind is pressing forward to
The great realization:
Eating's what comes first.
But I swear
You'll get your food and
You'll get through
Because right now we stand together
On the threshold of the land
That belongs to us.

Koch
That blanket there
I'll take that.

Therese Kaumann
And where am I supposed to sleep?

Büsching
In your bed where you always do.

Therese Kaumann
With you all lying there?

Kaumann
It's dark at night.

Therese Kaumann
Perhaps I might want to talk to you
It's been three years.

Fatzer
Tomorrow.

Kaumann
And where are we going to get
Food?

Fatzer
Tomorrow.

[B67(4)]

Koch
Of all our enterprises, now there is
Just the one: to live!
An enterprise of the greatest peril, with lousy prospects
If possible at all, only by rapine and desperate deeds
But from this hour on:
Every ounce of fresh meat is a victory
Every hour of the day we will rebuild the roof over our heads
And our only triumph – which we may not live to see:
At the waning of this year still
To be.
And let me tell you why
We should not return, each to our own hometowns:
For then we would disappear
In the crowd, secret loners trying
To shake off our outlaw state
But together
We stand incorruptible
With no name by which
They might know us
Irreconcilable
Four of a kind, thinking our thoughts and
Living
At the concourse of the enemy.
It might even be fine
To buy ourselves a house here
Waiting for the ruin
Of those who live here now
Illegitimately, but not:
For ever.

Fatzer
Of all of us, I am
Mentally and physically the most suited
To make it through alone, but I agree, I am
For sticking together.
Is that your chair? That's big enough
That chest there will do for me to sleep in.

Koch
What's the chest for anyway?

Therese Kaumann
I keep the coal in it.

Büsching
Where's the water?

Fatzer
When I go off in the morning to get you food
I guess you want food
I'd better have a proper suit of clothes like
Anyone else. Have you got a jacket?

Kaumann
It should be in the cupboard.

Therese Kaumann
Here it is.

Fatzer
That'll do. In that I'll look
Like one of them.

Therese Kaumann
Are you
All going to stay?

[B31]

Fatzer
If I am anything and if I am
He whose name is Fatzer
Then I shall raise myself up and rise
Out of this shithole.

[A9]

Chorus
But as for us, we shall
Sit down by the edge of town and
Wait. For there must
Come a good time. Soon now
A new beast will emerge
Born to unleash humanity.

Scene Five

[B84]

Fatzer's walkabout in the city of Mülheim.

Fatzer
Above all to know
At what point on the map we have
Crawled out of the dark and blood-smeared, blasted
Earth's crust
What they've got to eat here
What sort of people, and how many
Are still here.
For here, I feel it
We may stay quite a while.

In front of the town meat marketing board.

Fatzer (*asks a* **Woman**)
What building is this?

Woman
That's the meat market.

Fatzer
So you get meat here then?

Woman
Every man two ounces a day.

Fatzer
They'll have to give me four times that.

Woman
Are you as good as four men?

Fatzer
Why not try me and see.

Woman *goes off laughing.*

A Soldier (*to a* **Butcher**)
The whole train, it's food supplies for the army.

Like I said, there are five steers more than it says on the docket
And that's why I've come to you.

Butcher
OK, tomorrow you can have three of them. The day after
On Friday, we'll slaughter again.

Soldier
We've got to have the other two at the latest
By Friday evening
On Saturday morning we move off.

Butcher
Ah! To the slaughter yourselves!

The people laugh.

Soldier (*moves on*)
Stupid pig!

Fatzer (*trotting after him*)
I'd do well to follow this one!
The bloody smell of five steers
Will lead me on. And as I go
I'll cast an eye around, see how my old friend
The war, is getting along.
What clothes are the people wearing? People are wearing
Shitty clothes, I see that.
Their little bit of sheep's wool and linen they've
Stowed away behind the bayonets, eking it out
Thread by thread. This war is marching
On boots worn thin; he won't last long
Like that. Besides, I think I can tell:
The poor are poorer and the rich richer now, and
In between there's nothing: that's good too.
Children who weigh nothing at birth with
Pale mouths and
Won't put on weight. That's good.
Good too that it'll be winter again one day soon, all of that
Grinds down the war, when the people are cold.
Already they're sitting fifteen
To every little crack in the wall, because

No one's building anymore, and the more have to
Cram in together, the more
Enlightened they become.
And they still trot after their women
Just like in the old days, with such greedy looks
As if they had no other worries, other than how to
Get up a woman's skirts. That's not so good.
They're not quite enfeebled enough
Or worse:
They're growing used to the bloody times.
Everything takes its toll. Yes, even
With busted kneecaps they'll go crawling
After any hairy hole. As long
As they still have that, they'll
Put up with anything. We'll have to
Stop those holes too. The more I see
The more I must
Keep up with my good five steers.

A detachment of young recruits marches past.

Young folk, it shouldn't be.
Can't even feed themselves, and yet already
They're supposed to kill grown men. It all grinds the war down.
They should let them
Grow up first, and then wage war.

The **Soldier** *turns away and walks on.*

Fatzer (*trotting along after him*)
This one's got no opinions of his own
That's bad. That's why the war
Drags on so long when it should be
Long since over. But he'd better
Let me have the meat.
I know these people. This one
Will give up some of his meat.

In front of a baker's shop.

Four Women (*shouting*)
Give us flour!
Hand over the flour!

Fatzer
What are you shouting about?

The Women
We've got a chit
On which it says we'll get flour
But whenever we come to the baker
The door's locked and
There's no flour to be had.
But we know
There's flour behind that door.

Fatzer
So why don't you go and get it?

The Women
The rich get it all!
What's not snaffled by the army gets gobbled up by the rich
But we and our children
We get the bran.

Fatzer
So why don't you beat the door down?
Beat the door down and get yourselves the flour.

The Women
There's another loose tongue
People like you should be shot!
Why isn't he at the front where he ought to be?
It's the English won't let us have our food
And the French who murder our men
Here's one, he's hobnobbing with the enemy!
Look, an agitator!
Now he's running away!

Fatzer (*walking on, to the* **Soldier**)
These people are so stupid! This way the war
Will never end.

The **Soldier** *turns away and walks on.*

Fatzer (*trotting along behind him*)
As long as you've got a few strings of meat

Between your teeth
You won't stop the slaughter.
So we'll wait until the water
Turns foul in your mouths
And this December you'll die like flies
And by January you'll be food for the worms.

Two **Men** *walk by.*

The first Man
You still got wood in your storehouse?

The other
A thousand trunks.

The first
You'd do better not to hand it over, but
Hide it. Then when it gets
Cold we can let it out piece by piece and they'll
Have to pay
Whatever we ask.

The other
Right, and the same way we must
Get our coal out of sight
Bucket by bucket, the war had better
Not end.

Both off.

Fatzer
So there's still coal and still wood. But it's as well that
There are people who keep their pine forests
Stashed away. It all drains the energy out of the war!
These are good folk!
If there were more of their sort
The war would soon be over.
But there aren't so many, and the few
Still have it too good. As long as they can
Chew on boiled grass
And rotten horse flesh
They'll squeeze out a bit more war, without end.

We'd better fight our own
Battles and stock up on food
For some little while to come.
Oh, better watch out! Or he'll get away from me!
Now I see ever more clearly: we have to be
On the scavenge for more than just one day's lunch:
This war will last far longer.

Soldier (*turning round*)
Hey you! Why do you keep following me like a dog?
And why don't you speak when
I ask you a question?
Look, I've got a
Knife for your sort
Waiting for a chance to mug us.

Fatzer (*to himself*)
I'll have to try something different with this one.
If I want to get the meat –
And I need it, for the men I've led here –
Have to think! I promised. I'd better
Throw myself down in front of him and show my hunger.
Ho, Comrade!

He falls.

Soldier
What's up with you?

Fatzer
Give me something to eat!

Soldier
Get up! I've nothing for you!

Fatzer
Give me something to eat!

Soldier
Man, I don't trust you!
He lays himself down
You give him something to drink and
He stabs a knife in your back.

Fatzer
That's the way of the world these days.

Soldier
Don't think I haven't noticed how you've been
Following me. If you're honest
You wouldn't throw yourself down like that. You're
Not weak.

Fatzer
Think what you will, but
If I had something to eat
I wouldn't throw myself down either.

Soldier
What's that to me?

Fatzer
Nothing! I can just lie here and
Die a miserable death, and you say:
What's that to me?

Soldier
And why not?

Fatzer
Indeed, why not?

Soldier
Look, I've got nothing for you.

Fatzer
Right, nothing!
You'd better watch out: there are
Four of us and we have to have something
To eat, and if anyone
Finds us out, then we're already
Done for. But you've got five steers
And it's those I've been after
Running after you, and tomorrow
I'll come with my friends
And bring a cart
When it's dark, and you'll

Hand over some of your meat and
Flour and some dripping from your stores
All that's meant for the army; because
We're from the army too, see. So now help me up.

Soldier
I'm not helping you up. But
How did you get out?

[B15(3)]

Fatzer
Wasn't easy

Soldier
That I believe.

[B84]

If you're really from the army and
You've run off from this wretched war and tomorrow
If you wait at the butcher's with your cart, but
Where there are lots of people, then I'll
See what I can do.

Fatzer
Remember: for four!

Scene Six

[B85]

The street.

Koch
This is the place
He has to come by here
The man who'll help us, the man
Fatzer found
And it's nearly time.

[B15(4)]

Büsching
I wish Fatzer was with us
And not off on his own.

Koch
It's better he's alone. Lest
He gets caught.

[B85]

Büsching
If only Fatzer
Who knows him, gets here on time. He's a
Devil when it comes to timing.

Koch
Fatzer will be here all right.

Kaumann
When they sound the tattoo
His man has to be back in barracks.

Koch
So Fatzer will come
Before they sound the tattoo
And his man must be here already too.

Büsching
Yes, he must be one of these.
But which one?

A soldier walks by.

Kaumann
Him there! Perhaps it's him?

Büsching
Could be him, what do you think? He looks
Easy going enough.

Koch
Too easy going! A mite too affable. If he
Just looked a little tougher, at the upper lip
You couldn't say he looked like a grinder, and
Doesn't he have something grabby about him? The way he walks!
Affable yes – but affable to whom?

I tell you, the longer I look at him
Soft as the sweaty collar of a murderer: no
It can't be him.

A civilian walks by.

Büsching
And him?

Koch
That bullet head? Yes, maybe
He took his kit off so that he
Wouldn't be recognized, but look
Perhaps he's taken his skin off too, so as
Not to be recognized, and muscles and sinews
All not to be recognized?
That slightly sticking out ear has something vicious about it.
Believe me: he's not a one to stuff four bellies
Four bellies that – while the world above is lacerated by war –
Lie pegged out beneath the earth's crust waiting for meat.
No, not him.

Büsching
We'll never find him without Fatzer.

Koch
If Fatzer chose him, the man who's
To help us, then he must look
So that you'd know him, for otherwise
How could Fatzer know him?

The **Soldier** *from the other evening walks past.*

Büsching
Him for example, it can't be him
He looks like a pressure boiler
I wouldn't want to deal with him.

Koch
Yes, that's a
Hard man, you can see that.

Büsching
If Fatzer doesn't come now
It's all for nothing today.

Koch
The more you look, the less
A human being seems human. Not one of those
Who've walked past here looked like someone who would
Help us when we're in need.

They sound the call to quarters.

Büsching
So now we can go back home
He didn't come, I don't get it.

[B15(4)]

Koch
Something must have happened.

Büsching
I don't believe it.

Koch
Then he's a dog who deserves
To be drowned.

[B85]

Fatzer *walks up slowly.*

Fatzer
You there?

Büsching
Where were you?

Fatzer
I was detained.

Koch
Why, Fatzer, didn't you
Come? Like we agreed?

Fatzer
I had a little quarrel with a couple of butchers
They thought they could
Take me for dumb.

Büsching
So then it's all over with food
For the next few weeks?

Fatzer
Tomorrow's another day. Perhaps
You'll strike a different tone tomorrow
When you talk to me
When you need me.

Koch
We don't need a different tone, but you
You need to be there when you're needed.

Fatzer
So. I need to be there, do I?

Büsching
And how about tomorrow? Will you be there?

Fatzer
Yes.

Koch
And there'll be nothing detains you?

Fatzer
No.

Koch
Then, till tomorrow.

Scene Seven

[B74]

Back at the flat.
Bells proclaim a German victory.

Fatzer
Go on, crash the bells over our heads till they
Fall down! Starve yourselves
On to another victory! Hurl your hordes
Into the twentieth successive land and
Gnaw it to the bone!

Büsching
Oh, shut up!
What use would their defeat be to us?
Unless we survive it?
And will we survive? They sling us
Like hand grenades
At their enemies
Gripping us by the throat 'til the pin is pulled.

Fatzer
You won't survive. I see it in your eyes.
Look at those hollows
At your temples, I've often seen those
In people when they've croaked.

Büsching
You shut your mouth!
There's nothing at my temples. Ten years
Even if they win, I'll sit and laugh at the dead.

Fatzer
Laugh! Go on and laugh! You're dead and buried already.
Phew! You're getting smelly.

Büsching (*getting up*)
I'll tear his face off!

Koch
Sit down, Büsching!
He just wants someone for a punch-bag. Friends
Let's look
Our new defeat
Rationally, in the eye!

Büsching
Rationally?

You and your 'rationally'!
I piss on your 'rationally'! I won't
Be reasonable any more. It helps us not a jot.
I might as well
Chew on the wood of this stool.

Fatzer
Go on, Büsching, eat the chair! Just for me
Go on, get nibbling!
You're right. Koch can
Watch you while you eat! That'll be good for him!

He hurls a chair at **Büsching**.

Büsching
You bastards. You're the ones I blame! You
Are my enemies, and no one else. You'll
Kill me yet!

Koch
Büsching, Büsching, calm yourself!
I am not a
Stranger to these doubts either. The world's
In disarray, so out of joint, and nothing
Comes as we expect, so that
To be reasonable
Can be unreasonable
Or seem as much. You're a builder
You know what an angle is
But an angle's nothing
If the wall's not straight. These bells confuse us
Bringing us to thoughts that have
No purchase. In the presence of
Such great unreason it's hard
To think straight. Best
We don't think now, instead
We'll sit and mend our clothes. Agreed.

[B72]

Chorus
Stay rooted to the place
Of your defeat

Wait for
The last blows
Collect them carefully that they're not lost! On
The site of your collapse
Build your house
Sleep
Eat and test out
The hours in humbled abasement.
Don't change out of your bloodied garment
Speak with enfeebled voice
To the bystanders, ask
Calmly for water in the face of their laughter.
Stay at the place
Of your defeat, but
Flee swiftly (don't pause to pick up your hat!)
From the site of your triumph.

Scene Eight

[B85/2]

The street.

Koch (*to* **Fatzer**)
We have to have that meat
Don't start any quarrels today.
We can't stand by you.
As you've said yourself
No one must know us.
But we can't afford any more mistakes
Such a gift of meat
No one will offer us that a second time.

Two **Butchers** *approach.*

Fatzer
Here come those guys who insulted me yesterday
We have to
Show them they can't mess with us.

Büsching
Stay right here Fatzer, we have to
Have the meat.

Fatzer
I don't care about that. I have to
Have words with these men.

*Fatzer sets on one of the **Butchers**. Upon which other **Butchers** rush out of the shop and surround him.*

The Butchers
It's him, the one from yesterday whose
Skull we cracked! He's looking for
More of the same today.

Fatzer
Yesterday I was only one. But today
We're more. Hey Büsching!

A Butcher
Give him one in the mush!
Who is he anyway?

*They beat **Fatzer** to the ground.*

Koch
Stay where you are! Don't give
Anything away, act like
We don't know him.

A Butcher (*to the three*)
Hey you there!
Are you something to do with this one here?

Koch
No!

A Butcher
You were standing right next to him
You must know him.

Koch
No, we don't know him.

The Butchers (*going back into the shop*)
The better for you!

Büsching
Now we have to go and help him up.

Koch
Stop! We came here to get
Meat.

Kaumann
But for that we need Fatzer.

Koch
He'll have to get up on his own.

Fatzer *gets up covered in blood and staggers off.*

Koch
Fatzer!
Over here Fatzer!

Kaumann (*calls after* **Fatzer**)
Come over here!

Fatzer *goes off, as if he couldn't hear.*

Kaumann
Where's he off to, he's
Taken quite a beating.

Koch
When he comes back round
He'll be all right; we are
Still here and we need
Meat.

Büsching
The call will come any time now
Perhaps
We should have helped him; he's the only one who
Can get us through this.

When he was stretched out on the ground
I saw him look over.

The call to quarters sounds.

Koch
Time to go.
Let's not talk any more.
We'll sleep on it, but
Let me tell you: it's
Not good what I see coming.

The three exit.

[B59]

Chorus
You, Koch, plug your ears against
The din of the big guns and take no notice
Of the shells that whistle round you, but rather
Under the changing moons on your
Perilous route away from war, recognize
The error you have committed.
Step up once more
To that tank wall and improve
The sketch of your situation.
Draw through the dot Fatzer a long line
As long as the line of the enemy, for
Fatzer is not one, but
One of many. All obedient.
In the same way, and
Behind the line of the enemy runs a
Second line, the same length and disposition
Of that line that represents your bourgeoisie
For those who are drawn up opposite you also have behind them
Their own enemy, their own bourgeoisie. And then
Draw an arrow aimed against
Your enemy, exactly
The same as the arrow that is aimed at you.
This now
Is your true situation.
Now you
See what is to be done for you and for all soldiers

Who obey orders, whether for or
Against you.

[B59n]

The two long lines are
Soldiers and obedient subjects and
They all belong together, so join them
Top and bottom and
Write a 'P' in the middle of the square, for
'The Proletariat of all nations'.

[B59]

Turn around, and
Turn the war of the nations
Into the war of the classes and
Turn the World War into
Civil War – hold firm and carry
The war back into your own country, for until
You have driven out your bourgeoisie there
Will be no end to war.

Koch
So we should have
Stayed there at the front?

Chorus
Exactly. But because
You walked away from the mass
In grievous error, your
Ruin is now certain.

Chorus *advises the spectators not to take any further interest in the fates of the four.*

Chorus
Because these four
Have set themselves
Apart and defined themselves
Under a new and beastly sign and
Under constellations previously unknown to man
And have separated themselves
From us wantonly or unknowing, soon

Strange things will befall them, opaque events that
Whether good or bad, never
Before befell us and never will again. So
Shut your ears to them, for you will hear
Nothing human. Cut off
From a natural existence, they will wither and die without
Uttering anything worth hearing. What the sinking man says
Is worthless. What do we care for the deeds
Of he who is without hope? He is unlike
Any other human being.
What does it help to know
Who tears the flesh from whom, if both are
Certain of death?
The rambling of the unfortunate is worthless
Their lives are already concluded, and what they still
Have to say is of
No further interest.

[B60]

Anti-Chorus *points out that many still have an interest in the fate of the four.*

Anti-Chorus
The miserable of today
May be fortunate tomorrow, what does it matter if they
Are mortal still today?
We propose you watch
These four closely, for you will see
How, as they fall, they act as if
They were rising. No one makes such provision
Dying, if they are without heirs
No one examines so closely every stone
Of a building in which they can never live
Granted they
Do not walk away because some business calls them, rather
They walk into the void. What they do not do
That is their enemies undoing
And their real future will only unfold
After them. Listen
For what they have to say
Is much more important for *you*
Than it is for themselves.

Chapter Three: Mutual mistrust

Scene Nine

[B22]

Fatzer (*watches the others*)
I am stupefied by this 'tomorrow' and
Hobbled by a 'today' so non-committal! Squatting here
Between a 'not yet' and an 'already no more'
I no longer believe what I think!
It's a mistake, surely, tomorrow is already
An error! So why
Speak at all of today? What
Is the use of building a boat when the
River has run dry? When I watch you
At your food, I see others behind you digesting
Others quite unlike yourselves; but I don't see myself.
I can't make out your voices
Above the noisy tread of many
Footsteps, the footsteps of strangers. And
From out of so many round mouths tumble
Big square words; but where are they come from?
I am a forerunner, perhaps
But what
Runs after?

[B24]

Fatzer *hears the other three talking about him and behind them he sees a great crowd speaking.*

Büsching
Fatzer, he's our
Best man. What he says
He sticks to.

Kaumann
He's clever, he'll find
Something to eat all right, from out of
Some sewer
He'll conjure a cow!

Koch
Without Fatzer
We wouldn't be here at all. He found a
Way through the barbed wire and even
Through the people! He will
Help us through!

Therese Kaumann
I wouldn't trust him! He seems
Different to me. You lot may be just dim, but he
Is egomaniac, I know him! He'll
Betray you yet!

All three laugh.

Kaumann
The very idea that he'd betray us
Laughable!

Koch
That he's an egoist, that's surely
A good thing! He has a huge ego, enough
For all four of us, and for all four
He is selfish! He'll
Help us!

[B47]

Kaumann
That's what's so good about Fatzer, he
Has so much appetite that it'll
Be enough for us too. And he's such an egoist
That too will be sufficient for us all.

[B24]

Fatzer
Now they are talking
About me again and I
Listening to them, will rise up and become
The man they need.
Or maybe not!

Fatzer *joins them.*

Koch
Fatzer, that time you
Didn't come, when we were
To get our meal. Why not?

Fatzer
Yes, why not?
Think, Koch!
(*To himself.*) [B25]
When you speak, behind you
There are always others speaking!
And that's why your wide-mouthed chatter is
Important.
Behind you there are many others on the march
They tread in the same steps, and that is why
Your flat-footed walk is of any
Importance, don't you see.
Think: why [B24]
Didn't Fatzer come?

Koch
We don't know, Fatzer.

Fatzer
Hah, that's a shame!
The day before
I was there all right, you remember, I
Lay out
On the ground in front of you, had my
Eyes shut, and
Waited.

Kaumann
He thinks we
Should have helped him, I
Wanted to, I said straight out, Koch
Let's help him!

Koch
Is that what you mean?

Fatzer
Think about it!

Koch
I don't get you.
There we were, about
To get the meat. We had agreed:
We mustn't be recognized. If
Anyone is recognized then
The others must behave as if
We don't know him, so
We're not *all* done for! Then you started
A fight, although we
Had agreed to keep out of
Trouble. We
Saw you fall and wanted
To run and help, but I thought
Of what we had decided, and
Kept back, out of prudence! Was that
Not prudent?

Fatzer
Very prudent, maybe just
A touch too prudent?
Standing there, muscles clenched? [B33]
Things can't go wrong for folk like you
Prudence such as yours never needs a helping hand.
At most you might say, you're lacking
(Only a little, mind)
In impulsive affection
Foolish rage.
Perhaps, with more *lack* of self-control, you might have
Blundered in and
Perhaps you might have won through
Perhaps even with the help of your own
Dear Fatzer, touched by so much affection.
But maybe that is something you can still make up
Even if a shadow of a doubt
Will linger. With you, you have to rub your
Noses in what it is that should come naturally.
In a nutshell: Let me invite you, in future
To take your part in my disputes.
More brutish unreason please!

[B24]

Koch
And what's to
Happen now?

Fatzer
You really want to know? Well now
I challenge you: take up
This quarrel of mine
And come this same evening
At the same hour to the
Same place where I fell short. So
We
Can look each other in the eye again, and
So I can lay out those in turn who
Laid me out!

Koch
You surprise me. Frankly
We thought: you were going to tell us
How
We get the meat.
I thought: we wanted meat
And not a fight.

Fatzer
Frankly: I thought, we
Wanted a fight.

Koch
That's strange. But if you
Insist then we'd better
Take a vote. So:
Do you
Want to get involved
In our comrade's quarrel, in which case
You must ask yourselves, whether that's prudent, since
We dare not be recognized.

Fatzer
Or do you want to lay down fat for the winter?
Maybe I can remind you
Things don't always go to plan

In this world. Whatever may be
Prudent, we need what's human
Too: to eat is good
The question is: what sort of a man
Is doing the eating?

Koch
So do you want
Your meat or to fight?

Kaumann
Meat.

Büsching
Meat first.

Koch
So it's meat. Fatzer, we've
Cast our votes, and
Your quarrel is aborted.

[B77]

Fatzer
I refuse your mechanical ways
A human being is no machine.
Besides, I have a strong aversion to doing
Of all things, only those that are useful. Instead I'll
Shit on your good meat and spit
In the sweet water.
You go calculating to the fraction
What's left for me to do, and put it in the reckoning.
But no, I shan't do it! Keep on reckoning!
Calculate my ruin
Lay another five for the unexpected
Take of all there is about me
Only what is useful to you.
Everything that still lives on is: Fatzer.

[B15(8)]

Koch
You can rant and rage
While the world slides out of joint

And I
Sit here jealous of every bite
You get to eat! You
Should be shot in the
Night like a dog
Who knows no difference.

[B76]

Fatzer
Look at these poor souls, dug in
Hardly moving
Indistinguishable from the dirt
This walking slime, at
Every step the lime
Trickles from their eye sockets!

Exit.

[B26]

Büsching (*suddenly*)
I tell you, Koch, it doesn't look
Good for us, you, me and
Anyone, we can all be bought
For meat, which may not make us
Entirely despicable, but if this
Fatzer betrays us, then he'll have to
Go.

[A1/HM61]

Koch
The battlefield couldn't
Kill us, but
Here in the still air of a quiet room
We set about killing one another.

[B77]

Chorus
This is all the business of time.
He who dams the river will see, should he live long
How the dam crumbles or how

The river runs dry.
Be of good cheer, this stuff will stretch
Just rearrange it, there will be enough
Carry water into the desert and it will
Still be sand. Fear not:
The end is unreachable!

Scene Ten

[B6]

Fatzer (*brings a newspaper*)
Here's a picture
Of our city, New York
The one we built
Over the water, the
Atlantic Ocean, a new
City with the name New York.
Houses soar like a mountain range of steel and ore
And the golden light of electricity
Lights it up through the night.
All this was the work
Of our own kind, or of beings
Not unlike us.

[B15(6)]

Koch
But what was the use? Now
We scuttle round like rats in this
Hole, with nothing to eat.
They'll find us, they'll
Flush us out. We can't
Hold out against them all.

Büsching
Not like this.

Kaumann (*bringing a package*)
I've got some beets.

Büsching
Cook them! Where's that woman?

Koch
Get to work. Cook them yourself!

Büsching
Give here!

Kaumann
I'll just see if they're fresh!
(*He bites into one.*)

Büsching
Hey, two of them are nibbled.
Did you do that?

Kaumann
They were like that already.

Büsching
Like hell they were. You've
Been eating them.

Kaumann
Hey, it was me that found them in the first place!

Koch
What's that supposed to mean, you
Weren't supposed to eat them! Spit it out, what you've
Got in your mouth!

Kaumann
Fetch it yourself!

Büsching (*forces his head back*)
Spit it out!

Koch
This is a matter of principle!

Kaumann (*spits in* **Büsching**'s *face*)
There you are!

Fatzer (*starting to eat*)
You're one as good as the other!

Koch
You've got to cook it first!

Büsching
Here, have some! I'm not
Waiting!

Koch
You'll fart all over the shop!

Fatzer
And that's not allowed. It's a matter
Of 'principle'!

They eat.

Koch
It's so quiet, wherever we
Go! No sign
Nothing! And we're running on
Empty!

They eat.

[B47]

Fatzer (*eating*)
I don't really need food. I can hold out
Two days longer than the next man
But if you
Are slaves to this animal compulsion
And your bellies have no brains
Then you just have to do what I don't have to do
And it's all in my head that makes that possible.

[B15(6)n]

Büsching (*laughs*)
This is the new age.
I've seen a lot in battle
Men with red faces and so many
Crawling, men like beetles, but
A great man
I've not seen one of those.

[HM64]

Fatzer
I am your great man.

Enter **Frau Kaumann**.

[B15(6)]

Therese Kaumann
You all eating? Don't you want
A spoon, or
Two spoons? Are you
Happy now,
(*to* **Kaumann**)
Don't you need anything else?
But if
You won't speak, then I shall
Speak out, and if I can't ever get you
On your own, I'll say it in front of
This lot, while they stuff themselves.
(*To* **Fatzer**.)
But it's you I hate
Most, because you could
Be out looking for proper food.
So let me ask you this: if you don't intend
To get out and get a bit of air
Sometime, or just get out
To the outhouse, so I can see my old man
Alone, I'll say it in front of all of you:
I want him to take me again
Between the legs, it'll only take
Minutes, you'll excuse us that long
It's my simple right.

Kaumann
You shut your mouth! Have you
No shame?

Therese Kaumann
That's what I need, shame, to blush again. When
I take your food from you
You get angry. But
What else am I to do?

Koch (*to* **Büsching** *and* **Fatzer**)
Get up, take your
Plates and eat outside.

Kaumann
No, you can stay here
So long as I've only got grass and roots to eat, believe me
I have no thought
Of a woman!
That's that.

Exit **Frau Kaumann**.
Exit **Fatzer**.

Koch (*suddenly*)
There's one amongst us
Eats, and does nothing.
We can't know him for sure yet.
But the time is coming when
We shall have to know everyone.
Because no one can know
Whether tomorrow we'll still be of
This world! We
Have to test him.
So let me ask you this: are you
Ready to risk what
We have, so we can see
What's what with this man?

Büsching
You're like a bull
At a gate, no thought.
But a man is not like a
Flint and can never soften.
Be warned Koch!

Koch
But you're one who just
Let's himself be abused and
Puts up with anything! Don't
Do that with me, you
Talk but it doesn't mean a thing.

The truth is, I haven't
Slept since our comrade
Didn't show. He
Said: I'll be there. That
May yet cost him his neck.

Büsching
When you were in a fever
He didn't say a word and just
Carried you along in the platoon.

Koch
But why?

Büsching
Perhaps he just does what
He wants.

Koch
Then we must
Scratch him out.

Büsching
You're too hasty
Koch!

Koch
And because I know that
I'm also the slowest.
That's why I think we should test him and give him
The chance to prove himself. Let's
Give him our papers
And what money we still
Have, then he'll see
That we trust him
And he won't disappoint that.

Büsching
I don't see that
That won't mean anything to him.

Koch
You don't know a thing about him
But I think I know what makes him tick.

Büsching
If he's a traitor
He'll have to be executed.

Koch
Give me your things!

They get out their neck pouches.

Koch
Fatzer!

Enter **Fatzer**.
Where've you been!

Fatzer
Outside.

Frau Kaumann *enters behind him.*

Koch
We can't know what
Will become of us, and we've got
Nothing more to eat. So
We've emptied out
Our pouches and
Ask you to look after it all, one
Is safer than four
And you were always the
Surest.

Fatzer
Koch, you're
A sly dog, I
Know you.

Koch
Won't you take it?

Fatzer
Think it over yourself, I'll
Give you a minute.

Büsching
What does that mean Fatzer?

Koch
Take what we give you.
We trust you.

Fatzer (*takes it*)
OK. Give it here, whatever you have.

Laughs and leaves.

Scene Eleven

[B68]

Fatzer *takes the walk that endangers his comrades.*

Fatzer
Fresh air and the street belong to all and in equal measure.
To walk unhindered in the stream of traffic
And hear human voices, see faces
That must be granted me.
My life may be cut short, and soon, and I shall no longer walk
Amongst those who roam these streets. Even in the thick of the struggle
I must breathe, eat and drink. Perhaps this battle will last for ever
Longer than my life, and then, when I am killed
I shan't even have lived. And my body will shrivel up
In hiding in some lair, but why should I hide away
A man already so sadly diminished. No, I must walk
As I will and wherever takes my fancy.

[B69]

In a land where there is no honour
Every man is in dishonour. Do you mean
Stuck in the mud up to your neck
While dirt trickles in your eyes from above
Do you really mean to complain when one solitary passer-by fails

To doff his hat? You've been unwanted since you were in your
   mother's womb
Antagonized by your father while still a foetus
But sheltered at the cost of the state from
Your butchers
We'll have nothing to do with those people, other than
Throat cutting.

[B68]

The three others (*following behind him*)
Not a step further, Fatzer, you're not only walking
For yourself. You consume our air too
And cut short the years that are given us.

[B70]

The three (*as they gag* **Fatzer** *and tie him up and drag him away*)
So you can't just wander around like some anybody
We'll bind you fast. For your wandering, Fatzer
Is our ruination. You must wear a rope
Around your chest, to make you clever.
It's not a punishment, but rather: your only
Deliverance.

Chapter Four: The pivot

Scene Twelve

[B41]

Koch
As of yesterday I've been thinking: strange
How all that seems so lasting changes
And all that we were taught was fleeting
Remains unchanged.
I always used to think, the earth
Might split open at any time, and we saw
Fires blazing in the skies, but
We hoped to see the people that we knew unchanged
Familiar. Now their flesh and bone's all twisted.
The great Fatzer, who carried Koch out of the flames
In the bright light of day, lost his reason and became like a
Child, careless as a pebble in a brook, and weak
Whimpering Koch held out
A stick for him, like to a dog
But he can't jump over it now, and he
Has him recite the catechism, the iron law which
Addles his poor wits. And so
He, who at another time
Might have been no worse
Than many another
Is held, poised over an abyss.

[A9]

Chorus
This is the fearful pivot of the play.
While hunger falls upon them like a beast
The roof falls in over their heads
Their best comrade abandons them and
Sexual jealousy sows dissent.

Scene Thirteen

[B48]

Fatzer
To them I'm like a foot

That has died off and hangs on a gammy tendon
And which they drag along behind them, half-heartedly
Only not cutting it loose
For fear of losing more blood
This part of them is without feeling
You can step on it and they don't
Cry out, and although they need me
No one gives me their hand. They look on me
As a sickness.
In times gone by ghosts came from the past
So now they come from the future, and they're just like they used to be
Wailing, conjuring and unclutchable
Made only of the stuff of your fancies
And of your fears before all else.

[B25/*Fleischhacker* B9]

Most people say our time is old
But I have always thought we live in a new age.
Believe me, it's not of their own accord
That twenty years and more, houses have been springing up like
    mountain ranges
Thousands move every year to the cities, in fevered expectation
And on the laughing continents
The word spreads: the ocean they always feared
Is just a puddle.
The great cities lie in waiting for the third millennium
It's on its way. It won't be held back.
Many will die, for sure, in the upheavals to come
But what of it, if one man is crushed
When the cities clash together.
This new age of ours will last perhaps just four years
That is the most that will be given to humanity.

[A25/B49]

Chorus
And he lay there three days and nights. And the woman carried his food to him, and he asked her:

Fatzer
How do you live?

Chorus
And she said:

Therese Kaumann
I live miserably; for
You sit around day and night, so I cannot lie
With my husband.
Since he came back he has not touched me.

Chorus
He cajoled her and kindled her desire and told her, she might well blame the circumstances, and that Kaumann was weakened by hunger.

Fatzer
The circumstances, however, are not of your making.

Chorus
And he asked her:

Fatzer
Do you not, as you lie with yourself
Do it with everyone you think of
With strangers who happen to pass and wear their hats at a certain angle
With Koch no question
With me
Even with dogs?

Therese Kaumann
No! That is not true!

Fatzer
Do you believe in God? Or fear Him at least?

Therese Kaumann
Not anymore.

Fatzer
Why then do you fear that
Someone, without taking the time to take off his trousers
Might throw himself on you
Knowing that you are wet?

Therese Kaumann
Because it means such a lot.

Fatzer
It doesn't mean so much.
Or do you believe that two souls on an island
One of each sex, but
Without affection for one another
(Or no more than between you and me)
But without hatred either (also like us)
Or perhaps even *with* a bit of hatred,
Could live together for years, or days even, or even just a night
Together in a hut (like us)
Or even a day's journey apart, without
Lying down together?

Therese Kaumann
Yes, certainly.

Fatzer
That's good. In nature
This business is pure compulsion. But
Human intellect, discipline and so forth, may
Hold us back, as
In our case, for example, if
The woman has a husband then it's
Impossible.

Therese Kaumann
Of course.

Fatzer
Even if he wasn't around, although, no
It wouldn't be possible, even if
He was there and couldn't do it. Because
That can happen.
(*She laughs.*)
Of course an embrace such as that
Opportunistic, bodily urge, lust …
To stick your finger in a certain person's
Armpit
Wouldn't mean much; simply just
That the finger
Would be in the armpit.
(*She laughs again.*)

I see, you're fretting. Thinking first:
Because your man doesn't look at you any more, then thinking
Perhaps there's another reason, perhaps
Because he works too hard, then
That you look a bit grey in the mouth, a bit
Older than your years, not much ...
It needn't mean anything ...
I see too you're struggling
Against your nature, and that is
Praiseworthy. It's shameful
More than anything else
For a woman to need it, to melt
Just because someone takes a hold of her
In a certain way, or
To want to do it.
I see, you're cleverer
You know your husband is weakened
By hunger, and only because of that
Comes to you less often
Which is better than not at all ...
It's not so important ...
In nature it's an urgent business. And
Men and women, when they don't
Make love, for some reason, do something else of
Which we don't often speak, but
That's stupid because it's natural. I'll say
Frankly: I do it sometimes, I know, and you do too, it's
Natural and soon over, trivial
Almost, and often it feels like
If you're not sleeping with anyone, then
In your mind you do it
With everyone ...

[A25]

Chorus
And he called on her with wheedling words, that she untie him, and she did so.

She unties him.

[B34]

Chorus
And he took her breast under her blouse, and it was sweet
His rough hand coaxed it, took care that her breast
Stood firm and hardened under his touch, and he carefully
Took a hold of her rump and weighed it
Joyfully, and noticed how her
Thighs that were tight pressed together, opened and
Her hand drew him to her, and the ancient game
Was renewed and with it
That well-loved motion.

[A25]

Chorus
And he got her with child.
And she ran to her husband and thought how she might evict those from her house who were such a burden to her, and she made complaint about Fatzer, accusing him.
They came to him and said:

The three
Get up.

Fatzer
How can I get up when I am tied?

The three
You're not tied, for the woman has untied you and you have got her with child.

Fatzer
Have I? Then I must be stronger than all of you, though you bound me with ropes.

Chorus
And the man said:

Kaumann
Now all of you, leave my house
So I may live alone with my woman
For she asks that of me
And my house is her house.

[A9/A19]

Chorus
And so they discuss the situation and bicker, sitting round the table. In the meantime night has fallen.
Kaumann is angry and demands that they recognize his right of ownership over his wife.
Frau Kaumann demands that all three leave the flat.
Kaumann would be content if just Fatzer left.
Frau Kaumann laments the destruction of 'that beautiful creature Fatzer' but raises her hand to pass judgement on him.
Koch sets up revolutionary theses against property and about sex and freedom: what a man needs must be allowed to him.
Büsching defends Fatzer the longest, and he has a sense of humour. It is he too who warns him, but Fatzer seems not to hear him and despises him most.

[A9/A19]

Fatzer
I don't know who will win
In this dispute
But whoever is victorious – Fatzer is
Lost.
And from now on and for a long while
There will be no victors
In your world, but only
Vanquished.
As soon as you doubted me
I was lost.

Chorus
They argue over the woman. Then they even consider leaving the flat altogether, but as they are about to step outside they hear: Rain. The revolutionary theses are withdrawn. Rain drowns out the revolution. Then hunger once again joins the discussion.

Büsching
Oh yes, if only it wouldn't rain
And there was no frost and no
Chill in the morning air
Then everything could just take its course.

Fatzer
Since I committed what you
Call my crime, I have had
A clearer head and am
Stronger. It is as if
A man in straitened times has to provide for offspring
As if nature grants him the skills
To care for them. So let me offer
What I have thought up
For our situation.

[A20]

A little cottage industry, so setting ourselves up for a longer siege and making use of the woman ... to tempt in workers. In part to get the other tenants in this block, where we'll be living for some time, used to strangers. They'll say, they're going to the Kaumann woman. She's a whore. And partly so we can learn from them, how discontent in the factories is growing and so we can reinforce that discontent, on which so much depends.

[B54]

Koch
We are
Too sorely pressed, crouched here underground
Scarce able to breathe
It's too inhuman and this cannot last.
Everything changes, but we
Should we not also change?
Above our heads, every stone
Is changing, even the house
That shelters us is in flux.

[A10]

Chorus
And so the overheated discussions continue
Day and night. New
Resolutions. Immediately overthrown. Ever new
Constellations.
This way and that the decisions sway. [A9]
Anarchy?
Barbarism?

A kind of soviet emerges.
Disunity leads to system of majority voting.

Koch (*shouts*)
Too weak to defend ourselves we move over
To attack!

Chorus
Under this slogan
And under the threat of the public's growing curiosity
Koch fights
Desperately
For revolutionary action.
And begins to exploit
Every problem that arises
The desertion of Fatzer, the growing interest of their neighbours
Hunger, sexual individualism, Kaumann's assertion of his property rights
All consciously, cynically
To revolutionize the situation.

[B73]
Koch (*reads from the* Communist Manifesto:)
['The bourgeoisie, wherever it has got the upper hand, has put an end to all feudal, patriarchal, idyllic relations. It has pitilessly torn asunder the motley feudal ties that bound man to his "natural superiors", and has left remaining no other nexus between man and man than naked self-interest, than callous "cash payment". It has drowned the most heavenly ecstasies of religious fervour, of chivalrous enthusiasm, of philistine sentimentalism, in the icy water of egotistical calculation ... ']

Fatzer
Koch, you can't even
Provide for yourself and now you want to
Help the whole world.

Koch
Our situation, Fatzer, is so bad that
Nothing less than the whole world can help us now.
Any plan to help us must
Help the whole world.
['The weapons with which the bourgeoisie felled feudalism to the ground are now turned against the bourgeoisie itself ... ']

Fatzer *shrugs, laughs and leaves.*

Koch (*continues*:)
[' … in times when the class struggle nears the decisive hour, the progress of dissolution going on within the ruling class, in fact within the whole range of old society, assumes such a violent, glaring character, (*fading*) that a small section of the ruling class cuts itself adrift, and joins the revolutionary class, the class that holds the future in its hands … ']

[B62]

Chorus
Arise now Koch, and go your way
Through the town and
Discover if there's not
Something better than
Your own cause – Fatzer.
Look upon all whom you meet, and
Examine each one! Listen to their talk and
Feel the cloth of
Their coats and the stuff of their thoughts
Whether they're well fed or hungry
If they suffer hardship but
Are still prepared to bear yet greater
Hardships to end all hardship.
For if there are only five
In the entire town
Who are ready and capable
To prepare the revolution, then
Join them at once
Leave the old behind
And commit yourself to the new
That is: total revolution.

Scene Fourteen

[B78]

Fatzer
I don't know if I took my pound of flesh
Like every other man does – but I can't go back now
I must not get caught in
Their treadmill. It mills

Straw, not corn – I mustn't do it.
This flesh is foul and
It's no longer worth it for a man
Like me to take charge of something
That's foul today and tomorrow will be entirely lost to the world.
I was born with a compulsion to take
And make things mine.

[B11]

Man always
Thinks he stands in the world
Unchanged and unchangeable. The skies
May be aglow with fire above his head; the ground
Beneath his feet, he's seen how it may shake. But
He stands there, unchanging, constant, and round about
He likes to see
Other men, unchanged and unchanging.
Wrong!
The ground, it was always ground, the sky
Always sky, but man
Has withered away in fear, or stretched
Himself thin in his foolishness.

[B17]

Man cannot pass judgement
On man.
Like waste that has passed
Through some monstrous stomach
Which, by the action of its juices
Melts all skin and bone
So that in the shit you can't make out
What's fish, what's fruit.
In the same way, bedded in the murky broth
A human life
Lived out
Lies beneath the world's gaze.
And what his eager hand stretched out for, greedily
To still his misery
Is painted in the air and water
And
That he flew, a bird, was no more reason

Nor that he swam in his salty bath
A fish
But that he passed away, for flesh's sake.

[B3]

I'm sick at heart, believe me:
I'm sick.
I can't bring myself to do
What's good for me and for my destiny.
Things that mean nothing
To you – that the rain
Falls down from the sky –
Are quite
Unbearable for me. That in
The alphabet
A comes first, then B, and on
And on – you may be content with that
But for me it is the stuff of misery.

Fatzer *off.*

Chapter Five: The End

Scene Fifteen

In the flat.

[B5]

Büsching
The other day when
We were walking over the iron bridge
At seven in the evening and
Not knowing
What to do, we stopped
And watched the water
We, Büsching and Kaumann
Looked over to the light
While he, Fatzer
Looked over to the darkness.

[A16]

Koch
Of everything he's done to us, nothing
Riled me more than how
Before our eyes, blind as we were
He drew that plan out of thin air, in minutes
To put an end to our hunger. For half a year.

[B15(8)]

Büsching
Everything is as it was
Koch. When you've eaten
You shit. At night you fall
Asleep.
What is your problem?

Koch
You don't understand. But let me
Tell you: this here is a battlefield where
We're standing and by a long chalk it's
Not over yet!

What you do, Fatzer, just because [B38]
You want to, that counts for
Nothing, Fatzer, not here with us.

Büsching
So what do you say, let's kill him, so that
Those who come after us are warned?

Koch
There's nothing comes after us. But
So long as we're here, everything
Is for the best.
And it should profit no one
If I kill him because to me
He is abhorrent and
I want to see him stamped out
And there, where his face was
The dirt from my boot.

Büsching
Why are you yelling like that?

Koch (*yells*)
Because he's my friend.

[B18]

Büsching
No rope
Can hold out longer than
Its weakest strand.

[A14n]

Kaumann (*writes on the wall:*)
'1 dead man = 170 lb cold meat.'

[B39/B40]

Koch
To be weak is human, that's why it has to stop.
That just for once a matter should not run into the sand.
That what a man says might, for once, just mean
Exactly what he says.

This Fatzer cannot be a better Fatzer, or a worse
But simply
No Fatzer at all.
Enfeebled as we are, we'll set a marker in this earth
Not a stone, but just a hole
But still a witness that
Even in the dark times black was black and white was white.
We, who last night spent a restless night
For fear was in us, or, so over-full of new hope that we slept not at all
We know today: it's over and our day is done. And
This very day, when the victory bells
Intone our deadly enemy's greatest hour
Deferring his downfall to another year
Of which we know only this: that it will come long after our own deaths
Let us turn our attention to one of our own
Who's turned utterly to the bad, and
Order our worldly affairs.

[B75]

Koch, Büsching, Kaumann
We shall remain in darkness
But he
Shall be known to the world.
We will kill him, but
We will leave his name. And that
Is all that shall remain of him henceforward. Because
What we want
Is the natural course of things, only
His name, who departed in shame
Shall be recorded.

Scene Sixteen

Room.

[B14]

Girl
Devil knows why I invited
You in here
And why I enjoy watching you

Slurping my supper.
And in bed you treat me like
You can't wait for a smoke.
A man like you could be the last thing
A body sees.

Fatzer
There are some guys I know who stick to me
Like dirt to a dog. What
Binds them to me I don't know.
If they come
I'm not here.

Girl
Are you scared of them then, sweetie?

Fatzer
Not at all. Keep the door shut!

Girl (*has opened the door*)
Listen, shooting
And bells! Something's up!

Fatzer (*gets up*)
Open the door! Shooting?
That's it
That's what I predicted
It's us who are shooting!
They're coming and I'll
Take them!
Me, Johann Fatzer.

Therese Kaumann (*from outside*)
Is there someone called Fatzer lives here?
Then give him this letter!

Fatzer
Give it here! Therese!
Tell them, it's
All under control, we'll
Soon see each other again, they can
Start it rolling!

Girl
She heard you and
She's gone.

Fatzer (*reads:*)
Dear friend,
      Where are you?
We need you.
So come back and we'll
Talk it all through how things stand between you
And us, so there's no more
Trouble!
      Your friends.

Girl
Is that from the guys who stick to you
Like dirt to a dog?
And straightaway you get up?

Fatzer
I see, I've got up.

Girl
That's like it's the dirt
Whistling for the dog!

Fatzer (*hits her*)
Eat that, that's for
Talking when there's
Business between men
And now: get your suitcase
And pack
Your knickers, as if you were moving out
We're going
To an old flat and we'll live
There
Oh, for ever!

Girl (*packs the suitcase*)
And what am I supposed to do there?

Fatzer
What's great is
Not always quite so great, but it's no small thing either.
I'll tell you straight: I don't
Like being alone. That's why I'm going
To a place where
I'm expected
And on the way too
I don't want to be alone, that's why
You're coming too. Come!

[B40]

I don't believe they've got anything bad in mind
It'd be against all common sense, what use would it be to them?
And where will you ever find anyone on this pile of dried up dung
Who'd do something of no benefit to himself?
They need me, I can rely on that.

Both off.

[B58]

Chorus
But when all was done, there was
Confusion. And a room
Completely wrecked, and in it
Four dead men and
One name! And a door, on which was written
Something incomprehensible.
But you will now see
The whole thing. Everything that came to pass, we
Have set it out and enact it
In the very
Sequence in the very locations and
With the very words
That fell. And whatever you see
At the conclusion you will see what we saw:
Confusion. And a room
Completely wrecked, and in it
Four dead men and
One name. And we set it out like this, so that
You should decide

By mouthing the words after us and by
Hearing the choruses
What really went on, for
We were, in our judgement, divided.

Scene Seventeen

[B27]

Fatzer *enters.*

Fatzer
Here I am
Come voluntarily. No force.

Büsching
Sit down, Fatzer.

Kaumann
First, let's get this out: they're on to us
The people who want to kill us.
It was inevitable
They would find our den.

Büsching
Inevitable. And inevitable too
What's coming now.

Fatzer
Anyway, I'm here and
I'll speak openly:
It irritates me the hell, but I wanted
To come
To be with you in this hour
And even now
I don't want you to go away.
I tell you this: I never
Left you, just think: I
Am simply
Grown so used to you. This too
Now seems inevitable.
Besides, after all we went through, or so
It seems to me

This did not have to be, it's
More an accident that we're so backed into a corner.
What happened because of me
Gives me no pleasure.

Büsching
Your proposal?

Fatzer
To leave.
Whatever happened here:
Just to get away, together.

Büsching
Fatzer, we cannot
Accept your proposal.

Fatzer
You can't?
But if it were possible
Just once to clear
The decks, in one move
To see the matter in the cool
Light of day and just to sweep away the past.
To leave
Every account unsettled, simply to accept
What is, and then to walk away!
That would be something new.

Büsching
No, there's nothing new in
Prospect. That is: unless it's new to you
To settle accounts, in one move
To pay the bills. Nothing
Is just accepted, and no one walks away.
Rather we go on playing out
The whole thing, just as it's been set out. So
Fatzer, you have to change
Now, this very hour and in
This very place, and just for once do
What we say, simply because:
There are more of us

Two or three. Can you
Do that?

Fatzer
Is that what's written
On the wall?
(I get it.)
Something to do with a rope
That makes a life
Into 170 pounds of
Cold flesh. I won't do that.

Büsching
Oh yes, you'll have to
Change, at least
In this respect: that you will
Cease to be.

Fatzer
You animals! You want
To kill me! But I'll
Blow the whistle!
(*He goes over to the window and shouts out:*)
Come on in! They're in here!

Büsching
Grab him!

Fatzer
You lying hounds
You hooligans, you mangy scum!
Just because there are two of you and I am
One.

They tie him up.

Büsching
Move that thing into the window
Kaumann, and shoot
If they come
Before we're finished!
Fatzer, your end has come.

Don't bother yelling, right
Or left, there's nothing can
Save you. You were a good
Man, in whatever life you used to lead
But now you must die
Because you've turned
Turned sick and bad.
That's why you have to
Go, in fulfilment of the resolution
Of three men and one
Dead man, without delay!
Say that you are
In agreement.

Fatzer
Büsching! What are you saying?
Our butchers
They're on their way
To get us *all*? Didn't we
Lie together three years
In the trenches, and then …

Büsching
We did.
So what?
(*He calls out of the window:*)
Yes, we're here, but
Wait a while –
Or else we'll shoot –
Until we've settled something
Here that must needs be settled.
Then we'll come out
Quietly!
(*Shots outside.*)
So use your weapon, Kaumann!

Fatzer
I shan't!
Untie me Büsching!
I couldn't give a fuck if you
See I'm scared, I don't
Want to die!

Not yet! And
Not like this!
I am Fatzer!
etc.

[*Simultaneous shots. Black-out.*]

[B83]
Chorus
But we counsel you: Be
In agreement. Acquiesce. For so it comes to pass
As you have seen here, and no differently.
Don't try to escape. Whoever
Swims against the current, the water will
Flood into their mouth and
Drown them.

Epilogue

[B81]

Chorus
So it is good
Those who are born want not to die
It is good so
They eat and cannot fill their stomachs
And eat again
It is good so
But when their time comes, they perish and fall back into the holes that
    were dug for them
And in their place
Others come, sleep on their sheets and
Eat from their plates in contentment
It is good so.
What comes to pass, must come to pass, otherwise
Why would it happen at all?
Don't raise a hue and cry
About one man, he
Was born and he must
Perish, and his scope is brief.
Don't waste
Your breath, for you too
Must soon pass!

Anti-Chorus
Cry out to skies at the fate of our one man
Must he perish?
It is wrong so!
What comes to pass, need not come to pass
Alter it
Do not pass your plate on to the next man
Oh why would you?
It is wrong so!
Nothing is good, which is not
Made good by man!

[B82]

Chorus
Injustice
Flows like water

Misery rises
like the sun
And man tears at the flesh of man
Just as fish eat the fish of the sea
So it is and
So it is good.
And they will not return again and
The earth beneath which they lie broken
Will grow over
And it is good so.

Anti-Chorus
Injustice is
To us as water
It is bad so
And the rising of the sun is only as certain
As our misery
That is bad
Man tears at the flesh of man
Bad, bad, bad, it is bad so!

End

Appendix

[The following is a selection of the outlines, notes, scenes and commentaries, which clearly belong to the *Fatzer* material, but to which it was not possible to allot a place in the above version. A33 is one among several scene breakdowns and should not be understood as a definitive order of scenes. In the case of A20 (below) there is a very small overlap with our Scene Thirteen (above) which serves also to illustrate how, in the extreme case of an undrafted scene, we have exploited the available material for the stage version.

In addition to the more familiar sorts of sketches, at a later stage of composition (1929–30) Brecht conceived the idea of writing a range of commentary texts, the *Fatzerkommentar*, by which the project might be transformed from a more conventional play, possibly into some sort of a *Lehrstück* (learning play), a theatre piece for education and training. A selection of these commentaries ('C' texts), some of which are very fragmentary, comes at the end of the following group. We cannot know quite what Brecht proposed for them. Nor is it always clear what is commentary, what first notes towards a poem, chorus, dialogue, or the argument of a scene.]

[A32]
Downfall of the 'Egoist' Fatzer
In Mülheim on the Ruhr, at the time of the First World War, a time bereft of all morality, a tale unfolded between four men, which ended with the total destruction of all four, but which, in the midst of murder, false witness and debauchery, also bore the bloody traces of a new kind of morality. In the third year of the war, during a tank battle by Verdun, four men, a tank-crew, disappeared and were presumed dead. Then, at the beginning of 1918, they secretly re-surfaced in Mülheim, where one of them had a basement room. From now on, under the perpetual threat of being taken as deserters and shot, they had an extremely hard time securing the means of bare survival, all the more because there were four of them. They resolved, nonetheless, under no circumstances to separate, as their only prospect was that a popular uprising might put an end to the senseless war and so sanction their desertion. Together they hoped they might themselves participate in the uprising they were waiting for. For two weeks they tried, night after night, to procure provisions, and it was only towards the end of the second week that the most resourceful of them, Johann Fatzer – the very same who had persuaded them to desert in the first place and had led them, through French captivity, back home (or nearly home, for their hometowns were Liegnitz,

Passau and Berlin) – made the acquaintance of a soldier from the transport corps, who, in a moment of comradely feeling, promised to get them sufficient provisions from one of the catering wagons. The following night the four, under Fatzer's leadership, were to present themselves at the goods station. But, although they had discussed it all in detail, the enterprise, on which so much depended, failed, because Fatzer, having arrived at the meeting place, got himself mixed up in a dispute with some butcher's apprentices, in the course of which he was beaten up, in full view of his friends. It was only the self-control of the three that prevented them all from being arrested on the spot: They behaved as if they did not know Fatzer.

[A33]

1
Fatzer, Keuner, Büsching and Leeb break off from the war

2
Homecoming

3
Fatzer's walk through Mülheim

4
Fatzer's first deviation: copulation

5
Fatzer's second deviation: quarrel with the butchers

6

7
Quarrel in the cantine

8
Fatzer steals meat and kills

9
Victory bells

10
Fatzer's walk

11
Judgement

[A31]
Their Odyssey begins with the error, foisted on them by the individualist Fatzer, that they might, on their own, put an end to the war. Because of this, by which *they part company from the masses* in order to live, they squander their lives before they've even begun. They can never return to the mass.
Hence:
Perpetual efforts and resolutions to return!

Insights like this take on the character of literature. They cite these 'passages' later on, make changes.

Fatzer believes in blind chance, 'what exists is simply what is left', chaos. It is Koch who recognizes the necessity of the war and formulates the resolution to liquidate him.

The sentence they write on the tank: 'we're done' now gets improved (the character of literature!) by Koch, writing on the wall of their room: 'we're done with war'.

The tragedy of the last part is a dialectical tragedy!
in that Fatzer's pernicious nature (as a type) becomes evident when he involves all three in private affairs – in tempting them to destroy him, he destroys them. It would have been correct never to lose 'that connection to tomorrow', never to forget what is needed, to see everything else as an obstacle, not principally as something to overcome, which then becomes a goal, it would have been correct for them to clear off and to deny Fatzer and his sort any regard. They are confounded because they apply the principle of solidarity to someone who does not himself have any. For them it stands to reason: either they will all get out together, or none of them will. To the bitter end, they want to take him with them, whether he wants it or not.

To be content with the gesture
    Whatever you are thinking, don't say it
    Walk out of here with us, mechanically!
    Walk, like someone giving a greeting: because it's the done thing
    Execute the movement that
    Means nothing

[A20]

Therese Kaumann
In response to her demand for sexual satisfaction **Koch** gives her the assurance that, for the time being, she is free.

> For under these conditions
> Your roof was more to us than was your bed. Your pallet
> More important than that it's yours, since on it
> No rain falls, nor the eyes of others
> And if we can't repay your lodging with an embrace
> Weakened as we are by hunger, or because we are too many
> We must nonetheless, if driven by a meal of meat
> Or by the warmth of your body, still
> Come to you, if only for that
> And that is why
> We cannot
> Take the woman by the flesh and hope
> That she will bake us bread, but rather must
> Appeal to your wits, whether strong or weak

They decide the woman is free, but none of them are to do anything with her. Unity is more important, because that's a matter of life and death. As she goes out with the plates the man stops her to say he has no appetite to sleep with a woman as long as he's only got fodder like this. Whereupon the speech above by Koch.

Fatzer takes the woman. Probably in revenge for the fact they tied him up. 'Let's say, a woman was to untie me, and how then would I repay that?' This opening move is combined with the suggestion of a plan that would 'procure them food for weeks'. They debate and decide by a majority to listen to the plan. As their ideological argument they declare that 'the woman is free but holds what they need to be her own property, namely this lodging, and that they can only disabuse her of this belief by taking mastery of her body. For a man must have what a man must have.' Fatzer's suggestion of a 'cottage industry' follows.

Fatzer's assault of Therese is told by the **Chorus**.

Fatzer moreover augments his suggestion of a cottage industry, so setting up for a longer siege, with the idea of using the woman (whom he has just taken) ('you only say that cos you've had enough of her') to tempt in workers, 'in part to get the other tenants in this block, where we'll be living for some time, used to strangers. They'll say, they're going to the Kaumann woman. And she plays the whore partly in order to find out from her clients how discontent is growing in the factories, and to reinforce their dissatisfaction, on which so much depends.'

So all of this in *one* scene, which begins with Fatzer's entrance after the first time he fails to appear, and his suggestion they stand by him in his quarrel with the butchers, and which is interrupted by the recitation of the Chorus, which relates the sex act in the very moment that it's going on downstairs.

[B28]

Four men emerged from a great war. The city in which they surfaced was large. They wanted to partake of the life of this city. They wanted to rise in the morning at seven and do business in the midst of the bustle of people, take their meal at midday, and in the evening pay to watch a fight. They thought that they, as four together, could achieve this. But their fourth man made it all impossible. Although he was the strongest of them, from the outset it was clear that he was useless. He only asked them …

The fourth talked his neck into the noose.

It's easy to say: it's all
Without seriousness, fleshless, set to die
Of its own weakness – but
You shall not say that. Rather, you
Must take it seriously. Don't be high-handed, brothers
But modest, and beat it to death
Not high-handed, but: inhuman!

Don't do two things, but
Just the one. Not live and kill, but
Just kill. One is one
Black black, and loud not low.

[B12]

Fatzerchorus 1
And we saw, driving
Through our cities too swiftly and
So not clearly visible:
On urgent business
Its face smeared with blood

Justice
Surrounded by anxious guards
In steel hats.
And hearing a voice
Between the guns and the wolves
We asked and were told, this was
The voice of justice.

Fatzerchorus 7
1
Injustice is human
More human however
The struggle against injustice!
But here too hold your hand
Before the human, leave that
Unscathed, nothing
Can impart lessons to the dead!
Don't, knife, scrape off
The script with the dirt
Else you will have
But a naked sheet
Covered in scars!
2
Such a clean sheet
Scarred, let us
Insert at last into the chronicle
Of humanity!

[B21]

Who *is* the Chorus?
Before the ending:
But he too is
A man like you!
Uncertain in expression
Prematurely hardened
Attempting much
Saying many things:
Do not hold him
To what he has said, soon
He will change it …
It was nothing final that you saw and everything
Changed before it perished

Why
Do you take *him* at his word?
If you take him at his word, it will be
He who disappoints you!

Interludes: The People

[B16]

A

Soldiers *lead a* **man** *in chains.*

The man If you take me to the authorities, then remember: I am one who was on your side.

Soldier I'd know all right if you were on our side.

Man Just wait a moment.

Soldier Are you scared?

Man Yes I am. But that's not why I'm talking. I only want you to wait a while so I can tell you how things stand in the world; for you have no idea.

Soldiers (*laugh*) All right, so tell us how do things stand in the world!

Man The poor are exploited, and the ...

Soldier Fine, now let's get moving again.

Man Stop! But the exploited of all nations are beginning to realize that they belong together and that this war is being waged against them.

Soldier Is there anywhere where they might be doing something about that?

Man Yes, in Russia.

Soldier But they're criminals aren't they?

Man No. Poor people.

Soldier I suppose you want us to let you go?

Man Don't you understand? You just need to know that for you too it will soon be time.

Soldier But if it's like you say, and if the poor are so many, how come you, who are so smart: how come you are going to be shot?

Man Because otherwise *you* will be killed!

Soldier But you're the one who's going to be shot now, aren't you?

Man Yes.

Soldier So can we move on?

Man Yes, let's move on.

B

Train.

Soldier They've got a new plan now, the top brass, and they're saying: this one's so good it's *got to* work. So they're going to gather all the squadrons and everything at one point and finally break through and then they'll reel in the whole front. That's a plan, subtle, you'd be amazed the human brain can come up with something so brilliant.

Second soldier But it won't help them, Josef, all their artistry is in vain. And for why? Because they can never do away with the people, not with any plan in the whole wide world. 'Cause the people can withstand anything, even the finest plans, anything. Even when they hobble the sons of the people and tether them down, the sons of heroes, and then blow them high into the sky, none of it helps, the people don't even twitch, they put up with it, and even the cleverest plan that the generals cook up over their coffee, they'll withstand even that. And that's because, if you've been bred for obedience, your guts will wear out long before your patience wears out.

First soldier If you want to shout that any louder it'll be your guts that give out.

Second soldier When we were in Poland you know what we found in the knapsacks of the Ruskies we'd done in: those leaflets with the seditious stuff in them, all printed in German. That was all we knew about what was going on in the world, and to read that we first had to shoot them. We're not so clever you know.

First soldier We've never been able to stand on our own two feet.

Second soldier That's a stupid thing to say! It's the ones who stand on their own two feet who deserve to be shot first. It's the ones who keep us on the leash, they're the stand-alone ones. But there'll never be a revolution where everybody stands for themselves, and you don't understand that. That is our whole strength that we're not self-reliant. And those amongst us who carry on so wild and headstrong, they'll be the first who have to go if we're to keep ourselves pure, the first. Otherwise this world will never change.

First soldier You're just saying all that because you can't see work out they get their cut!

Second soldier That's our hope, that there are those who don't understand what they'd have to understand if this cesspool's *not* to change.

[C2]
Fatzer document
The purpose for which a piece of work is made is not identical with the purpose for which it is taken. So the Fatzer document is made primarily in the first instance so that the writer may learn.

If it later becomes a pedagogic piece, then the students will learn something quite different from what the writer learnt. I, the writer, have no need to finish anything. It is enough if I educate myself. I only lead the investigation, and it's my method in doing that that the spectators in turn may investigate.

[C6]
Fatzer commentary
Part of the Fatzer document is the Fatzer commentary. The Fatzer commentary contains two kinds of directions for the players: those concerning the presentation, and those concerning the meaning and use of the document. The study of the directions about the meaning is not necessary for an understanding of the directions about the presentation, and so not for the presentation itself, whereas the study of the directions about the meaning may even be dangerous without the study of the former and in the absence of the acting out itself. So the directions for the acting out should be read first, and only after the student has presented the document

should the study of the meaning and the use follow. The student should copy the presentation following the example of the first artists of the time. This presentation by the first artists of the time should be criticized both orally and in writing, but in any case it should be copied so long until it starts to be changed by that critique. Suggestions to modify gestures or tone of voice should be made in writing; they are not to impact on the exercises themselves. In this way also the directions of the commentary may be changed at any time. They are full of errors in respect to our time, and the merits of the commentary may not be applicable to other times.

[C7]

1) When is Fatzer's walk through the town of Mülheim a reality – even though no man Fatzer ever walked through the town of Mülheim?

Answer:
If sufficient people and sufficiently good people who are sufficiently enlightened have recognized it as truthful.

Explanation:
As well as the deeds of man that were, there are those that could have been. These latter deeds are just as dependent on the times as are the first, and there is equally a story about them which reveals contextual relations, across the ages. Certain images, such that people make for themselves of themselves, are particular to a certain age in which just these gestures may be evident to people observing one another, because it is these gestures that are important. So, by particular characteristics, people recognize the most truthful images of their lives, by the juxtapositions of figures in certain attitudes, which reveal the true interests of the people of that particular time. So now, if sufficient people and sufficiently good people who are sufficiently enlightened have recognized Fatzer's walk as truthful, then it is just as much a reality as the speech advocating the end of the war by our comrade Lenin.

2) When do sufficient people and sufficiently good (useful) people who are sufficiently enlightened recognize Fatzer's walk through the town of Mülheim as truthful?

Answer:
When Fatzer's walk seems to them possible for sufficient, or sufficiently good, or for sufficiently enlightened people.

Explanation:
But there must be sufficient people, because nothing is true that is not in the interests of many, and they must be sufficiently good people, because

nothing is true that is not in the interests of people who are as good as they can be, and they must be sufficiently enlightened, because only such people can recognize the truth.

3) But when do they recognize it as useful?

Answer:
If it is of use to them in their daily, or yearly, lives that they themselves, or as many others as possible, have taken cognisance of this walk; that is to say, in their struggle for food, lodgings and clothes, in their manner of eating, living and dressing, as also in their encounters with other people, their walks through cities, their conversations and their plans.

They may also derive use from it if they can show that they are good and sufficiently enlightened people, of whom there must be sufficient numbers.

[C14]
Our attitude derives from our actions, our actions derive from necessity. If necessity is sorted, whence then do our actions derive?
When necessity is sorted, our actions derive from our attitude:

Our thoughts come from

Why does the state ordain to students that they study the commentary? In order to give them thoughts that are useful to the state.

[C16]
When the thinking man teaches a teaching he does so because such is needed. The thinker is tasked to think. It is not the point to propagate a particular insight by means of the teaching, but to perform a particular attitude.

Where is truth to be found?
Truth features in the doctrine of assent [*Einverständnis*], that is the doctrine of the correct attitude. In adopting the correct attitude, truth, i.e. the correct perception of relations, will be manifest.

Truth is a weapon in the struggle of the exploited classes.

Knowing the truth means knowing: what it is that helps whom?

[C23]
Theory of Pedagogies
Bourgeois philosophers make a big distinction between the doer and the observer. This is a distinction the thinker does not make. By drawing this distinction, you end up leaving politics to the doers and philosophy to the observers, whereas in reality politicians must be philosophers and philosophers politicians. There is no distinction between true philosophy and true politics. The recommendation of the thinker follows from this insight, namely to educate young people by making theatre, that is to say, to make them simultaneously into both doers and observers, as the precepts for the pedagogies suggest. Delight in observing on its own is damaging for the state, as equally is delight in just doing. In that young people, through their playing, perform deeds which are then subject to their own observation, they may be trained in the service of the state. This playing must be so designed and so executed that the state derives a use from it. So the value of a sentence or a gesture or an action is not determined by its beauty, but whether or not the state benefits when the actors speak the sentence, perform the gesture, engage in the action. The use that the state has may, however, be very much diminished by dimwits who, for example, only let the actors execute such actions as seem to them social. Whereas the state may derive use precisely from the representation of the asocial by its emerging citizens, especially if it is executed according to exact and outstanding models. The state may best correct people's asocial urges, which are the product of fear and ignorance, by extracting the asocial from each and every one in its most consummate form, a form which is more or less beyond the reach of the autonomous individual. This is the basis of the idea of using theatre making in pedagogics.

[C29]
The fourth chapter
The fourth chapter is the chapter of crippling visions. Fear is the herald of the advent of great changes in the spirit of humanity. By their own fear or by that of others, those in position of leadership recognize the coming of great changes. These are changes that they are expected to implement. In our own times there is great fear at the growing dominance of the cities, and many hanker after some way of escape. The leadership, however, knows that all such thoughts are bad, and they strive to actualize the great cities. It is the same with mechanization and collective morality. The leaders explain the sense of mechanization and the usefulness of collective morality. Swimming against the stream is foolish, but it calls for wisdom to recognize the direction of the current.

The fourth chapter is also the chapter of the shattering of perceptions by circumstances.

Many draw a distinction between reason and feeling, and subordinate reason to feeling. There is no distinction that could engender conflict between true reason and true feeling. Those in a position of leadership, however, subordinate feeling to reason in that they never employ reason without some material for it to interrogate.

The Bread Store

With Elisabeth Hauptmann, Emil Hesse-Burri
and Hermann Borchardt

Translated by Marc Silberman and Victoria Hill
Edited by Marc Silberman

3 Caspar Neher's sketch of the chorus of unemployed workers, from *The Bread Store*.

Introduction

The Bread Store (German: *Der Brotladen*), like *The Judith of Shimoda*, is one of the few 'almost' completed fragment plays among the stage works attributed to Brecht. Like many of the projects he initiated in the waning Weimar Republic, it was a team effort that emerged over several years of gestation, interrupted by other endeavours but not abandoned as the issue of economic crisis that crystallized in the market crash of October 1929 consumed his attention. In this respect we might regard *The Bread Store* as a transitional text in which characters, songs, and dialogue migrated among several concurrent projects. Brecht's critical assessment of his collaborator Elisabeth Hauptmann's musical *Happy End* (1929), for example, inspired him to produce its 'correction'. This led to their work on *The Bread Store*, which was to provide a general social critique of religion, specifically the Salvation Army as a capitalist enterprise. Ultimately this topic yielded the major play *Saint Joan of the Stockyards* (1932). While none of the scenic fragments related to *The Bread Store* were published during Brecht's lifetime, two young directors at the Berliner Ensemble, Manfred Karge and Matthias Langhoff, created a stage version from the relevant material housed in the Bertolt Brecht Archive, and they mounted a production in April 1967 with original music by Hans-Dieter Hosalla and stage design by Karl von Appen. This version has been translated into and performed in a number of languages.[1]

The new English translation presented here follows the Karge/Langhoff text to a large extent. At the time they described this version as 'one possible suggestion' for their own production, and we do introduce a number of changes. Based on the fragments and notes published in the *Berliner und Frankfurter Ausgabe* of Brecht's works (*BFA*) and the extensive archival material, we have first and foremost added dialogue, text passages, the stage directions, and several brief but thoughtful commentaries by Brecht about the nature of the play's conflict.[2] There are also modifications in the attribution of choral passages and dialogue as well as in the sequencing of some plot events. We believe this version provides readers and potential directors with a coherent story constructed around three main actions: the battle for one dime of profit on the part of the newspaper boy Washington Meyer that depicts the miserable conditions of the unemployed; Mrs Niobe Queck's unsolicited negotiations for the wood to heat a bakery oven that leads to the loss of her apartment, her five young children, and her life; and the battle for bread that results in Meyer's death. Using masks, hats, accessories, and some imagination, as few as ten actors can perform the play, taking on multiple roles; with more actors it is possible to include a separate chorus for the intervening commentary passages.

The team of Brecht's collaborators on this and other projects evolving in these years included most importantly Elisabeth Hauptmann as well as Emil Hesse-Burri and Hermann Borchardt. After the unexpected success of *The Threepenny Opera* in August 1928, Brecht – at the bidding of theatre manager Ernst Josef Aufricht – convinced Hauptmann to author another musical with song lyrics he would contribute and, once again, with settings by Kurt Weill. Following an outline he provided, she completed the three-act play titled *Happy End* under the pseudonym Dorothy Lane, and it opened in Berlin at the Theater am Schiffbauerdamm in September 1929, on the first anniversary of that already legendary beggar's opera. It was, however, a failure and closed after only seven performances.[3] Set in the underworld of post-First World War Chicago, it confronts the gangster Bill Cracker with the Salvation Army lieutenant Lil Holiday, who fall in love and decide to join forces and fight for the poor against the rich. Inspired partially by George Bernard Shaw's *Major Barbara* (1905), it reflects the ongoing interest on the part of Brecht and Hauptmann in the history of the Salvation Army as an idealistic institution that wedded its 'spiritual' practices to those of capitalist profiteering.

When the 'Brecht collective' began thinking about *The Bread Store*, it was conceived as a counter example to *Happy End*. Their work proceeded more or less in two well-defined phases, beginning in winter 1929 and continuing later in 1930, at which point the project was abandoned. The folios with *Brotladen* material housed in the Bertolt Brecht Archive contain 245 leaves, mainly typewritten pages, many with handwritten notations or corrections, but also some brief, scribbled notes and sketches.[4] This material includes entire scenes, early drafts of sections of some of these scenes, notes on the scenes, various plans for the sequence of scenes, sketches of the stage design, and leaves with choral texts, poems, songs, and theoretical notes. Notes from the later phase are almost all clearly marked with the title 'Brotladen', and although the plans still seemed to call for a three-act structure, by this late phase there are no longer any summaries or lists of acts and scenes, suggesting that there was still neither a coherent idea nor a plot-line. Theatre critic Herbert Ihering, a promoter of Brecht, mentioned plans for a play called 'Der Brotladen oder Die Macht der Religion' (The Bread Store or The Power of Religion) in February 1930, noting the quality of the choral passages in contrast to another play he was reviewing in an article.[5] Moreover, two regional newspapers reported in June of the same year that Brecht was working on an opera libretto for Kurt Weill with this title![6] Finally, in the issues of *Versuche* (Experiments), the pamphlet-style publications of his own works that Brecht began to issue in 1930, he listed *The Bread Store* as forthcoming in number 2 (with the subtitle 'Ein Lustspiel' or a comedy), again in numbers 3 and 4 (1931), and once again in number 5 (1932), although the team had stopped working on it by the end of 1930 and completed – instead – *Saint Joan of the Stockyards*, which was broadcast as a radio play in April 1932.

The close connection between *Happy End* and *The Bread Store* is most evident in the characters' names, which undergo a series of transformations in the course of the project. In the earliest planning stages Gorilla Bagsley, Lil, and Cracker are still the names of the main characters adapted from the musical. Bagsley ultimately becomes Janushek, although in some notes he crops up as Jeffers and Jefferson. Similarly Lil becomes Miss Hippler after being variously referred to as Miss Falladah Heep and Mary. Finally, Cracker – the gangster in the musical – disappears entirely, although some of his traits are shared with the newspaper stand owner Schmitt in the later fragment. Like the musical, *The Bread Store* was initially set in the United States, in New York City rather than Chicago, and references in early notes to President Warren Harding, who held office from 1920 until 1923, indicate a time frame of the early 1920s. The names of Washington Meyer, Janushek (alias Jefferson), and Mrs Queck (alias Mrs Jackson, probably a reference to President Andrew Jackson) allude to American leaders who helped shape the young republic during difficult times. This suggests that from early on the team's work was oriented towards a plot-line about the challenges facing the Weimar Republic after 1919, using Brecht's signature technique of displacing topical political developments in Germany to faraway, exotic places. The consequences of the October 1929 Wall Street Crash and its effects in Germany, however, led them to set the action in Berlin during 1930 in the second writing phase. Moreover, some of the names now took on the patina of antiquity with references to Homer's *Odyssey*: Janushek became Ajax Janushek; Mrs Niobe Queck was variously called Helena and Hekuba Queck and was even mentioned at one point as a mythical siren; and Schmitt, who in the earliest drafts was called Swiney or Sweeney, finally became Ulysses Schmitt. These changes go hand in hand with the shift from prose to blank verse for many of the dialogues and all of the choral passages in the completed scenes.

While Brecht was a prolific writer during his entire life, the years between 1927 and 1932 are especially rich in this respect. The global economic crisis as well as Brecht's introduction to Marxist texts at this time stimulated his interest in getting class struggle onto the stage and finding new formal means of bringing it to life in the theatre. Faced with the fundamental questions of how to change the world and where to find the energy to do so, he was testing artistic forms that could give shape to two dialectical contradictions: first, the need for collective action and the function of the creative and potentially destructive individual within the collective; and second, the longing for an end to violence but the need to use it to achieve its rejection. Like the fragments of *Fatzer* and *Fleischhacker*, *The Bread Store* remained unfinished because Brecht was exploring political and theatrical contradictions so radically that he failed to find an adequate form for the material. It is no accident that he was experimenting precisely with the *Lehrstück* (learning play) form because the theatre of the Weimar Republic was in crisis, just as the entire society was losing its grounding in the traditional concept of the individual subject. Hence the tendency of the learning plays to demonstrate how and why the individual must consent to the demands of the collective, even if it leads to the extinguishing of the individual. Later, in exile, Brecht characterized the *Fatzer* and *The Bread Store* fragments as 'of the highest technical standard' in the theatre (*Journals*, 25 February 1939), a standard he could no longer meet as a refugee without a theatre or audience to address.

The play was conceived in 'the grand style', with declamatory verse in classical metres, and aimed to make visible class attitudes during the economic crisis of those years.[7] In contrast to the learning play model, *The Bread Store* does not focus on the hoped-for utopia of a collective society but on a religious collective and the false consciousness of (unemployed) workers. Founded in Great Britain in 1865 as a religious sect growing out of the Methodist Church, the Salvation Army developed an organizational hierarchy with military ranks and titles. Their mission was to convert and help the poor, and to accomplish it they implemented a number of activities: small groups of soldiers who sang in the streets and the hangouts of the impoverished, publications, cheap homeless shelters, and low-paid work.

Brecht and Hauptmann were drawn to the Salvation Army because it represented for them the most modern of all religious collectives, one which drew on a model of class struggle embedded in early Christianity and which recognized the misery of the underclasses, but then displaced the revolutionary potential by interpreting their oppression as individual failure. Their interest had already been sparked in 1927 and peaked while they were working on *The Bread Store*, with excursions to Salvation Army revival meetings and research into their publications.[8] The play is not so much a critique of the sect itself; instead it intends to show the social function of religion in capitalism, and how this false collective adapts to capitalism by transforming social injustice into an individualistic, humanistic ideology and thereby blocks revolutionary change. If the Salvation Army spontaneously helps the impoverished by feeding and sheltering them, at the same time it manipulates the systemic economic chaos of capitalism's crises to increase profits for its own ends.

From this perspective Mrs Queck emerges as a rather passive figure, and Washington Meyer is the real protagonist and counter figure to Miss Hippler. As his name implies, he will become a statesman with the vision of a battle for independence, although he is unable to save Mrs Queck. Yet that is part of the lesson to be learned here: helping the individual, Mrs Queck, out of pity for her plight can only lead to failure under the conditions of advanced capitalism. In early drafts the collaborative team actually distinguished two groups of unemployed labourers and their different attitudes: those who receive weekly unemployment benefits and have food to eat ('Stempelarbeitslosen') and those who are so dependent on the informal labour market that they do not qualify for such payments and go hungry ('Stempellosen', in our version the UPs or unemployed). The former criticize the latter's willingness to accept degraded labour conditions and depressed wages, but in the later drafts, written after the market crash consequences were becoming apparent, this distinction disappears. Now a new element becomes ever more important: the underdeveloped sense of class struggle among the unemployed, which makes them susceptible to petty-bourgeois tendencies and moral explanations for their own oppression. The Salvation Army functions as a disruptive element, preaching the early Christian idea of asceticism with high-minded exhortations that the unemployed improve themselves by searching their souls for a lack of piety.

This is where the chorus – a classical theatrical device that Brecht was employing at this time in his learning plays as well – intervenes. Here, however, the chorus is refunctioned into the collective voice of unemployed workers who speak in rhythmic free verse on a Berlin street corner. In the earliest drafts referred to as the 'core chorus' ('Kernchor'), it later becomes the chorus of the UPs and sometimes a separate chorus distinct from the UPs that comments on appropriate and wrong actions. For example, the chorus establishes a central motif in the play: the concept of false pity as a destructive motivation in the class struggle. Both Washington Meyer and Mrs Queck fail in their responses to the economic crisis insofar as they both assume this attitude of pity. Meyer tries to use cunning to escape his poverty but then empathizes with the plight of Mrs Queck and thereby risks his livelihood and ultimately his life; and Queck acquiesces to her immiseration as a means of leveraging help from her neighbours.

Responses of pity to the contingent effects of dependence on the capitalist system are shown to be an expression of a lack of class consciousness, hammered home by the chorus's refrain: 'Stuff wax in both yours ears.' Mrs Queck's desperation and the sympathy of the unemployed are transformed into the hope that the Salvation Army will save the day, but that hope is revealed as a betrayal, and disappointment leads to a spontaneous uprising, represented both as a kind of nonsense and – in the choral commentary – as a new quality of consciousness on the part of the unemployed workers. To this extent *The Bread Store* belongs to Brecht's ruminations about the nature of collective violence, as explored, for example, in the learning play *The Decision* or the later philosophical text *Me-ti: Book of Interventions in the Flow of Things*. Indeed, the play that evolved out of this fragment, *Saint Joan of the Stockyards*, comes to the conclusion: 'Only violence helps where violence rules.'

The fact that the uprising in the last scene includes slapstick elements situates *The Bread Store* within the early experiments of Brecht's epic theatre, before he began to theorize the concept. The entire play is saturated with aspects of travesty and caricature that undermine any sense of fourth-wall realism, and its comically grotesque tone recalls nothing if not the tradition of *commedia dell'arte*. We might even consider the play to be a first 'model' of epic theatre in the sense of 'The Street Scene: A Basic Model for an Epic Theatre' (1938). But here, instead of a random car accident, a group of unemployed workers depicts aspects of their everyday life on a street corner, thereby making visible the contradictions of their social existence and provoking those who watch to develop a critical attitude. Here we can already see the almost documentary-like, un-dramatic presentation of events that construct the play's argument (what Brecht referred to as the *Fabel*) and reveal contradictory attitudes. Thus, there are repeated incidents of 'reporting': The prologue tells how the poor themselves do not understand the laws of capitalism; the real estate agent explains at length the power of the big banks; Meyer describes the offstage negotiations taking place between the baker and the Salvation Army lieutenant concerning the woodpile; and the battle and Meyer's death are narrated as they happen by those involved. These are examples of *Verfremdung* effects that aim to challenge the audience to articulate class positions rather than to awaken sympathy, to force them to judge situations and reactions as right or wrong.

Finally, there are numerous plot elements and incomplete dialogue passages that could not be integrated into this version of the play. These include a planned boxing match between Schmitt and Meyer (a favourite device of Brecht's that we know, for instance, from *In the Jungle of Cities*); a short scene in which Meyer learns how to sell newspapers; references to a subplot about Mrs Queck's eldest son William who goes off on his own in the big city; and a possible encounter between Mrs Queck and an astrologer (another false ideology?). Moreover, among the material in the Brecht Archive's *Brotladen* files are eleven songs and poems or choral fragments, some of which were also used in *Happy End* and/or *Saint Joan of the Stockyards* (see the two optional songs included at the end of the translated text).[9]

MARC SILBERMAN

Notes

1 See Bertolt Brecht, *Der Brotladen, Ein Stückfragment: Bühnenfassung und Texte aus dem Fragment* (Frankfurt am Main: Suhrkamp, 1967). The East German journal *Sinn und Form*, 10.1 (1958) published the Prologue and two scenes from the *Brotladen* material (6–27), and volume 7 of the 1967 edition of Brecht's *Gesammelte Werke* included these as well as a third scene and several of the song texts intended for the play (Frankfurt am Main: Suhrkamp), 2913–49. There is an extant English translation of the Karge/Langhoff version by Eugene Schlusser and David Illingworth titled *The Breadshop* that was published in the London journal *The New Review*, 3.33 (December 1976), 11–23. There are also translations into French, Spanish, Portuguese, Swedish, and Japanese.
2 See Bertolt Brecht, *Der Brotladen*, *BFA* 10.1, 565–659. The primary folios with scenic material in the Bertolt Brecht Archive at the Akademie der Künste in Berlin are *BBA* 1352–6.
3 *Happy End* was published in German for the first time in 1977 under Hauptmann's name (Berlin: Aufbau); Michael Feingold produced an English adaptation of the play and songs (London: Methuen Drama, 1983).
4 There are also several folios (1860–4) with relevant *Brotladen* material in the separate Elisabeth Hauptmann Archive at the Akademie der Künste in Berlin, but this consists mostly of carbon copies of the material to be found in the Brecht Archive, although there is a folded, poster-size leaf with a hand-drawn sketch of the play's structure arranged as three acts with nine scenes (Elisabeth-Hauptmann-Archiv 1861).
5 Herbert Ihering, *Von Reinhard bis Brecht*, 3 (Berlin: Henschel, 1961), 46.
6 *BBA* 474/98 includes notices clipped from *Wiesbadener Tageblatt* (2 June 1930) und *Münchener Neueste Nachrichten* (4 June 1930).
7 Elisabeth Hauptmann quotes Brecht in the brief introduction to the fragment scenes published in *Sinn und Form* as follows: 'Das Stück war im großen Stil gedacht und sollte v.a. gewisse Haltungen während der Wirtschaftskrise jener Jahre sichtbar machen' (5).
8 Hauptmann published a story under the title 'Bessie Soundso. Eine Geschichte von der Heilsarmee' in the popular magazine *Uhu*, 4.7 (April 1928), 26–39; and at the same time they were authoring *The Bread Store*, Brecht worked with Hauptmann on a film scenario called 'In ein berüchtigtes Lokal' based on her play *Happy End* (*BFA* 19, 322–9).
9 In addition, the Salvation Army song in Scene Two ('March ahead to the fight … ') is included in *Happy End* and is taken here from Michael Feingold's translation; and in Scene Six, 'Onward into the fight …' was written for *Happy End* (Salvation Army Song I) and used in *Saint Joan* as well (Scene Two).

Characters

Niobe Queck, *widow with five children (William, Henry, Ana, Leopold, Frederick)*
Washington Meyer, *newspaper boy*
Unemployed Persons, *called* **UPs**, *also numbered* **UP 1** *through* **4**
Masher, *another of the* **UPs**
Flamm, *real estate agent*
Meininger, *baker*
Reuter, *wood merchant*
Ulysses Schmitt, *newspaper vendor*
Mr and Mrs Dittmeyer ⎤
Mrs Franzke | **Meininger**'s *renters*
Mr Bolke |
Mrs Janushek ⎦
Ajax, *her son, apprentice to* **Meininger**
Salvation Army troop
Ms Hippler, *Salvation Army lieutenant*
Policeman
Physician
Social worker
Alfons, *wood merchant's assistant*
Chorus

Prologue

[B9]

Chorus (*To the audience.*)
You there who just have
Come from your meal
Allow us please to render for you our
Ceaseless struggle for food like you enjoy
Even simpler fare would suit us.

We beg of you: behold us
In ceaseless search for work!
Alas both food and work
Are subject to unchangeable laws
Unknown.

Evermore they fall
Downwards
Through the grates in the street
All manner of people without markings
Or attributes, downwards
Suddenly, silent and swift, downwards
Walking beside us, cheerful, downwards
Out of the midst of the stream of people
An imprecise selection
Six of seven downwards
But the seventh
Enters the dining room.

Who among us will be spared? Who
Is ordained to be saved?
Who is marked?
Where is the grate, the next one?
Unknown.

Scene One: The battle for a dime

Schmitt (*Turns to the* **UPs**.)
Hey you there! I'm looking for someone to deliver my newspapers and hunt for new customers for my newsstand because lately my regular clientele hasn't been growing and I can't leave the stand.

UPs
Choose among us, oh mighty one
We all are eager
To sell your papers.

Schmitt But I don't need just anybody. You there, do you have a family?

UP 1 (*nods*)

UP 2 (*stands in front* **UP 1**)
I've got nobody.

UPs
He drinks.

UP 3 (*stands in front* **UP 2**)
I could
Put up with a lot, I was
A baggage porter.

UP 4 (*stands in front* **UP 3**)
You're too old.

Meyer (*crawls between his legs and stands in front of him*)
I'm younger.

Schmitt
Come along. (*He gives the boy a pack of newspapers.*)

Chorus
Ulysses Schmitt, seasoned in battle
Instruct the novice now, explain to him
The laws of your business.

Schmitt
See those ten newspapers.
(Wipe off your paws!)
Make them into ten dimes.
One for you, nine for me.
(Stand up straight!)
Who are you?
You are nothing.

Nothing but a hole screaming for bread
One more gaping mouth, wanting grub!
But here you have the newspaper:
These ten papers are your all:
The straw you clutch, your rope, island and anchor
Food, shelter and boots for your feet
In any case everything
The world has to offer you.
(Wipe your nose!)
Whoever takes them from you is
Your enemy.
And you have no other, but he
Wants to kill you.
(Listen!)
So ten times you'll be tested
For strength, endurance, courage
Should you fail just once
Better you had never been born
For even one sip of sludge
Would be wasted
On such a man.
You are not the toughest. I
Gave you a break. Others tougher
Than you failed to get their money, but
If you don't get it together
I'll knock off your head
Like I did the others.

Washington Meyer *leaves to sell newspapers.*

Chorus
Now you are on your own and off you go
Prove yourself!
That your time has come, you know
What awaits you, you have heard
Now take action!

Trial run: Selling newspapers
Washington Meyer *sells his newspapers on the street, a moving conveyor belt on which he walks.*

Meyer
Paper! Paper! (*He sells nothing.*)

Chorus
Tell them what's in it for them.

Meyer (*to a* **UP**)
Protective measures by the police for
Christmas Eve in the west! (*He sells nothing.*)

Chorus
Know that there are two kinds
Of people! Their wishes
Are different, different too their views
Different are their deeds.

Meyer (*the boy looks in the newspaper*)
Then I must figure out what the one kind wants and what
The other. Stock market reports! Help wanted ads! (*He sells.*)

Mrs Queck (*to* **Washington Meyer**)   Watch out for Mr Janushek on this street corner, he's brutal by nature and he won't want to pay. (*Exit.*)

Meyer   We'll see whether he pays me or not. I have the papers here, and if he takes one, he'll hand over a dime. (*He places the newspapers at the corner of the building.*)

Chorus
Step forth, Ajax Janushek!
Shatterer of men!
You old shatterhand!

Ajax *takes a paper, pays nothing, leaves.*

UPs (*laughing*)
Now your taskmaster's going to knock your head off!

Meyer
What's the point of running around
When at the end of every day
Janushek appears, the seasoned fighter, and
Takes a paper for free

If for every ten papers the value of
Only one belongs to me
And Janushek steals it in public view
Only because he is strong.
Discouraged, he sits down and cries. He calls up to a window.

Mrs Janushek! Mrs Janushek!
Your son, Mr Janushek, took one of these papers here
And didn't pay!

Mrs Janushek (*at a window*)   I just can't believe that because, if my son takes a newspaper, then he pays for it. (*Exits.*)

Meyer
You old biddy! (*Stops to think.*)
Now I know what I'll do.
Cunning helps.
There's a trash barrel. That's my salvation!
The straw I clutch, my rope, island and anchor.

He fetches the barrel, rolls it to a certain spot and places the newspapers near it.

There is my enemy who wants to kill me.
I'll show him.
Anybody else would put
The papers down where the old woman is looking
But I'll lie down there myself because
I know I can never
Convince her, the mother,
Even if she sees that her son
Doesn't pay for the paper. She
Can't see it. What's it to her
If I'm missing a dime, to her
I have to show my severed head.

He sits on the ground and with his pocket knife cuts out the bottom of the trash barrel and tries sticking his head through it.

Chorus (*turning to the audience*)
Now he's acting like a statesman
Washington Meyer, the statesman

And following the law of the lower depths:
Faced with force, go into hiding!
For if force strikes empty space
Then it weakens itself.
So now he devises a ruse
With this trash barrel.

Trial run: The struggle
Ajax Janushek *returns and tries to take another paper.* **Washington Meyer** *jumps on him.*

Chorus
Still he is weak, for he fights.
Weak is the weakling as long as
He fights.
Soon he is defeated and grows strong
And deploys his ruse.
Falling into the trash barrel
Under the blows of the enemy
He will pretend his head
Has been driven by force
Through the iron-riveted bottom of the barrel
Poor head. After which
A man is dead.
All this he plans under the very eyes of the mother
This is how he frightens the bully
So he's willing to pay.

Meyer   Mrs Janushek! Look out the window, Mrs Janushek!

Mrs Janushek   Ajax!

Ajax Janushek *turns around in alarm. At this moment* **Meyer** *lets himself fall into the barrel so that his head comes out the hole cut in the bottom, as if it had smashed through it.*

Ajax
I'll pay two dimes!
I'll pay three dimes!
If only you'll come back to life!

Meyer
Three dimes!

Ajax
I'll pay three dimes!
I can't bear
That my mother in her old age
Had to witness my vile behaviour.

Meyer
Three dimes!

Mrs Janushek
Ajax, into the bread store this minute.

Crying, **Ajax** *pays a single dime and at the stern call of his mother goes back into the building.*

Meyer
One dime!

Bloodied and tattered from the fight, he shows the **UPs** *the coin.*

UPs
One dime.

Meyer
But at least I have a dime!

UPs
Such a happy man.
He has his dime.

Scene Two: The wood of the widow Niobe Queck
In front of the bread store. [B10]

Mrs Queck   I am the widow Queck with rent in arrears. I do all the errands for Mr Meininger, the master baker who owns the building where I live. Since my husband died, I support my five dependent children with these small errands, including my William, who is a very lively child. There are five because my deceased husband never ever in any way exercised self-restraint, and I would not have taken the liberty of not satisfying him in every way, immediately, totally and completely, for ever and ever. (*Exits into the house.*)

Meininger   Mrs Queck! Come here!

Mrs Queck   Yes, Mr Meininger! I'm coming. I would never take the liberty of not satisfying you in every way, immediately, totally and completely, for ever and ever, Mr Meininger.

Meininger   I need 100 Marks' worth of wood for the ovens in my small bakery, which are heated by hand. Run to the wood merchant Reuter and fetch the wood immediately. As usual, we'll take uncut logs and have them chopped by the unemployed – the neighbourhood is crawling with them – that's a good 30 Marks cheaper than buying chopped wood.

Mrs Queck   Yes, Mr Meininger. So I'll order wood for 100 Marks, uncut logs, as you say, and pronto. (*Exits.*)

UPs (*rushing in*)
Everything's coming up roses today! Work!
Right here we are expecting
A load of wood that needs chopping!

Meininger
Who told you that, you vultures?

UP 1
The news spread like wildfire, Mr Meininger.

UPs
Where are the axes, where's the splitting block?
And we need saws as well!

Meininger
Good. It is true, we do expect a load of wood.
So there will be work. Line up over there.

UPs (*They line up.*)
Everything's coming up roses today!
Steady work!
Everything's coming up roses!

Flamm (*enters*) I'm Flamm the real estate agent and I'm making my rounds. Good morning, Mr Meininger.

Meininger Good morning, Mr Flamm.

Flamm At last a real winter again, beautiful! With snow and ice. Actually, people never feel more alive than in winter. Thanks to the crisp air you go home for lunch with a real appetite. So how's business, Mr Meininger?

Meininger I'm pleased to make your acquaintance. A real estate agency is of course an incomparably bigger business than mine, Mr Flamm. And you negotiate directly with banks.

Flamm Yes, but times are terrible. Our situation as a smaller real estate agency, which to you may seem wonderfully strong because we agreed to a second mortgage on your building, is in fact absolutely horrible. We deal with small banks, which have us by the throat and themselves are in the clutches of the big banks, while the big banks are smack dab in the middle of a crisis because even the big national banks are shaky, what with industry devouring huge sums without really getting ahead, because now the state is even playing with the idea of taxing industry, and what's more – something that hasn't occurred since time immemorial – it has a plan to actually collect the taxes because America, to whom Europe is in debt up to the hilt, is wrestling with its own terrible crisis, and even the most learned experts have absolutely no explanation. I can in fact only touch upon the extremely complex connections between industry and commerce, which I myself hardly understand, because you haven't studied political economy. All you need to know, Mr Meininger, is that you're washed up.

Meininger That's all very interesting, Mr Flamm.

Flamm So how's business, Mr Meininger?

Meininger The Meininger Bread Store, established in 1848, owes its good reputation among its customers to the hand-made method it has consistently maintained.

Flamm Yes, the Meininger Bread Store is considered one of the best small bakeries on this street. It's a shame that the neighbourhood is crawling with bakeries like yours. I see that you employ as many people as a big corporation. Siemens is laying off workers, and you're hiring. That's decent of you, now before Christmas. The people will have something to eat. And when New Year's rolls around, you'll pay us the interest you owe. We're at the limits of our patience, Mr Meininger.

The Meininger Bread Store, with its unpaid interest, will be closed on January 1 unless at least the interest on the mortgages, which are hereby terminated, has been paid. If you pay the interest on January 1, you can continue to peddle your hand-made bread for another year.

Meininger   Mr Flamm, I've seen the light. I wouldn't take the liberty of not satisfying you totally and completely in this matter on January 1. (**Flamm** *exits.*)

UPs
The most powerful man we've ever seen.
And he's complaining!

Meininger (*entering the bread store*)   When I see you bums, I start to see red. (*Yelling from inside the bread store.*) The light's on again in the bakery. This extravagance is going to bankrupt me! Two of you are fired. You don't know what a penny is any more, you've got no respect for a penny any more, there'll be no more beer for supper and we'll throw the Christmas carp in the trash so at least we'll save on the butter.

UPs
Alas, our giant begins to totter.
When giants totter
It's the bystanders who are the victims.

Mrs Queck (*enters*)   Mr Meininger, I executed your order in the greatest haste as best I could totally and completely in every way. The wood will arrive in a moment. Uncut logs. Uncut logs worth 100 Marks.

Meininger   100 Marks for uncut logs in my situation.

Reuter (*enters*)   I'm Reuter the wood merchant with the uncut logs for Mr Meininger. This deal is an important opportunity for me because I must pay Mr Flamm the outstanding interest on my mortgages by January 1. Hello, Mr Meininger.

Meininger   Hello, Mr Reuter.

Reuter   Here's the wood.

Meininger   What wood?

Reuter   Pine logs.

Meininger (*picks up a piece as if it didn't belong to him*)   Nice logs you have there. Who ordered the wood?

Reuter   You, Mr Meininger.

Meininger   You mean me? You're joking. Do you think I have money to throw away? Do I look like the head of Siemens?

Reuter   Mr Meininger, don't play games with me. Mrs Queck ordered this wood for you, and here it is. I came with her to collect the money right away because a rumour has spread like wildfire that not everything is in order here. Here is the invoice.

Meininger   Wait a minute. Mrs Queck!

Mrs Queck   Something else, Mr Meininger?

Meininger   Mrs Queck, I ask you now in the presence of Mr Reuter, the wood merchant, whether I instructed you to order wood for me. What do you have to say, Mrs Queck?

Mrs Queck   Yes, Mr Meininger.

Meininger   What do you mean, yes? Did I instruct you to or not?

Mrs Queck   No, Mr Meininger.

Reuter   Mr Meininger, I don't believe my own ears.

Meininger   Yes, Mr Reuter, you shouldn't have believed your ears when Mrs Queck ordered this wood supposedly for me. I must ask myself, Mr Reuter, how could you listen to Mrs Queck. Mrs Queck is less than nothing.

Mrs Queck   Yes, how could you, Mr Reuter. If I say you should deliver wood, you can't simply turn around and deliver wood. Who am I after all.

Reuter   I would never dream of handing over a truckload of wood to Mrs Queck.

Mrs Queck   Never.

Reuter   Am I an idiot or what?

Meininger   This is a question only you can answer, Mr Reuter.

Mrs Queck   Yes, you have to answer it for yourself, Mr Reuter.

Meininger   Yes, Mr Reuter, as you see, the wood belongs to Mrs Queck. The invoice goes to Mrs Queck.

Reuter   Well, Mrs Queck, Mr Meininger refuses to accept the wood you ordered. As far as I'm concerned it's your wood, Mrs Queck. Here is the invoice.

Mrs Queck I ordered the wood for Mr Meininger.

Reuter Did you have a purchase order in writing?

Mrs Queck No.

Reuter Don't you have some kind of proof that Mr Meininger ordered the wood?

Mrs Queck No. Wait. Mr Meininger hired those men to chop the wood, they have axes.

Reuter Mr Meininger!

Meininger Mr Reuter?

Reuter (*pointing to the* **UPs** *and axes*) So, Mr Meininger, the fact that you ordered the wood is beyond dispute at this point, don't you think.

Meininger Can't you just take the wood back, Mr Reuter?

Reuter No, in these times the rule is we don't accept returns on anything. You ordered the wood, Mr Meininger.

Meininger Anyway, those are uncut logs. Since when have I ordered uncut logs?

Reuter For the past five years, Mr Meininger.

Meininger I'll tell you when I stopped ordering logs – I stopped this morning.

[B4]

Reuter Really! In our little town we have a way of handling cases like this, you know. So what have we got?

Meininger The police.

Reuter The police. The police are charged with guaranteeing law and order, and what's happening here, you must agree, is not law and order. I'm turning you over to the police, Meininger.

[B10]

Meininger But Reuter my friend, we're not going to come to blows just because of the wood.

Reuter Mr Meininger, I agree, it's embarrassing to argue with you in front of this rabble.

Meininger May I invite you to step inside, Mr Reuter?

Reuter Thank you, Mr Meininger.

Exeunt to the bread store.

UPs
Alas, among the giants
Struggle breaks out anew
Who will pay the price?
Surely not the giant.
Alas our giant totters!
On whom
Does his expiring eye alight with greed?
Surely it alights on us!
For the giants struggle, but
It's the bystanders who are the victims!

Meininger (*standing in the door*) Mrs Queck, can you pay your outstanding rent on New Year's day? Mrs Queck, your lease is terminated.

Mrs Queck Do I have to move out, Mr Meininger?

Meininger Exactly.

Mrs Queck Then the furniture has to be carried downstairs.

Meininger Get the axes!

UP 1 Too bad, we won't be chopping the wood after all. But we've been standing around in the cold for half an hour, someone has to pay for that.

Meininger Why only half an hour? You've been standing around in the cold for days, I suppose I should pay you for that too?

UP 2 No.

Meininger You see what I mean.

UP 3 Hold on, just hold on, you owe us for the half hour. We just stood around for the last half hour because you told us to.

A Chorus Member Here rules logic, here rules hunger.

Meininger Can someone show me exactly what you have done? You see. Carry the woman's furniture down. (*Exits to the bread store.*)

Mrs Queck What a day!

The **UPs** *carry down a chest of drawers, a sofa, two chairs and five children.*

Mrs Queck   Be careful with the chest of drawers. Watch out on the left it still has one leg left.

Masher   Okay, we'll bump it on the right then, Mrs Queck.

Mrs Queck   Thank you, Mr Masher.

Frederick   Mama!

Mrs Queck (*sits down on the furniture*)
Shut up, Frederick! Well, at least that's done.
Dwelling in this house full twenty years
We had begun to love our cosy home
Even the leaking pipes
I would not be without them in my old age
Without the dampened wall –
Even the mould to me
Is precious in the floor boards –
My life would be a life no longer.
The blast of wind through the wall
I know it
Even the toilet's stench
Didn't bother us
We are accustomed to the smoking, but
Wood-devouring stove
And accustomed to
The trembling of the house
Below the elevated trains and
Above the subway trains.

Reuter (*coming out of the bread store with* **Meininger***, both with thick cigars*)   Mr Meininger, you know that I would like to come to an agreement with you, but the problem is that Mrs Queck owns nothing.

Meininger (*pointing to the furniture*)   Mrs Queck has very little but not nothing, Mr Reuter.

Reuter   So, this furniture belongs to you, Mrs Queck.

Mrs Queck   Indeed, Mr Reuter.

Reuter (*examines the furniture*)   Junk! You will have to pay for the wood, Mr Meininger.

Meininger   Why should I?

Reuter   Of course, you have certain claims on Mrs Queck. And Mrs Queck does own the furniture.

Meininger   Junk! Mr Reuter, I refuse to pay for the wood because Mrs Queck owns furniture.

Reuter   I won't accept this junk, Mr Meininger. And what is that?

[B12]

Mrs Queck   This is the bass tuba of my deceased husband Mr Queck, made of real brass. I'm saving it for my boy William who is very musical.

[B11]

Reuter   Mind you, I want to make clear that if I confiscate your furniture, I am not acting in the capacity of a social worker but solely as a private businessman. I say that to prevent another stink in the newspapers, which unfortunately are always mean enough to turn the straightforward acts of men who sacrifice themselves for the public good into something devious. I believe that after this explanation no one will be able to use this against me, Mrs Queck. Alfons, you can take the furniture away immediately. (**Reuter** *exits*.)

[B10]

Alfons   So, Mrs Queck, I'll have to take away your chaise longue now.

Mrs Queck   Henry, get off, you too Leopold.

Alfons   I'm sorry I have to do this ...

Mrs Dittmeyer (*coming out of the house*)   What's going on here? You can't be serious about taking away Mrs Queck's last pieces of furniture. That's the limit. Mrs Franzke! (**Mrs Franzke** *looks out the window*.) Now they're even taking away Mrs Queck's furniture.

Mrs Franzke   Honestly, that shouldn't be allowed, taking away the woman's furniture on top of everything else.

Mrs Queck   No, that really shouldn't be allowed.

Mrs Dittmeyer   So, what will you do now, Mrs Queck, no apartment, saddled with the children. Mrs Janushek! Mrs Queck's furniture is being taken away.

Mrs Janushek *looks out the window.*

Mrs Franzke Mr Bolke should do something!

Mrs Dittmeyer Mr Schmitt! (*To* **Mrs Franzke**) That's the newspaper man at the corner.

Bolke What's the matter, Mrs Franzke?

Mrs Franzke Mrs Queck has been put out on the street and now her furniture is being taken away.

Mrs Janushek Ajax, see if everything's okay.

Ajax (*coming out*) So what's up with the furniture?

[B4]

Mrs Franzke Mrs Queck, send your Henry to the police station right now.

Mrs Queck Henry, run to the police station, quick.

Mr Dittmeyer Now we'll see whether a human being can just disappear into quicksand right here on the spot, at five in the afternoon.

[B15]

Policeman Break it up! Who owns the piece of junk?

Mrs Queck Please, Officer, that's a chest of drawers.

Policeman (*exiting*) Get the chest out of here immediately, it's blocking the way.

[B10]

Alfons I have strict instructions from Mr Reuter to take the furniture away, but if you want to interfere and you speak softly to me, then I'll go without it.

Bolke In that case then we would indeed by all means speak to you softly.

Ajax So, I think we all agree that the furniture stays here, right?

Alfons Okay, fine. (*Wants to leave.*)

Schmitt (*enters*)
Stop! What are you doing? Lunatics
Ready to rush into battle
Yet without weapons, blinded by pity! Would you
Retrieve
A single pebble that

Fell into the sea!
Who are you? They hear you talking five streets away
Like millionaires who determine the fate of the world
As they see fit. But hardly able
To fend for yourselves, with half-filled stomachs
Begging for clothes
And still not ready to hold your tongues!
Return to your homes, hold on to what's yours
Stuff wax in both your ears so you
Can turn back.

Pause.

Chorus
Now they come to their senses.
Warned of the consequences
They hesitate to express their pity.
Soon
You will see them leave with a handshake
Seeking their own
Warm homes.

Mrs Dittmeyer (*leaving*) She still owes us a milk jug, we'll never get it back now.

Mr Dittmeyer (*leaving*) I kept asking you: did you get the milk jug back?

Mrs Queck No, I wouldn't have believed it either that one day I couldn't return a milk jug.

Mrs Franzke
Oh, Mrs Queck
Now you're sitting out on the street. Just this morning
You spoke to me so kindly.
You always kept the stairwell so clean
And often you said: such and such
You would never take the liberty to do.
What will you do now. Where will you
Go tonight.

Chorus
Wait! Ask no more
If she answers, what will you do?

You cannot help her!
Stuff wax in both your ears
Or you'll be lost for years!

Mrs Franzke *exits.* **Ajax** *shakes hands with* **Mrs Queck** *and leaves.*
Schmitt *shakes hands with* **Mrs Queck** *and looks at her silently.*

UPs
That guy there is right!
He says nothing!
He asks nothing!
And he gives nothing!
For he knows his place.

Chorus
Stuff wax in both your ears
Or you'll be lost for years!
Don't ask! The answer of the unfortunate
Only entraps you in misfortune
You who are too weak to help
Are not strong enough to hear the death cry
Unlike the battles on high are those in the depths!
For those in the depths sink
For almost no reason. The slightest blow knocks them
Fully flat. Seven times seven mishaps struck them
Ere they were born. Each misfortune that strikes
Is for them the final one.

Alfons
So should I take the furniture away? (*Silence.*)
So I'll take the furniture away.

Alfons *exits with his handcart.* **Mrs Queck** *runs around the stage like a chicken with its head cut off.*

UPs
Gone too the furniture! The third mishap!
Those struck not by just one mishap lose
Not only the prospect of rescue but also
Their dignity. Easily we forsake those
Who can no longer be helped. Thank God, they are gone
They could no longer be helped.

This we know:
He who is afflicted with boils
Seems himself like a boil.
We don't rid him of boils; instead
We get rid of him.

Chorus
Yet breaking away is hard, especially for him
Who dwells at the edge of an abyss and in it
He scavenges for bread. Threatened himself, he is loath
To abandon his own kind. Who signs a death sentence
Where the name is left blank? Perhaps it's his own.

UP 1 Mr Meininger! We carried down Mrs Queck's furniture, we have to be paid. You can't argue with that.

Meininger Yes, so you carried down Mrs Queck's furniture?

Mrs Queck Yes, they did, you can't argue with that Mr Meininger.

Meininger (*leaving*) So, you're paying, Mrs Queck. That's good. Well, folks, I've got my own troubles.

Chorus
Unlike the battles on high are
Those in the depths. The defeated giant
Goes home to eat after the battle.

Masher So, Mrs Queck, that makes one half hour per person 25 cents: comes to 1 Mark 25.

Mrs Queck 1 Mark 25, you say? Okay.

UPs (*holding out their hands*) So, 1 Mark 25.

Mrs Queck You know what, I don't have any cash.

Masher Yes, Mrs Queck, but that's not the end of the story.

Mrs Queck Yes, yes. Now I owe you 1 Mark 25. Last week I was at my wits' end because Leopold needed socks, and now just like that 100 Marks out the window. If the gentlemen could perhaps lend me 30 cents, then at least I wouldn't be completely without means for the time being.

[B4]

Meyer (*enters*)   So, gentlemen, Meyer's contract with Schmitt is now on a different footing. Washington Meyer has taken over the mobile newsstand.

Mrs Queck   Congratulations, Mr Meyer. Couldn't you hire my William? I'm in a fix now.

Meyer   I can't do it, Mrs Queck, I'd be putting my contract at risk. I'm not allowed to hire minors.

UP 1   Washington, the woman was thrown out in the street.

[B10]

Meyer
Yes, Mrs Queck, I regret to see you
In changed circumstances, which surely will not
Last for long. I myself
Barely found shelter and work
And I would be happy if I could say to you: Here
You take my first dime!
But I can do nothing for you.

Chorus
Stop! Don't offer the dime
From your pocket! You who rise
Plug your ears to the lament of those sinking
Stuff wax in both your ears
Or you'll be lost for years!

Mrs Queck   I myself find it really unpleasant to sit here in the street. You know I dislike being dependent on people. They don't actually do anything for you. They don't raise a finger when someone has some bad luck, although their heads are full of their own worries. I couldn't even tell you right now what I plan to do in the next half hour.

[A27/A25]

Chorus
Just when the need is greatest, something will turn up.
And here comes – the Salvation Army: Mrs Queck's heavenly opportunity.

Salvation Army (*enters singing*)
March ahead to the fight

Where satan's pow'r is at its height
Sing ye now, use your might,
Let your song ring
through the night.
Soon you will see the morning light,
And with the morning our Lord Jesus Christ,
Hallelujah!

[B15]

UP 1 (*impudently*)   The woman is lying in the street, Lieutenant.

Mrs Queck (*impudently*)   I'm lying in the street, Lieutenant.

Hippler   Why are you out in the street, sister?

Mrs Queck   I said: you ordered the wood, Mr Meininger.

Hippler   And what was the truth?

Mrs Queck   That Mr Meininger ordered the wood.

Hippler   That can't be the reason you were evicted, look into your heart, why has God punished you?

UP 2   Because Mr Meininger is bankrupt.

Hippler   Tell the truth, sister.

UP 3   She already did.

Mrs Queck   I didn't pay the rent, just imagine, five months.

Hippler   Oh, you didn't pay your rent. But that can't be the truth either. The truth is that you have sinned, in the eyes of God. We will sing No. 27: Lift your eyes to the Lord.

[A4]

UP 1   Excuse me for saying so but this woman's not short on piety, she's short a place to sleep. I think she's fine on the inside, it's the outside that's the problem.

[B42]

UP 2   Is there no chance for the woman?

Hippler   Yes, there's a chance for her in heaven.

UP 3   But that's not a chance she can really take.

Hippler   Indeed it is hard to get into the kingdom of heaven. In fact it is easier to get into a bank.

Mrs Janushek   Just imagine, I hear Mrs Queck is going to a bank.

Hippler   Mrs Queck is not going to a bank. She must go into herself and become a fully mature person. Concentrating on external matters won't help Mrs Queck at all.

[B16]

Mrs Queck   But can't we talk about external matters?

Hippler   No, we don't want to discuss external matters. We want to discuss what is inside you, sister, and what it looks like in there. Are you inwardly so mature and so certain that you are as you should be, and that there are no deficiencies in your relationship with God? So that you can just stand up and just ask him: now help me, God.

Meyer   Let's assume that she can say it about herself, or one of her five kids can say it about himself: does that get them off the street? Mrs Queck, I'm asking you now, what do you want? Bread or solace?

Chorus
What will she want? Bread or solace?
What will she get? Solace!

[B5]

Hippler   Just get your own house in order, Mr Meyer. Leave Mrs Queck to our good Lord. And now, Mr Meyer, what is your attitude toward God?

Meyer   Well, Miss Hippler, it's positive, very positive. Only he seems to have very little influence in the city. We always hear that he has a lot of rich friends, Mr Rockefeller and Mr Siemens. But unfortunately his friends often seem to leave him in the lurch.

Hippler   Oh, you mean because he never buys your newspapers?

Meyer   That too.

Hippler   God is invisible.

Meyer   Yes, he is, he's damn invisible. We would all like to surrender Mrs Queck to the good Lord, but not to the snow and to hunger.

[B16]

Hippler Well, the external problem, that's easy, who owns the building you were evicted from?

Salvation Army girl (*pulls her back by the sleeve*) Don't get mixed up in this, sister, the people should settle these worldly things among themselves.

Meyer The building belongs to Meininger, the baker, he threw her out, Mr Meininger.

Hippler Mr Meininger is a very decent man. Every Sunday he sits in his usual seat at our service, right, sisters? It's easy to have a Christian conversation with Mr Meininger.

Salvation Army girl What are you thinking, sister. Don't get mixed up in a situation like this.

Meyer Then go ahead, have a Christian conversation with Mr Meininger.

Salvation Army girl (*mumbles*) Stuff wax in both your ears, or we too will be lost for years.

Hippler (*to those behind her*) What is it you want from me? (*To those in front.*) You only think about worldly things.

Meyer (*Pulls out a dime.*) Yes, but we don't just think, we also act. Here is a dime, a very common, lowly, ugly, dirty dime.

Meyer (*holds up two closed fists, one with a dime in it*) Mrs Queck, I ask you now: Bread or solace?

Mrs Queck I'll close my eyes, Mr Meyer. (*Taps the dime.*)

Meyer Bread.

[B28]

Chorus
Behold, it reaches
The foundering woman, the bread store's
Final gift! A meagre hard roll.

A Chorus Member
So now, what about the power of religion?

[B29]
Hippler Our text today is: Although you neither see nor taste him, yet he is present everywhere. You understand, God is ever-present, even if we do not perceive his works at this moment. Now a related parable –

A Chorus Member We understand, either God exists or Mrs Queck does.

[B30]
Hippler
Vice vaunts itself, but soon passes away!

Salvation Army girl
Let's go, sister.

Hippler (*exiting*)
Sin sits clothed in scarlet, and her breasts are never empty!

[B4]
Meyer Mrs Queck, I have decided to help you move ahead. I will put you back on your feet as quickly as possible. In my trade I come into contact with all kinds of people, I'll see whether I can find a buyer for the wood.

Mrs Queck That's very kind of you, Mr Meyer.

UP 1 Hey, Washington. What about us? Is there nothing in it for us?

[B10]
Meyer Mrs Queck, we'll sell the wood chopped up.

UPs

Now there'll be work! Roll up your sleeves!
Washington Meyer is looking for a buyer.

Meyer What should a buyer pay for chopped wood?

Masher 140.

Meyer What do you get for chopping the wood?

UP 2 Eighty cents an hour.

Meyer How many hours do you need?

UP 3 With five people two hours.

Meyer That leaves 32 Marks for you, Mrs Queck. And you'll get your furniture too.

Mrs Queck I'll have 32 Marks, Mr Meyer, that's more than I expected.

Masher You see, Mrs Queck, you should never give up, something always turns up.

Mrs Queck
God never forsakes his own, Mr Masher.

UPs and Renters (*singing and dancing*)
A miracle has happened! The poorest of the poor
Get a chance: they are the ones who
Fetch the booty, they gather up the spoils
The defeated giants' abandoned goods.

UPs
A miracle! When two rich men argue
The poor man laughs! As if a frightened giant shits
In the middle of the square and an anguished cry
Arises too soon from those upon whom
It falls. Behold, they see when morning dawns:
Dung can be sold.

UPs and Renters
Thank God, there is help for Mrs Queck!
Thank God, she is not without resources!
She is not without prospects, she has a wood pile!
That really takes a weight
Off our minds.

Scene Three: The return of Washington Meyer

[B24]

UP 1 What do you see?

Masher (*standing on the woodpile on the look-out*) Still nothing.

UP 2 If only we had agreed on a signal so that right away, when he turns the corner, we'd know if he had succeeded. You still don't see anything?

Masher Sure, I see a lot: the stream of people from the subway and the line there in front of the employment office, but no sign of Meyer. Since he left to find a buyer, the earth has swallowed him up, but now I see something: Meyer!

UPs
Now there'll be work! Roll up your sleeves!
Grab an axe and a splitting block, grease up the saws
Chop the woodpile into neat little pieces and
Then we'll buy bread!

Mrs Queck Is he alone?

Masher Yes.

Mrs Queck Fast?

Masher Slow.

Mrs Queck What's he got in his hand?

Masher Nothing.

Mrs Queck That surprises me.

Meyer *enters, sits silently on the woodpile.*

A UP Well?

Meyer *shrugs.*

Masher Hey man, speak! – So nothing.

Meyer So, now you're surprised.

Mrs Queck Let him alone, Mr Masher, we have the pile of wood, someone will have to buy it from us sooner or later.

Scene Four: The night

A child It's so cold, mama.

[B15]

Mrs Queck There's no real winter anymore. When I was your age, winter began in October and it lasted until April 15, and that cold was another thing entirely. The toilet was a solid piece of ice. I can still hear grandpa saying: it's too cold. The man had 90 years under his belt.

[B34]

Meyer Although it's forbidden and can cost me my job, for tonight come in here, into the newsstand.

[B50]

Chorus
Washington Meyer, statesman
Do you no longer know that
Cheap pity's no help to the pitied but
Weakens the person who pities, and that
In such times one single
Humane thought can suffice
To shatter the ground on which
Fate has set us up, therefore
Stuff wax in both your ears
Or you'll soon be lost for years!

[B25]

Meyer Quiet, police. If he sees you, the plan for spending the night here is off, and besides I'll be out on my ear and can start again from scratch.

Mrs Queck Don't worry, I'm literally holding my breath. No one's heard me yet.

Policeman Hey, who's in that newsstand?

Meyer Nobody.

Policeman Who's in that newsstand, I asked.

Mrs Queck's voice Nobody.

Policeman All right, let's take a look at the nobody who's spending the night in your newsstand. So, you rent out your newsstand, and if something happens, then it's the fault of the police.

[B36]

A Chorus Member But Mrs Queck shouldn't have to freeze to death on a park bench.

Policeman   No, because when it's this cold she's not allowed to sit on the park bench.

A Chorus Member   I see, freezing to death is forbidden.

[B26]

Policeman (*pushes* **Mrs Queck** *out and says*)   And now get out of the stand. At night people belong at home.

Mrs Queck   We don't have a home, Officer, that was our home.

Policeman   Sure, and now I'm the monster. And if I don't follow the rules, what happens to me? And I have three kids.

Mrs Queck
You didn't need to have so many kids
Now you're trapped.

Policeman (*exiting*)   The stand has been confiscated.

Mrs Queck   Don't worry, Mr Meyer, we have the pile of wood, someone will have to buy it from us sooner or later.

Scene Five: A loaf of bread

[B22]

Mrs Queck   It's almost 1 o'clock. I see that everyone's eating lunch, and I'm hungry too. After all, I still have the woodpile here.

UP 1   But at the moment you've got almost nothing to eat.

Mrs Queck   It's true, I've got nothing to eat.

UPs (*singing*)
Well, what's up with you, Mrs Queck. You
Have the wood and yet nothing to eat? Well
Can that be true? What
Does the wood merchant live on if not on his woodpile?
Oh, but it isn't the wood that pays for his grub
It's the woodcutters
What a revelation, Mrs Queck!
The world is not what it seems!
It takes your breath away! And your bread as well.
Well, what's up with you Mrs Queck?

Well, your woodpile is nothing but dreck!
Well, what's up with you Mrs Queck!

Mrs Janushek   Ajax, come up here, the soup is on the table!

Ajax (*enters*)   Just a minute, mama!

UP 2   Hey, Ajax, it's feeding time.

Masher   Mrs Queck, there is a man who, if he wanted …

Mrs Queck   But Mr Masher!

Masher   … you'd get your loaf of bread right away.

Mrs Queck   Do you really think so, Mr Masher?

Masher   Mr Janushek, there's a pretty woman here who'd like you to give her something to eat.

Ajax   Who is it?

Masher   The young woman may not want me to tell you her name yet.

Ajax   Can I look at her with my own eyes?

Masher   What would that be worth to you?

Ajax   Offer her one loaf of bread at the most.

Masher   Could you bring it out here?

Ajax   I can't just give away one of Mr Meininger's loaves of bread here on a public street.

Masher   You're not just giving it away.

Ajax   Well, then, the person in question will have to come and get the loaf of bread herself.

Masher   Where?

Ajax   In this case I'd give it to her inside the bread store.

Masher   Just a moment, Mr Janushek. (*To* **Mrs Queck**.) Mrs Queck, the other party is offering a loaf of bread. Do you accept the offer?

Mrs Queck   Of course.

Masher   Then you can get it in the bread store.

Mrs Queck   Thank you very much, Mr Masher.

Masher The other party accepts the offer.

Ajax I've had second thoughts, Mr Masher. I can't just give her a loaf of bread for that.

Masher Well, what will you give her instead?

Ajax Mr Masher, in a deal like this I'll give a woman all the pleasure she wants, but not a loaf of bread.

Masher Mr Janushek, the young woman is not in the mood for pleasure.

Ajax Leave that to me, Mr Masher.

Masher What if the young woman doesn't enjoy it?

Ajax *smiles.*

Masher And if she really doesn't enjoy it?

Ajax Then I'll give her a loaf of bread.

Masher Mr Janushek, I want to see whether the young woman is willing to accept this proposition. (*To* **Mrs Queck**.) The other party isn't willing to stuff a loaf of bread down your throat too – pleasure on top of pleasure. Make up your mind.

Mrs Queck I'm not in the mood for a good time, Mr Masher.

Masher Then you'll get a loaf of bread.

Mrs Queck A loaf of bread is what I would like, I only care about the loaf of bread.

Masher Then that's all you'll get, Mrs Queck. (*To* **Ajax**.) It's a deal, Mr Janushek. Mr Janushek, kindly proceed into the bread store.

Chorus
Into the bread store, Niobe Queck
And be mindful as in ancient times
That you withstand the omnipotence of love
And resist the primal urge.

Mrs Queck I only care about the loaf of bread. (*Enters the bread store.*)

Chorus
Behold how inconspicuously
The pair of lovers meets

The room behind the baking trough is waiting
Impatiently for the
Obliging visitor, but
Slow is her step and, as we said, inconspicuous
So it should be.
Now show tact and restraint, all of you
Talk about the weather, for who really
Knows what is happening now, who
Can know it. Perhaps he's reading to her from the newspaper.
Surely she's just sorting his laundry.

Mrs Janushek (*from the window*)   Ajax, the soup's getting cold.

Ajax (*in the bread store*)   Just a minute, mama.

Masher   Watch him closely when he comes out.

UPs
Will his face most likely
When he emerges now
Reveal triumph or failure?

Ajax *comes out of the bread store, casually checks the temperature of the air, and goes up the stairs.*

UPs
Iron countenance!
His face reveals nothing
So it should be.
Hail Ajax!
Now emerge, Niobe Queck
Show what you accomplished
Triumph or failure!

Mrs Queck   *comes out beaming, hiding something under her skirt, and then holds up a loaf of bread.*

Masher   Mrs Queck, you kept your promise.

Mrs Queck   For me the loaf of bread was all I cared about. Henry!

The children enter.

Mrs Queck
Here, Henry, your bread.
And here, Leopold, yours.
Pay heed as you eat it. For
An inner voice tells me:
This is the last bread
I will slice for you.

Scene Six A: The heavenly bread store

[A26]

Masher Mrs Queck, we've been waiting five days for work, but now the hunger and cold are too much for us. Mrs Queck, we must now leave you to your own sad fate.

Mrs Queck I feel very bad about holding you up for so long, just imagine, five days.

A group from the Social Welfare Agency arrives.

Meyer Social Welfare Agency. Mrs Queck, now they'll get you off the street.

[A8]

Physician Well, what's the matter?

Mrs Queck My hands hurt and my feet are swollen.

Physician Mrs Queck, eat an egg and some chicken broth every morning and soon we'll have you back in shape. Your children need a healthy mother, Mrs Queck.

Mrs Queck A very good doctor.

[B32]

Social Worker Oh, those must be the little children. I certainly hope they're all younger than four.

Meyer Mrs Queck, you did tell me that all of them are under four, didn't you?

Mrs Queck Henry is just four. Anna would be three and a quarter. Leopold two and a half. And Frederick one year old.

Meyer (*to the fifth child*)   Yes, and what will we do with you? You must be a twin, that settles that.

Social Worker   Well, Mrs Queck, now say goodbye to your children.

Mrs Queck   Do I have to take leave of my children now?

Social Worker   Yes, children, now say goodbye to your dear mother.

Chorus   Now, Niobe Queck, take leave of the children you raised with so much effort and many a sleepless night.

Mrs Queck   Bye, children.

Children   Bye, mama.

[A9]

Mrs Queck   That's one less worry. But there's still the pile of wood.

[B35]

Meyer   To get her off the street, well, something would have to happen in this country. We would have to march from one end of the world to the other. Not a stone could remain of the city as it now stands.

[B8]

Chorus
Behold, Washington Meyer, the statesman
Young still in years he could not
Bear to see them lying in the filthy street
The unfortunate ones.

[A12/A4]

Meyer (*calls to the* **UPs**)   We've waited much too long. We must turn to stronger measures. Then, I think, we can present you with a small fruitcake, Mrs Queck.

Mrs Queck   But Mr Meyer, surely you aren't thinking about doing something harmful to Mr Meininger. That wouldn't be right, after all, I've lived in his building for twenty years.

Masher   You see, Meyer, she doesn't want to join us.

Meyer   All join in or we starve, all of us.

[B42]

Hippler (*enters*)   Oh, you want to do something wrong.

Chorus   Disputation.

Masher   Is a person bad for wanting to eat?

Hippler   No.

UP 1   But if the person gets nothing to eat?

Hippler   God feeds the birds of the air, and so will he feed you too.

UP 2   Yes, but if somebody just sits on his hands and waits for God to give him everything, just sits back and takes it easy, that's not right either, is it?

Hippler   No, that wouldn't be right either.

Masher   That's right. You have to hustle, if you want help from God. So you should be allowed to hustle for your food, and if they absolutely won't give it to you, it's alright to take steps to force it out of them – one way or another.

Hippler   Stop, you shouldn't do anything illegal.

UP 3   Yes, but if you have to use force to get something to eat, is it wrong? Don't we also have a right?

[B41]

Hippler   Someone who doesn't work has no rights.

Masher   Well, if we only have rights when we work, then we must have the right to work, because otherwise we have no right to any rights.

Hippler   No one has a right to anything. What you receive is a blessing and not a right.

UP 4   Well, then we must have a right to be blessed, otherwise we need a blessing to get blessed.

[A27]

Hippler   If you don't wear a crisp, high collar for all to see, that's fine. But if you're hiding a limp, loose collar on the inside – that's monstrous.

[B42]

Masher Enough of this.

Hippler You can't just do whatever you want.

[B17]

Meyer Why are we the ones who can't do what we want? Mr Meininger can throw Mrs Queck out, he does whatever he wants.

[B17/B19]

Hippler Put your own house in order, Mr Meininger can't just do whatever he wants because there is something in him that tells him what he must do, and that is his conscience. And if Mr Meininger did not have that, then all the police in the world couldn't prevent him from doing whatever he wants. The rich control the state, and they have money and are also smarter than you and they also don't drink so much. They've gone to the university and considered everything and don't simply vegetate like animals. What can you do against them in the shape you're in: poor, abject, stupid and full of urges I don't even want to talk about. And yet there is something that speaks to them and that stands above them and speaks to them privately in their little rooms.

Meyer They don't have little rooms, they have palaces.

Hippler Yes, in their palaces of marble and gold something speaks to them and says: who are you? And what is it that is speaking? It's conscience. And so it can happen that a rich and powerful man suddenly becomes humble and recognizes: he's only human, just like you, and he can't do whatever he wants, just as you can't do whatever you want. Only in your case it takes the police to make you recognize it. The poor have to be in favour of religion because only religion prevents the rich from making mincemeat of the poor.

[B18]

Meininger (*enters*) What Miss Hippler just told you is very true, I can subscribe to every word.

Hippler Oh, good morning, Mr Meininger.

Meininger Good morning, Lieutenant Hippler.

Hippler By the way, Mr Meininger, couldn't you take Mrs Queck in again, it would be a big help to her.

Meininger Miss Hippler, that's impossible. You see, I've taken in another family, I can't just put them out on the street.

Hippler No, Mr Meininger, it's true, that won't work, but just ask your conscience. The apartment belongs to Mrs Queck.

Meininger No, no, no, the apartment belongs to me. I can't do whatever I want. I have to pay the interest on my mortgage, whether I want to or not.

[B16]

Hippler Mr Meininger, the people are all so angry because no one is helping Mrs Queck. You will take her in again, don't you agree?

Meininger What do you mean? They're angry? Agree to what? Let me tell you something, Miss Hippler, keep your hands off my property, understood. Since when has this become the fashion at the Salvation Army? That's bolshevism, that's what it is.

[B18]

Hippler Mr Meininger, as a Christian, you simply can't talk like that.

Meininger And what's more, its noon and time for lunch, consequently I don't have the time to argue with you about who owns my property.

Hippler It belongs to the Lord Jesus, Mr Meininger!

Meininger (*exiting*) You are not the Lord Jesus, Miss!

Hippler (*following him*) Where is your conscience, Mr Meininger!

[B24]

Masher Now I ask you: what is she doing in the bread store?

Meyer She's saying good morning, Mr Meininger, you have a pile of wood there. Mr Meininger, what is its value? – Miss Hippler, the wood cost me 120 Marks. – Mr Meininger, do you need cash? You do need cash, don't you? For Flamm, your business associate? You don't need wood, and look here, here's cash. 50 Marks. But we need the wood, and we'll have it chopped for 20 cents an hour by our deserving poor. – The deal is done, Miss Hippler. That's how it works, Mr Meininger.

Masher   I can't believe it. That would be illegal.

Hippler (*still at the door*)   That's how it works, Mr Meininger. Come with me, Mrs Queck, there is shelter for you at the Salvation Army.

Mrs Queck   And the wood?

[B31]

Hippler   Mrs Queck, we've now arranged the wood business so that we'll take over the wood ourselves, it's better for you this way. Why should you waste your time on such things?

Mrs Queck   That's what I always said, why should I?

[B24]

UPs
Welcome friends! Liberators all!
Behold in us willing workers
With hands poised we stand
Ready to work!
Double time will be our pace
Triple the power of our firm grasp!

Hippler (*while the* **Salvation Army troop** *tunes its instruments and opens the hymnals*)   Let us begin with a prayer.

UPs   Excuse us, Miss Hippler, but where are the axes? Where's the splitting block! We don't see the saws either.

Hippler   We will now sing No. 27.

Salvation Army troop (*sings*)
Unto the Lord lift thine eyes!
Seek nothing other than God.
Things of this earth are but lies
Hence unto the Lord turn thine eyes
And not to this earthly abode!
Hark to the words of our Lord
Not to the voice of this world
Let Satan be put to the sword.

Masher   But what are they doing there?

UP 1   Why are they carrying off the wood?

[B10]
Meyer They're having it chopped on the cheap by their own poor. I guess at the Salvation Army they know how to balance their accounts.

[B24]
Salvation Army troop (*sings*)
... We hear only God and his word
That he may be pleased by our deeds

UPs
Alas, they are carrying off the wood!
Only through work was there hope for bread
And they are carrying off our work
The soldiers of heaven!

Hippler
Take just a moment now listen
For three minutes only to the voice of heaven!

UPs
In the service of capital.
Hallelujah slut, now you're carrying off the wood!
Put the wood down! You bloodhounds!

Hippler (*to the troop*)
Hold steadfast against this hostility, even if
They throw mud at you, and hurry up!

UPs
You musical jackasses! Singing and trampling!
Take your hymnals and leave the wood here!

Meininger (*rushes out*)
Whoever disrupts Miss Hippler's singing will answer to me!
Abusing harmless young ladies!
Starving trash, you are nothing and you own nothing
And you know nothing and only want to stuff your faces!
How dare you crawl forth in broad daylight
From your mouldy hovels, filthy
Like bedbugs and legion like bedbugs. You bloodsuckers!

Lazy rabble! Lowlifes!
Stinking troublemakers!

UPs
You're no troublemaker but you
Sure do stink. Bloated fat ass!
When a letter comes from the bank
He shits in his pants!
But he kicks the widow out
With his filthy feet!
Dirty little shopkeeper!
Puts plaster in the bread and then raises the price.

Meyer
Now look how he shits in his pants
When the mighty fist of the masses threatens!
Smash in his windows!

Meininger
What, you want to start a riot here?
Hey, you renters! Bolke, Mrs Franzke and you Dittmeyers
And you tenants and lodgers too, get out here!

Renters
What's up, Mr Meininger?

Meininger
A riot!
They're attacking the bread store!

Meyer
If they don't give you work
Then use force and take the bread.
Straight from the store!

[B19]

Mrs Queck Mr Meyer, how can you be so wicked. You ought to know that religion is in us all and that only religion can help us. I would not allow myself not to obey our dear Lord and his commandments in every way, immediately, totally and completely. If you want to do something illegal, I will have nothing more to do with you, gentlemen.

Hippler Quite right, for there is not only this world but also another, and you should turn your attention to that one. There is not only an earthly bread store but also a heavenly one, and that is your bread store, Mrs Queck. What ails you, sister?

[B33]

Mrs Queck I feel weak.

[B27]

Hippler
Oh sisters, she is overcome by weakness
Which in truth is strength, and
Her earthly body, suffering too much deprivation
Is failing, while in truth
The soul is rising up from her body and cold fear
Which strangles her breath
In truth is hope.
And now those things are clear that had been obscure.
This hunger, never satisfied,
Tears her apart, yet in truth
Is the least of her sufferings.

Mrs Queck
And now I see too
The bread store, beckoning me.

Hippler
The further away, the clearer she sees it.

Mrs Queck
Transfigured by light I can see it now.
Long was it clouded over, but now the cloud lifts.
Bread is nothing! Manna is everything.
Brief was hunger, eternal the feast.

Salvation Army girl Oh, no! She's dead!

Hippler Come all of you and behold how this simple woman has become beautiful. It is obvious that this woman simply needed a spiritual awakening. Now she has gained experience, she has found her faith again.

[B24]

Meyer
Let's go to the new building, bring stones!

Masher
Take sticks too!

Meininger
Sticks! I'll give it to you!
Just you wait, I'll crush you! (*To the* **Renters**.)
I'll evict anyone
Who refuses to help me
Protect the windows now and doesn't grab
Whatever's at hand.
And you too, Hippler, I expect you to stand by me.

Salvation Army troop (*sings*)
Onward into the fight
Fear not, for God is your sword!
Sing loud, sing out with might!
Still reigns the night
Yet will the dawn bring us the light
Soon cometh to all of us Christ our Lord.

Renters (*come out of the building*)
It's not enough!

Meininger
Then take the loaves of bread! And the cakes!
Fetch the rolls, the old ones, stale now
And aim at their eyes!

The Renters *behind the barricades. The* **UPs** *with* **Meyer** *in the lead approach with sticks and stones.*

Meyer
Ha! He's taking cover!
He prefers to use the hard rolls as ammunition
And the loaf of bread to protect his window pane
Than to feed the hungry! Come forth, you dregs
Of humanity! You capitalist!

Meininger
You cowardly bums! Twenty of you!
Mr Bolke, you know what you owe me!

Mr Bolke
Fourteen Marks fifty.

Meininger
Get out there and punish those who insult me.

Masher
That's Bolke, the bastard! Before he was with us
Now for a filthy room he turns against us.

The **UPs** *with* **Meyer** *in the lead storm the barricade.*

Scene Six B: The battle of the bread

[B24]

UPs
And weakened by hunger, they grab for sticks
Hurl with wearied knuckles the paving stones
But their anger is just and makes up for costly weapons.
Ever in weakness constrained from one defeat to the next
Fighting for barest existence, they will
Nonetheless achieve
Total collapse of the monstrous
Enemy. They know it.

Meyer
Do not grow weak!

Meininger
Now climbs the mighty Meininger himself
The wall of bread eyes flashing with rage.
Bellowing: Save
Save the state, Bolke and Dittmeyer!

Renters
And frenzied the renters seize the
Well-baked loaves of bread to protect their
Property.

Bruises from blows with edibles, even
With hard rolls, stone-like.
Seeking the eye not the mouth of the foe, so
Must he fight off his food.

Meininger
Advance!

UPs
Bring on the grub, shrieked the un-
Employed, as trembling they transform their weakness to
Valour.

Renters
And defend the property, shrieked the
Owners and redoubled
Their projectiles –

UPs
Not baked by them!

Renters
– hailstones, so that the
Hard rolls darkened the heavens.

UPs
But the hungry ones fought in the hard rolls' shadow.

Renters
Many an eye, cast too greedily
Upon our property, our hard rolls
Under our siege it sneaks out
From its homey hollow, flowing
Like oil into mouths that sought
Other nourishment.

UPs
Back and forth
The battle surged.

Renters
Lo, even Janushek, behold the old hag

Even she is enraged. With a mighty
Sweep she empties the pitcher, boiling hot,
On the heads of the storming
Starving masses
The last of her salad oil.

Mrs Janushek
Stay the course, Mr Meininger, I see the police!

Renters
That's Mrs Franzke's doing!
Stealthful she fled
The endangered abode to summon with haste
The guardians of law and order.

UPs
Alas!
You stupid asses, you think if
You storm a bread store
Bash in the face of this baker or that
It will change things for the better? That
Is surely hopeless; but
Not without hope is our struggle
The permanent one, for control
Of the state itself and the power of dictatorship.

Policeman Mr Meininger, you summoned me. Mr Meininger, I'm here. Mr Meininger, what can I do for you?

Meininger I want law and order.

Meyer That is widow Queck's wood intended for removal by the Salvation Army, unlawfully.

Policeman And what is the truth, Mr Meininger?

Meininger The wood belongs to the Salvation Army, according to law.

Meyer Mr Schmitt, testify that the wood belongs to the widow Queck.

Schmitt
Of course it belongs to Mrs Queck, but
What does that mean? Don't believe for a minute
A calculation that shows something

Belongs to you. Even if
In your calculation every number is right, never
Will you be paid what is owed
If you have nothing.
So the wood disappears now, on its way
From whispering pine forest to cast iron stove
Changing from tree into warmth
For a time your debt and your prospect, but
Never your property.

Policeman
Quite right, Mr Schmitt. You are a sensible man.
Miss Hippler, take the wood away.

Meyer
Then I say: while I'm alive, the widow's
Wood will not be taken from her.

Renters and UPs
As long as he's alive, he says, the widow's
Wood will not be taken from her.

Meyer
You gangly brainless blockhead
Come here and in the service of capital
Take the wood from the widow.

Policeman
Quiet!

Washington Meyer *hits the* **policeman** *on the head several times with a stick.*

Policeman
Hitting me on the head, that's against
The law!

Chorus (*to* **Meyer**)
Having been warned, step forward, take leave of the masses who hide you!
You have been seen, now
Your destruction will be enforced!
Infinitely remote they sit the targets of blind attack

But right here is the iron heel that will smash you.
Of course, you know well, unteachable as you are:
The problem of the wood that is taken from her
Does not end with its removal.
You resist, and you will die at the street corner
At seven in the evening and three days later you are buried
Long after the wood has been burned, but
Your cause is not brought to an end.
Washington Meyer, statesman
You who could not bear to see misery lying on the street
Disorder and violence –
Die now!

Washington Meyer *hits the* **policeman** *two more times on the head. Shaking his head, the* **policeman** *picks up a hard roll and kills* **Meyer** *with it.*

Chorus
Thus fell Washington Meyer this evening at seven o'clock
On the street corner. Battling for
The interests of a woman, herself in a downwards spiral
He without family, supporters, or shelter.
Sinking down from the lowest rung
For reasons of justice
Downwards.

Optional songs

1) May be inserted at the end of Scene Three

[B49]

If no one chops the wood
Then the baker bakes no bread
And if the baker bakes no bread
Then the wood choppers all fall dead

And if the wood choppers all fall dead
For whom do we bake the bread?
And if no bread is getting baked
Then no wood is getting chopped
Etc.

2) Epilogue: The Path Downwards

[B52/B54]

Don't ask, comrade
Where your path leads.
Your path leads
Downwards

When you were one year old, comrade
You began to walk
You walked –
 Downwards.

You went to learn
You went to work
You went briskly
You went painfully
Comrade, do not go too fast
You're going downwards.

You take a wife, comrade
You have children
You go together on the path
Downwards.

But on Sundays you march with comrades
You sing, you wave our flag on high
You go to the beat of a drum
Downwards.

We marched together, comrade
We demonstrated together
We discussed the new times
We went our own ways.

Where
Will we meet?
Down there.

For you too, comrade
Will not always go
Downwards.
When you lie under the ground
You'll no longer go downwards.

Additional notes by Brecht

[A17, l. 36–39]

Meyer wants to abolish the external misery
The Army wants to abolish the internal misery
Both want to leave the State as it is
Therefore neither will succeed, for the Army at least externally ...

[A30]

The Communist Party	The Salvation Army
At first helps no one	Helps the individual
Guides the individual to the masses	Separates him from the masses
Uses violence as a tool	Opposes violence
Thinks materialistically	Thinks idealistically
Successful because of the bad situation	Despite the bad situation
Is interested	For idealistic reasons is uninterested in changing the situation

[A31]

The Salvation Army assumes only a modest place among social welfare institutions but the preeminent place among Christian organizations for this purpose. Poor people's own materialism as well as that of their exploiters has helped them more than religion, their own religion or that of their exploiters. But the Salvation Army's history is itself a history of the most modern, active, and likewise 'Christian' Christianity, showing perhaps most blatantly the fate of all 'idealistic', religious corporations and activities in advanced capitalism. It is the history of a horrible shift from a corporation based on personal renunciation to one that merely makes claims, from one that opposes profit to one that earns profit, from one that is fundamentally poor to one that is fundamentally rich, in short, from one that is anti-capitalist to one that is capitalist. Even Engels spoke in the introduction to the English edition of *The Development of Socialism from Utopia to Science* (1892) of 'the dangerous aid of the Salvation Army, which revives the propaganda of early Christianity, appeals to the poor as the elect, fights capitalism in a religious way, and thus fosters an element of early Christian class struggle, which one day may become troublesome to the well-to-do people who now find the ready money for it'. The element of unchristian class struggle has long been choked off. Today there remains only the image of a grotesque abnormality, precisely the image of early Christianity in advanced capitalism, an image that should not be lacking in any collection of bourgeois habits and customs.

[A34, l. 15–19]

Scheme 1 = The Funnel
Setting of the plot: like a funnel
On three levels one above the other from bottom to top 1. the Salvation Army, 2. the street with the woodpile, 3. on the top the bread store

The Real Life of Jacob Trotalong

With Margarete Steffin

Translated and edited by Charlotte Ryland

Introduction

The Real Life of Jacob Trotalong (German: *Das wirkliche Leben des Jakob Gehherda*) was to be a comic play in three acts, portraying the life of a waiter who dreams of heroic and chivalrous deeds while living a life defined by submission and weakness. The play's title sets up that focus on submission with a southern German flourish, the name 'Gehherda' recalling a local phrase for somebody who simply does as they are told.[1] In this way, Gehherda/Trotalong embodies the subservience that is at the core of Brecht's characterization throughout the play.

Thought to have been written in the mid-1930s while Brecht was in Denmark, Trotalong stands chronologically between his *Lehrstück* (learning play) phase and the genesis of his most important pieces of epic theatre. Its own genesis shows experiments with monologue, comic dialogue, slapstick, projection, and dramatic interludes, making it a staging post in the development of Brecht's theory and practice of epic theatre. An alternative opening scene – probably a first draft of the play's beginning – is particularly interesting in this respect, showing how a relatively expressionist scene with multiple characters and a great deal of humour was pared down and reimagined in the epic style. The whole fragment was written in close collaboration with Margarete Steffin, with evidence to suggest that she could be considered the work's primary author, as outlined below, and her involvement in the composition of the alternative opening scene is particularly intense. That scene is included here, as well as the main typescripts as published in the *Berliner und Frankfurter Ausgabe* (*BFA*) and a selection of additional notes and outlines.[2] The full English text presented here thus offers a comprehensive, stageable fragment, indications of how the play might be expanded for a production, and the alternative opening scene.

The action

The holdings relating to the fragment in the Brecht Archive comprise a total of 127 leaves in 4 folders. Two of the folders (527 and 2195) contain almost identical typescripts of a first and part of a second act (though in 2195 there are some pages missing towards the beginning). The outlines and notes that accompany these typescripts suggest that Brecht's intention for the whole play was a survey of the 'everyday life of the petty bourgeois', or – as in a draft title – 'The True Life of Jacob Trotalong or Dreams of a

Dime-a-Dozen Man'. His everyman is to be shown from various angles: in conflict with his employer and with his colleagues; and as a waiter, spouse, father, and political entity (see A2 and A3, in the text below). In each case he is compelled by circumstance to undertake activities that degrade him, never managing to assert his own agency but remaining the object of others' demands.

The completed scenes do show Trotalong in conflict with his employer and with his colleagues, but from only one of these angles – that of the waiter. Trotalong is second waiter in an inn which could be on 'the Alster, the Thames or the Hudson', in other words, in the centre of any major capitalist city. Later details in the completed scenes, as well as in the outlines and additional notes, suggest that Brecht favoured the American setting: with references to the Waldorf Astoria hotel in New York City, to Philadelphia, and to the US president, and with the appearance of gangster characters. Nonetheless, these elements are not integral to the plot and the action certainly lends itself to being transported elsewhere.

By contrast, the historical setting is fixed: The inn is suffering from the effects of an economic crash, with references made to the late 1920s, and its employees are rendered vulnerable by the insecurity of their jobs. Their behaviour, and the level of humanity and compassion which they can muster, is repeatedly shown to be subordinate to this economic pressure. The first act centres on reports by the inn's 'washing-up girl' that she has been raped by a guest of the inn, and on the staff's collective refusal to corroborate her story in case it deters the wealthy guests from returning. These scenes are interrupted twice by a sudden change in the stage lighting and the onset of music, marking the transition into Trotalong's dream world. In these dreams the waiter becomes increasingly – ridiculously – chivalrous, rescuing Sylvia's honour by challenging the supposed rapist, Maschner, to a duel. The dreams form interludes, akin to Wang's dreams in *The Good Person of Szechwan*, and make use of the epic techniques of projection and music familiar from *The Threepenny Opera* – both marking a radical shift in mood.

The second act returns to the inn, under changed circumstances: The first waiter has resigned, and Trotalong finds himself propelled into a position of relative authority. His third dream is in the style of a gangster movie, with Trotalong transformed into a *Godfather*-esque benevolent provider, using threats and extortion to bring everybody into line. It is no longer the guest Maschner who exercises influence by throwing his money around, then, but Trotalong himself.

This is as far as the fragment goes, but it appears that, as was common in his working practices, Brecht also drafted a final scene (B2). That scene depicts a father and son standing before a monument to Trotalong, praising him as 'an example for us all'. The scene is also described in one of Brecht's draft outlines (A9).

Additional archival material

Plans of individual scenes show how the original ideas shifted and developed into the final typescript. One note, for example, states that Trotalong owns the restaurant but disguises himself as a waiter in order to keep an eye on the management, subsequently firing all but the washing-up girl because they behaved in either a brutal or a cowardly manner. In the next scene, Trotalong saves a young girl from being seduced by some young men, and accepts nothing in return (A4). This would appear to be an early version of the first act. Another note (A6) gives an indication of how the fragment might have continued, with the inn's staff arriving at the Astoria and hearing the news that the military has been deployed. In the subsequent scene, 'Normandy is blown up' and 'Jacques-Trolong' ('Jacques-Gehda') is mentioned. This 'Trolong' appears in the archival materials as a shadowy hero who promises some kind of salvation, and it seems likely that he is a new iteration of Trotalong, another dream-self with the power to help those around him.

Steffin's involvement in the alternative opening scene is particularly prominent, with extensive handwritten text and annotations. Comprising a far greater cast of characters, the focus of this scene rests more on the figure of Trotalong as dreamer than on the economic exigencies that determine his behaviour in 'real life'. Trotalong is presented as a strong character, driven by a sense of his own self-worth and a desire to find 'the truth' (a desire that is more closely reflected in an alternative title for the play, *The True Life of Jacob Trotalong*; see A3 and the song 'The new Don Quixote'). This idealism nods to Brecht's expressionist roots, recalling in particular the protagonist of Georg Kaiser's play *Von morgens bis mitternachts* (*From Morn to Midnight*, 1912), a bank clerk who shuns his comfortable yet monotonous life and embarks on the search for a more fulfilling sense of 'value' than that offered by capitalist society.

There are differences in the characterization of other figures, too. The first waiter is more vicious and intolerant, appearing to take pleasure in presenting Sylvia as a willing participant in her own rape. This scene and two additional notes offer alternative ways of portraying the first waiter (see *BBA* 527/62, below). Sylvia, too, is rendered differently. Whereas in the later version her vulnerability has come to the fore – her fear of losing her job outweighing her desire for justice and self-protection – here she is far more assertive and gives details of the crime committed against her. It is striking that, despite the manuscript being fairly polished, Sylvia's report of her rape is left out completely – with simply the placeholder 'tells the story' ('erzählt den Vorfall') instead – and is handwritten on a separate sheet by Steffin (*BBA* 527/84). As well as confirming Steffin's intense involvement in the play's composition, this gives an insight into the writers' working practices. Perhaps the harrowing episode conflicted too much with the comedic tone of the rest of the scene, and was therefore written separately.

There is a marked difference in the style, too, with this alternative scene presenting a more colloquial, pacey, and comedic dialogue than the later version. Here the washing-up girl and her boyfriend, later called Sylvia Schmitt and Klaus Joppe, are Miss Capp and Mr Hat, and this ridiculous tone is reflected in their interaction, in particular Klaus Hat's repeated ejaculations of 'Sylvia!' as he gradually loses his grip on the proceedings. There are initially absurd names for a number of characters in this scene, which are all subsequently naturalized except that of the protagonist, who remains 'Trotalong'.

The typescripts of the first and second acts vary most prominently in the name of the inn, which is either The Two Knights (*BBA* 527) or The Black Knight (*BBA* 2195). In both versions the inn is referred to later in the play as The Black Knight. This English version calls the inn The Black Knight from the outset, ensuring consistency and making more sense of Trotalong's daydreaming: While undertaking dull and menial work in The Black Knight, unable to come to the aid of the washing-up girl, he dreams of becoming a chivalrous 'Black Knight' and rescuing her honour.

Brecht also sketched out a number of songs for the play (A10), most of which either do not feature in the typescripts or are present as prose. The play was to open with a 'song of the good old days, the time before the crisis', which was also intended to bring out the darker side of that era. Brecht noted that the song could be sung later by the first waiter, and this links it to the first waiter's litany of complaints in the opening scene of the typescript. Although that passage is not presented as a song, the waiter's swaggering monologue could easily be performed as such. The mention of a song called 'Everything is fine' also makes sense of the emphatic use of that phrase in the typescript, at the end of the first act. Another song, 'Something has been asked of you', was to be placed before the first dream to articulate the core of the play's philosophy: the submission ('kuschen') of the working man to the demands of capital in an era of mass unemployment (A10).

The completed scenes contain short verses, and four songs from Brecht's archive are thought to belong to the fragment: 'Song from *The True Life of Jacob Trotalong*', 'That great man Ford', 'At times like these / The new

Don Quixote', and 'Before the leaves fall'. The first three of these lend themselves clearly to insertion into the extant scenes and so are included here in translation.[3]

Genesis and context

Despite being one of the more comprehensive fragments in Brecht's archive, the play is not mentioned elsewhere – in letters or others' writings – and the archival material itself gives scant indication of the time of genesis. Many of the documents, including both handwritten and typed scenes and handwritten annotations, are written by Steffin, and the mention of 'Korsch' in one of Brecht's notes on the play suggests that he was writing it during his intense engagement with the philosopher Karl Korsch. The latter lived close to Brecht in Denmark from July 1935 to autumn 1936, and Steffin was in Svendborg at this time, too. Korsch's wife reports that the two men would spend most mornings together, and the note in question appears to be a list of comments from Korsch on the play – perhaps noted down by Brecht following one of their morning sessions (*BBA* 527/63).[4] Given that during that period Brecht was in New York from October 1935 to February 1936, and London from March to the end of July 1936, it seems likely that *Trotalong* was written either in late summer 1935 or in late summer 1936.

As well as being of substantial interest in its own right, *Trotalong* takes an important place within Brecht's oeuvre, pointing both backwards and forwards and marking a point in the development of his theory of theatre. It also lends insights into Brecht's working practices, into those of his collaborator Steffin, and into the nature of their intense collaboration. Indeed, archival work by Steffin scholar Stefan Hauck has revealed significant doubt as to the authorship of the fragment. In an essay published in 2001, which draws on compelling archival and biographical evidence, Hauck concludes that the fragment had been drafted by Steffin earlier in the 1930s and was taken up again during her stay in Svendborg, then with Brecht's involvement.[5] Brecht worked intensively with his 'co-workers' throughout his oeuvre, as outlined in the General Introduction to this volume, but *Trotalong* clearly presents a particular case where, as Hauck argues, the conventional structure of citing Brecht as author and then naming his co-workers may be reversed: *The Real Life of Jacob Trotalong*, by Margarete Steffin. Collaborator: Bertolt Brecht.

Whatever the attribution, the fragment reflects many of Brecht's core concerns and interests during the 1930s. In thematic terms, the depiction of a post-crash economy harks back to his writings during the late 1920s and early 1930s, attested to in this volume by *The Bread Store*. His portrayal of Trotalong's moral compass as being offset by economic constraints has strong echoes of *The Threepenny Opera* (1928), recalling Peachum's 'We should aim high instead of low / But our condition's such this can't be so', and one of Brecht's best-known aphoristic lines, Macheath's 'Food is the first thing. Morals follow on'.[6] The introduction of gangster characters in *Trotalong* also recalls *The Threepenny Opera*, though the London mobsters are reincarnated as American villains and in this way figure as precursors of characters in *The Resistible Rise of Arturo Ui* (1941). In general this development reflects Brecht's long-standing interest in film, and in particular American gangster movies, as well as in crimes happening on the streets of American cities at the time.

Notes in the archive folders confirm the distinctly filmic influences of the planned three-act play. The most comprehensive outline is full of references to Hollywood actors, from Maurice Chevalier to Mae West, and shows the play moving through various settings, taking in gangsters and a 'disguised detective' (A1). Here Brecht names one male Hollywood actor for each act, reflecting the shifting modes of the play: Act One, the charmer Maurice Chevalier; Act Two, the gangster Edward G. Robinson; and Act Three, the 'everyman' comic Harald Lloyd. These could either refer to the character types for key figures in the play, or represent Trotalong's self-projection in each of his dreams, or both.[7]

The archival materials also suggest that the gangster element would have been developed in the second act. Brecht's outline for Act Two mentions 'Robison [sic], the gangster chief', which probably refers to Edward G. Robinson, a tough-guy Hollywood actor who played many a gangster during his career, and another outline of that act makes reference to a gangster character named Giaguera, scheduled to appear in Act Two, Scene One (*BBA* 527/58). During the mid-1930s Brecht spent time in New York. Hanns Eisler reports that the pair went to the cinema regularly, in particular to see gangster films. At the same time Brecht was collecting material about gangsters and murder, extortion, and corruption, and he took these newspaper cuttings with him when he returned to Denmark.[8]

The mid-1930s were a crucial time for the development of what would become Brecht's most important and well-known concept: that of *Verfremdung*. This and other key concepts developed partly out of his engagement with his own oeuvre, as he sought to ground and define his works. So when *The Mother* was produced in New York for the first time in 1935, for example, Brecht published an essay in English that made frequent use of the terms 'non-Aristotelian' and 'epic' in order to explain how his theatre worked.[9]

Trotalong shows Brecht experimenting with 'epic' devices, while also retaining elements of the learning play, and thus looking both ways in the development of his oeuvre. The opening monologue in the completed first scene has Trotalong speaking to the audience, outlining the situation that will give rise to all the conflicts and contradictions in the action. As the play progresses, this *Lehrstück* style gives way to experimentation with 'epic' techniques, in particular the use of dreams and the split character. This duality makes visible precisely the dichotomy that Brecht outlined in his essay 'Theatre for Pleasure or Theatre for Instruction': 'People's activity had to simultaneously be *as it was* and be capable of being different'.[10] The frequent shifts between Trotalong's real-life persona and his dream character display this dichotomy, while also making clear a second strand of Brecht's theory: that man is always 'a function of the milieu'.[11] Trotalong's 'real life' behaviour is dictated by the economic conditions, and his only defence against this is through solipsistic escape into a dream world.

A third strand of Brecht's theory also comes to the fore in *Trotalong*: the importance of fun in the theatre. In his theoretical writings at the time he takes pains to emphasize the importance of lightness and humour, and this comedy certainly falls squarely into that category.[12] That fun is not for its own sake, however, but is bound up with the production of *Verfremdung*. In a reflection on Chinese acting techniques and their estranging qualities, Brecht highlights the role of the clown in the popular German fair as embodying 'an act of *Verfremdung*'.[13] There is a clear link between clowning and the absurd, slapstick behaviour in *Trotalong* (in particular the jousting/boxing/pantomime-horse scene in the first act), in that they both thoroughly estrange the events they represent.

Chinese acting techniques, in particular the use of masks, were prominent in *The Good Person of Szechwan*, which Brecht began writing three or four years after *Trotalong*. This fragment anticipates *The Good Person* in its use of dreams and a split character, although in the later play these are distributed across two characters – Shen Teh and Wang. Wang's dreams give him the opportunity to speak to the gods, while Shen Teh's split character reverses the format in *Trotalong*. Her essential and instinctive benevolence is shown to be incompatible with the prevailing economic conditions, and an alter ego is needed to redress that balance. This alter ego participates fully in the 'real-life' action of the play, distant from Wang's dream world. Conversely, Trotalong is so oppressed by those conditions as to be unable to act out his fantasies of benevolence in anything but his dreams; and in those dreams his chivalrous behaviour is pushed into absurdity and is full of contradiction. Thus the *Doppelgänger* remains outside the main action, existing only in Trotalong's dreams and casting into relief the protagonist's incapacity to become that dreamed-of hero. The solidarity and chivalry that he desires is completely absent in his real life, which instead shows repeatedly that humanity and compassion are impossible when living under such economic constraints.

The *Doppelgänger* structure is more complex than a simple doubling of the protagonist. Rather, multiple characters are doubled and the masks periodically slip, implying that it is impossible to shrug off the constraints of real life completely – even in your dreams. The first scene sees the cook, Mrs Lange, stating plainly, 'For 20 Marks a week, and that not even guaranteed, surely nobody can demand chivalry of you.' The relationship between Trotalong's real life and his dreams becomes evident when that lack of economic security is repeated in the second dream. This time Trotalong has become the chivalrous Black Knight, buying a lance from a pawnbroker who is presented as Mrs Lange's *Doppelgänger*. The Black Knight refers again to his twenty Marks a week, to which the pawnbroker replies: 'Yes, and that not guaranteed, isn't that so?' The restaurateur and other characters from the inn also figure as doubles, taking on various roles in the jousting match, including that of Trotalong's pony. Trotalong of course plays the Black Knight, challenging the guest Maschner, yet he remains subservient to his opponent. When the latter suddenly calls for schnapps, and later for a whisky soda, the Black Knight/Trotalong rushes off to fetch him one. The relationship between the restaurateur and Trotalong is similarly maintained when his boss peeps out of the pony to say, 'When you're done, come into my office. It's a scandal how you're loitering around.' But the impossibility of Trotalong leaving behind his economic inferiority when he dons the Black Knight's armour is made most palpable by the 'business discussion' that forms the joust's second round. Here Maschner seizes the advantage by reminding the Black Knight/Trotalong of the hope promised by the sailing club, thus reinforcing the power that comes from his financial security, along with Trotalong's relative poverty and impotence.

The final doubling is of a different nature. When the Black Knight finally wins the joust, his solution for rescuing Sylvia's honour is not to banish Maschner but to force him to marry her. Sylvia readily agrees to this, and when Lange points out the absurdity – that Sylvia really wanted to marry her boyfriend Mr Joppe, not her rapist – it is implied that those characters are one and the same. Joppe walks with a limp, and as Maschner walks off with Sylvia into their future as a married couple, he suddenly begins to limp, too. 'He *is* Mr Joppe. Yes, Mrs Lange, you've underestimated me once again', cries the Black Knight, suggesting that his chivalrous behaviour has both done away with Sylvia's abuser and ensured that Sylvia's wish of marrying Mr Joppe is realized.

That limp brings us back to the fragment's historical context: a play about power relations written by a playwright in exile from a fascist regime. Nazi propaganda minister Joseph Goebbels walked with a limp, and Maschner's sudden transformation here might be seen as an allusion to that figure, and in particular to his seduction of the petty bourgeoisie. Indeed, the imperious behaviour of the sailing club throughout the first act and the authority that they project through an explicit group identity (their 'club sweaters' and badges) introduce shades of proto-fascism. Raimund Gerz notes that productions of the fragment have sometimes emphasized this aspect, portraying the members of the sailing club as representatives of a burgeoning fascism and the inn's staff as subjugated 'fellow travellers' (*Mitläufer*).[14]

Production history

Trotalong was not performed during Brecht's lifetime, but there have been several posthumous productions. Milan's Teatro del Sole premiered the piece in 1971, followed by productions at the University of Utrecht (1977), in Rostock in 1978, and in Düsseldorf in 1983. The Düsseldorf production was directed by Peter Palitzsch, who had been one of Brecht's assistants at the Berliner Ensemble. This version of the play was subsequently published in the journal *Spectaculum*, 41 (Frankfurt am Main: Suhrkamp, 1965), 125–44. Palitzsch's version follows that published in the *BFA* almost exactly, but inserts the songs 'The new Don Quixote', 'That great man Ford', and 'Song from *The True Story of Jacob Trotalong*' into the action. Director Piet Drescher produced the play three times during the 1980s and 1990s, culminating in a well-received production at Berlin's Renaissance-Theater in 1997. A contemporary review indicates that the production was of significant scope with a great deal of music, mentioning 'the songs, ensembles and choruses, composed by Uwe Lohse'.[15] One of the song performances from that production is available online.[16] This, the cook's 'marriage song', is not evident in the archival material, suggesting that the production contained several embellishments and additions. Drescher's production thus serves as proof of the fragment's latent potential, to be taken up, imagined, and reimagined on the stage. Brecht and Steffin's work on *Trotalong* has left us with a series of texts with precisely that potential, resonating with the aesthetic and political concerns of their era and of our own time. This English version now opens up that reimagining to new linguistic possibilities.

CHARLOTTE RYLAND

Notes

1. The word 'Gehherda' appears repeatedly in Brecht's oeuvre, including *Die heilige Johanna der Schlachthöfe* (*BFA* 3, 176), *Coriolanus* (*BFA* 9, 75), *Flüchtlingsgespräche* (*BFA* 18, 246), *Der Messingkauf* (*BFA* 22.2, 809), and *Die Tage der Kommune* (*BFA* 8, 280).
2. See Bertolt Brecht, *Das wirkliche Leben des Jakob Gehherda*, *BFA* 10.1, 719–52. The folders with *Gehherda* material in the Bertolt Brecht Archive at the Akademie der Künste in Berlin are *BBA* 327, 328, 527, and 2195, with the vast majority in the last two.
3. The translation of 'Song from *The True Life of Jacob Trotalong*' is by Tom Kuhn. A song in the alternative first scene, with the opening line 'In times like these ...', became known as 'The new Don Quixote' ('Der neue Don Quichote') and is also translated here by Tom Kuhn. Both poems are in Bertolt Brecht, *Collected Poems* (New York and London: Liveright/W. W. Norton, 2018).
4. Raimund Gerz, 'Das wirkliche Leben des Jakob Gehherda', in Jan Knopf (ed.), *Brecht Handbuch. Stücke* (Stuttgart and Weimar: J. B. Metzler, 2001), 326–31 (326). Werner Hecht notes that – according to Korsch's wife – during this period Brecht and Korsch worked together for several hours most mornings. Werner Hecht, *Brecht Chronik 1898-1956* (Frankfurt am Main: Suhrkamp, 2003), 491.
5. Stefan Hauck, 'Wer schrieb *Das wirkliche Leben des Jakob Gehherda*?', *Dreigroschenheft* 3 (2001), 10–19.
6. Brecht, *Collected Plays: Two* (London: Bloomsbury, 1994), 124 and 146, respectively. See Gerz, 'Das wirkliche Leben des Jakob Gehherda', 329.
7. The editors of the *BFA* suggest that Maurice Chevalier is being considered here as a model for the character of the guest Maschner (*BFA* 10.1, 1204).
8. These details of Brecht's trip to New York are reported by Hecht in his *Brecht Chronik* (471). Eisler's comments on their cinema trips are from *Brecht, Music and Culture. Hanns Eisler in Conversation with Hans Bunge*, edited and translated by Sabine Berendse and Paul Clements (London and New York: Bloomsbury, 2014), 87. The newspaper cuttings are held in the Brecht Archive, in folders 469 and 470.
9. Brecht, 'The German Drama: Pre-Hitler', in Marc Silberman, Steve Giles and Tom Kuhn (eds), *Brecht on Theatre* (London and New York: Bloomsbury, 2015), 119–24.
10. *Brecht on Theatre*, 111 (Brecht's emphasis).
11. Brecht, '*Verfremdung* Effects in Chinese Acting', *Brecht on Theatre*, 151–8 (157).
12. See Brecht, 'The German Drama: Pre-Hitler', *Brecht on Theatre*, 122.
13. Brecht, '*Verfremdung* Effects in Chinese Acting', 151.
14. Gerz, 'Das wirkliche Leben des Jakob Gehherda', 329.

15 'Maul halten für den Arbeitsplatz', *Neues Deutschland*, 30 September 1997. Available online: http://www.berliner-schauspielschule.de/gehherda.htm (accessed 13 November 2017).
16 The 'marriage song' sung by Heike Jonca in Piet Drescher's production of *Das wirkliche Leben des Jakob Gehherda* (Renaissance-Theater Berlin, September 1997), music by Uwe Lohse: https://commons.wikimedia.org/wiki/File:Ehesongbrecht.ogg (accessed 13 November 2017).

Characters

Trotalong, *the second waiter. Also* **The Black Knight**
The Cook, Mrs Lange. *Also* **The Pawnbroker**
The First Waiter, Franz
The Bartender
The Washing-Up Girl, Sylvia Schmitt
George Joppe, Sylvia's *boyfriend, in the alternative first scene*
The Boyfriend
The Proprietor, *in the alternative first scene* **The Manager** and **The Director**
The Guest Maschner, *in the alternative first scene* **The Young Man**
The Second Guest
Maschner's friends, *members of the sailing club*
The Boatsman, *a guest at the inn. Also* **The Umpire**
An Old Woman
A Photographer
A Reporter
Spectators *in the grey ravine*
Two Men, *in top hats*
The Cauliflower, *a man with a cauliflower ear*
The Hairdresser
A Short Man
Two Philosophers, *large men with revolvers*
Four Gangsters, *athletic figures with violin cases*
A Father, *in the final scene*
A Son, *in the final scene*
The Cashier, *in the alternative first scene*
Mrs Krüger, *the cleaning lady in the alternative first scene*
The Porter, *in the alternative first scene*
Leopold, *the bellboy in the alternative first scene*

[B1]
Act One

The bar room of a small inn on the Alster, the Thames or the Hudson, called The Black Knight. *The staff consists of* **The First Waiter Franz, the second waiter Trotalong, The Cook Mrs Lange, The Bartender and the Washing-Up Girl**.

It is nearly evening, and the bar is being prepared for the arrival of guests.

Trotalong   Life in this inn is very dull. Especially now that there are so few guests, because everybody's broke these days. Though we've got a lot worse too, to be honest. The meals aren't cooked properly any more, but they're more expensive. I'd never have used a table cloth like this in the old days. Truth be told, we don't know why the proprietor doesn't just close up. Probably just because he's in so much debt. As of last Saturday, though, things seem to have taken a turn for the better. A small group – we must assume they belong to a sailing club – spent the weekend here. We have high hopes that these young people will eventually bring the whole club here. It's a really pretty area, after all. Hopefully the young people will come back today.

The Cook   Are you sure you remember rightly, Franz, did you really hear them talk about a club? Otherwise it's just going to be another disappointment.

The First Waiter   One of the young men made explicit mention of a club. And didn't you notice their club sweaters?

The Cook   Yes, you're right, they did have club sweaters on.

The First Waiter   Last week the old man was a whole day late paying the bills.

The Cook   Hmmm …

The First Waiter   Yes, that is a bad sign.

The Cook   But he seems to be hopeful again now, this time he chose the meat himself.

The First Waiter   How does he look today, then?

The Cook   Bad. The man is not at all well. He really ought to call a doctor. Can't you tell him, Franz?

The First Waiter   It's not a doctor he needs, it's a banker. He's the biggest rascal that ever ran an inn in this town. Top of the class when it comes to exploiting his staff. And now we're worrying about his damn health, for God's sake! It makes me sick!

The Bartender (*enters*)   Their boatsman just rang, they're coming!

The Cook   Thank God! (*Exit.*)

The First Waiter   I didn't really think they'd come back, to be honest! Isn't Sylvia here yet? I'll bet my bottom dollar it's her that's drawing the customers in, rather than our Lange's cutlets. (*Grinning.*) Do you see, Trotalong, the proprietor chose the meat himself! Doesn't it make you sick, all the effort we're making for just a few guests? I can't even bear to think of the times when business was good here. The benches were so full, not even a knife could fall to the ground. And think of how we treated them!

If I didn't like the look of someone, I just whipped their roast away from them. If a guest who'd been waiting two hours became impatient, I simply said: Sirs, there's space here, this gentleman is in a hurry.

Back then we spoke man to man, eye to eye: can I get you anything else, you piece of shit? Another glass of water, perhaps, rammed down your throat? How else can I help, you bastard?

On my way to the table I would cut one portion of beef into two, and I'd get a right look when I served up only one of them. They would say: Mr Franz, don't forget about me, and then I'd be annoyed for the rest of the day.

If someone had ordered goose à la mode, they should have caused a stink when a cream cake was served up instead. And if a chap like that got all saucy, I sometimes wondered whether it wasn't a case for the criminal court.

It was pure philanthropy, call it sentimental, that we didn't make use of rubber truncheons in our dealings with the guests. But we did use looks of such crunching contempt that the guest would have preferred the earth to open up, at his own expense, and swallow him completely.

There was a time – a whole six months during the summer of 27 – an unforgettable summer, when I didn't even hear a guest say: the beer is too warm.

If we'd had the space for it, all the ladies would have thrown themselves at me, seeking my patronage when the whipped cream was being ladled out.

Things like mustard, pepper, toothpicks were nowhere to be seen. They ate like pigs, without tablecloths! Forks, knives, coasters, everything cost extra. I'm exaggerating here a bit, but only a tiny bit.

And if it looked like somebody was scraping together something like ten per cent for a tip, then I saw red.

I only roughly totalled up the bills, in any case, my handwriting at this time – good God! All the numbers looked the same, you know, the 3 like a 5, the 1 like a 7, the 4 like a 9. I always just shouted what they owed back over my shoulder, and the money ended up in my pocket.

Oh, summer 27, dawn of a new age, where have you gone?

Trotalong Perhaps things will improve again if we get a club coming here?

Enter **Sylvia**, *the washing-up girl, in casual wear, accompanied by her boyfriend.*

Trotalong Hello, Sylvia.

Mr Joppe I want to talk to the proprietor.

The First Waiter And what do you want from the proprietor?

Sylvia (*pointing to* **Joppe**) He is my boyfriend.

Mr Joppe It's a private matter. Fetch him immediately!

The First Waiter Right away. I'll bet he's already waiting for you in the back room. Surely been there for days.

Mr Joppe (*to* **Sylvia**) Well this is a nice sort of place for you to spend your time.

Sylvia Don't say that. These are my colleagues.

Mr Joppe I want to talk to the proprietor. Don't stop me.

Sylvia But if you talk to him when you're so furious, you'll ruin everything. Promise me you won't get angry and shout, because otherwise I'll get the sack. You've only got an assistant's post yourself, and you've never suggested we might get married.

Trotalong The old man!

The Proprietor So what do you want from me? (*To* **Sylvia**.) And why are you so late for work? The day before yesterday you left early, too. I've been keeping an eye on you all week, don't push your luck! (*To* **Joppe**.) So what do you want?

Mr Joppe I want to know, amongst other things, why you have been keeping an eye on my fiancée all week.

The Proprietor   I don't believe that I owe you an explanation for that.

Mr Joppe   Perhaps you do. Calm down, Sylvia – My fiancée has informed me of an incident that is an utter scandal. Sylvia, tell me again what happened here last Saturday.

Sylvia   It's the thing with the young people from the sailing club.

The Proprietor (*sharply*)   What happened with the guests from the sailing club?

Sylvia *is silent.*

Mr Joppe   She was taken to a guest's room and molested, as well you know. Because your head waiter told her she had to accept the invitation.

The Proprietor   Franz, did you tell Miss Schmitt that she *had* to go to the guest's room?

The First Waiter   Me? No chance!

Sylvia   But Mr Franz, you did …

The Proprietor   Was that all you wanted to know? Trotalong, fetch me the staff regulations.

Trotalong *brings a box.*

The Proprietor   These, young man, are the instructions to which my staff adhere, if they don't want to get thrown out. You can read here: 'Female members of staff are forbidden from accepting invitations from guests to drink etc., the staff are expected to act with the greatest reserve.' I think that suffices.

Mr Joppe   When she was in the room, she was forced to drink. She didn't want to. She came out again and went into the kitchen, and asked the cook, Mrs Lange, for some coffee. You said explicitly: could it be very strong.

The Proprietor   Your boyfriend is certainly very worried about your moral conduct. (*He calls.*) Mrs Lange! (**Mrs Lange** *enters.*) Mrs Lange, our Miss Schmitt's fiancé is telling us a terribly gruesome tale that apparently took place here last Saturday. She was thoroughly inebriated, and apparently asked you for a coffee in the middle of the night.

Mr Joppe   So you do know about it! You know that it was in the middle of the night.

The Proprietor   Mrs Lange, what's the story with this coffee, then?

The Cook But young man, there was nothing to it.

Mr Joppe I want to know if she asked you for a cup of coffee, very strong.

The Cook In the evenings none of our staff is allowed coffee.

The Proprietor Anything else, young man?

Mr Joppe (*to* **Sylvia**) I don't believe what the head waiter says, I don't like the man, but the cook doesn't look like she's lying.

Sylvia (*cries*) Why don't you all tell him what really happened? Don't you see that my boyfriend is starting to think badly of me?

Silence.

Sylvia Mr Trotalong, did I not cling to you before one of the guests and the bartender put me in the car? I beg you, just tell the truth.

Mr Joppe Gentlemen, you must understand that I come here without prejudice, but that there must be clarity between me and my fiancée. I have made my peace with the situation, I know that in the hospitality trade you have to put up with certain things, but it does matter to me whether my fiancée was telling me the whole truth when she said that she defended herself.

The Proprietor Trotalong, you were asked something.

Trotalong I ...

Change of lighting. Music begins, lending a sense of unreality to the scene. The following words are projected onto a screen:

FIRST DREAM OF JACOB TROTALONG: JACOB TROTALONG TELLS IT HOW IT IS

Trotalong I cannot keep silent. Others may make bones about it. Thinking only of their trivial, superficial interests, they forget that it is their duty always and in all circumstances to tell the truth, especially if another party would be damaged by the untruth. I, Jacob Trotalong, do not do so. What is going to prevent me from talking? This miserable existence in your inn, Mr Friedrich? Oh no! Send me out onto the streets if you can, but let me first have told the truth, just as Galileo Galilei, at the stake, hurled his 'And yet it moves!' into the face of an astonished crowd, as can be read in the famous novel *At the Stake*. That's how I behave, too. Yes, Mr Joppe, your fiancée didn't lie to you, she was not driven by wanton lust. Here in this corridor she clung to me and begged me to defend her against the seducer. Inebriated as she was (your coffee, kindly offered but here so fearfully denied, Mrs Lange, had not sobered her up), she clung to me, crying loudly: I don't want to! And now that what had to be said has been said, Mr Friedrich, dismiss me! I know it's inevitable. I would have been happy to stay here, but now I'll happily set off into the shadows, for who is going to employ me after this? Don't cry for me, Miss Sylvia, just look at the shining eyes of your betrothed, that alone will be my reward. Thunder away, Mr Friedrich! No? You say nothing? Your expression softens? You hesitate? Rattled by so much self-sacrifice, you forget your inn, you step up to me, I can barely believe it, you reach out your hand to me, you look me in the eye, you say to me ...

Change of lighting. The music stops abruptly.

The Proprietor Chop-chop!

Trotalong Of course, Mr Friedrich! – I don't think I can come to your aid here, Miss Sylvia. Much as I would like to, I really can't remember your calling on me.

The Proprietor Well, Mr Joppe? Would you like to hear what the bartender has to say too?

Mr Joppe I don't think that will be necessary.

Sylvia But George, they can't get away with lying to you.

Mr Joppe You shouldn't cry so much, Sylvia, you're casting doubt on the gentlemen's chivalry, and that makes a bad impression on me.

Sylvia *goes out, crying.*

The Proprietor If you weren't so young, young man, you wouldn't get off so lightly. In any case you won't object to my staff finally getting on with their work. This can't go on much longer, anyhow.

Exit, with **The Cook** *and* **First Waiter**.

Mr Joppe (*to* **Trotalong**) If these people come back today, Mr Trotalong, would you be so kind as to telephone me? I am an usher at the Admiral Cinema, 33-333.

Trotalong I'll call you, but I don't think anyone will come. The weather is too bad.

Mr Joppe Was he at all good-looking, the guest?

Trotalong I believe that women would call him a good-looking man.

Mr Joppe That's bad, because my fiancée told me he had a paunch. (*Exit.*)

The Cook (*comes back*) Has he gone at last? And did you see, by the way: he limps. She says we've ruined her chances of getting married.

Trotalong Do you think I should have behaved differently? For a moment I did wonder whether I should give a different answer.

The Cook For 20 Marks a week, and that not even guaranteed, surely nobody can demand chivalry of you.

Trotalong I'm just worried it will carry on. The young man made a request of me; but perhaps they won't come this evening.

The Cook (*on her way out*) Let's hope not.

Trotalong Or, if they come, perhaps they won't call for the girl tonight. Or, if they ring, perhaps she won't go in.

Four young people enter. They go into the lounge. In the doorway one of them turns around.

The Guest The same as last time!

Trotalong Certainly, sir.

The First Waiter *brings four bottles and glasses.*

The First Waiter Bring the cards and the cigarettes!

He goes in. **Trotalong** *brings what he requested.*

Trotalong (*coming out with* **The First Waiter**) It looks like they just want to play cards today. So I don't need to telephone, thank God. Why do people always believe the worst of others, anyway?

A ring from the lounge.

The First Waiter (*going in*) I'll serve them myself.

The Proprietor (*entering*) Everything OK?

Trotalong They're playing cards.

The Proprietor There. You see, they're just playing a quiet game of cards. I do not like scandal. *He goes to* **The Boatsman**'s *table, who is drinking a beer.*

The Proprietor I suppose the young people are from your yacht club?

The Boatsman No chance. They are their own yacht club.

The Proprietor I see.

The Boatsman You had high hopes, I presume?

The Proprietor Me? No. You can't make a living off a yacht club at weekends, either. (*Exit.*)

The First Waiter (*comes from the lounge*) They are definitely from a club. They're wearing badges. (*Exit.*)

Trotalong So shall I phone the young man now or not? I promised to phone him if they came back, but if she doesn't go in to them, then perhaps I don't need to phone at all. Then it's just as if they hadn't come at all.

The Washing-Up Girl *comes out of the kitchen. She arranges her hair in front of a small mirror.*

Sylvia I tell you, Trotalong: I'm not going to stand for anything this evening. Even if they drag the whole yacht club along with them, I shall rise above it. You all drove George away from me, but that doesn't mean I'm just going to take everything lying down. I don't want to lose my job, but I'm not going to ruin myself for this crappy inn. You are fine colleagues. One can depend on your chivalry! (*She goes in.*)

Trotalong But if the same thing happens as last time, then I will …

Change of lighting. Music begins, lending a sense of unreality to the scene. The following words are projected onto a screen:

SECOND DREAM OF JACOB TROTALONG: THE BLACK KNIGHT
In the darkness we hear **Trotalong** *shouting.*

Trotalong
Abuse and injustice! How much more
must the poor downtrodden endure?
Must they be constantly beaten and crushed,
Will nobody cry out 'enough'?
No one dares reach out their hand
To try to rescue the drowning man.
Where is the one with water for the thirst?
Who will shield the victim from the worst?
Where is the one with not stone, but heart?
Who is there for the wretched, who takes their part?

The stage lightens, **Trotalong** *has disappeared. The four guests and* **Sylvia** *come out of the lounge, all drunk.*

Sylvia   Leave me alone! I don't want to! When the need is greatest, is not help closest at hand? Will nobody protect the pure of heart? Is there nobody here to take my part?

A muffled voice (*loudly*)   There is.

One of the guests   Did I hear something? Has somebody here got a problem with a little late-night fun?

The Black Knight, *who was standing to the right in front of the entrance, suddenly steps down from his pedestal.*

The Black Knight   'Twas I.

The drunken guests stagger backwards, as if there has been a thunderclap.

The Black Knight (*strides forward a few steps*)   So hear me now, Egon Maschner, you who have debased this pure, innocent girl for your sport, the hour of judgement has come! You will wed this girl. And before the cock crows in the courtyard of the inn.

The Guest Maschner   But what gives you the right, Sir, to meddle in my affairs?

The Black Knight   If you do not agree, then I will simply have to challenge you to a duel. What that means for you must be clear as day, for I am the Black Knight and I make short shrift of people like you.

The Guest Maschner (*querulously*)   And where is this splendid duel to take place?

The Black Knight   The contest will naturally take place where it has always taken place, that is …

The First Waiter (*who has entered with* **The Proprietor**)   I'm sure he'll summon him to the grey ravine. The duels always take place there.

The Black Knight   It will take place in the grey ravine.

General movement.

The First Waiter   There lie the graves of the seven fallen.

A Second Guest   Everything must proceed fairly. The fight continues until the decision, and the weapons will be supplied by the fighters.

The Guest Maschner   A suit of armour and a lance! (*To* **The Black Knight**.) I trust you are in a position to acquire a lance? I trust you're not short of cash.

The Black Knight   Do not worry about it. (*He turns to leave.*)

The Guest Maschner   Waiter, a double schnapps!

The Black Knight *walks off and serves the* **Guest Maschner** *a schnapps.*

The Guest Maschner   Are you really never going to learn not to spill it?

The Black Knight (*on leaving*)   Soon you will talk quite differently, and before the cock of this inn crows. We'll meet again at 11.45 in the grey ravine!

A small pawnbroker's. A large wall clock shows 11.40, its hands moving fast. An **Old Woman** *is buying some bread rolls, so* **The Black Knight** *has to wait at the counter. They pay him no attention.*

The Old Woman   I didn't know you sold rolls here too.

The Pawnbroker (**Mrs Lange**)   Lots of poor people live round here, and every now and again they pawn a roll with us, when they unexpectedly need money for a nice book, and then of course they can't redeem it again.

The Old Woman   I hope they're very hard, otherwise my Emil will gobble the lot of them in one.

The Pawnbroker   Just in case, I'd soften them in good spring water first.

The Black Knight   Do you perchance have a well-maintained lance here? I did not expect to have to provide my own for the contest, and now I'm in a tight spot.

The Pawnbroker   After the crusades, a whole load was pawned and never redeemed.

She fetches two long lances.

The Pawnbroker   This one has got a bit brittle, but it's cheap. I could let you have it for 43 Marks 50.

The Black Knight   I tell you, my life depends on it being good.

The Pawnbroker   Then you'll have to invest a bit. This is a good one, but more expensive. 49 Marks 95.

The Black Knight   Yes, I'll take it. It's too late to be picky, anyway.

The Pawnbroker   I can only take cash, naturally. And you have a weapons licence, I presume?

The Black Knight (*searches carefully in this pocket*)   No, but I see now that I'm rather short at the moment, so I would prefer the cheap one after all. It looks pretty good, actually.

The Pawnbroker   You'll know what your life is worth to you.

The Black Knight   Naturally. So please go ahead and wrap up the cheap one. On 20 Marks a week you can't go all out, you know.

The Pawnbroker (*exiting*)   Yes, and that not guaranteed, isn't that so? Please just keep an eye on the till while I'm out.

The Black Knight   Right, I'll take it out of the till.

He breaks it open with a dagger and pockets the money.

The Pawnbroker *returns with the lance wrapped in brown paper.*

The Black Knight   Here's the money. You can't let me have it for less, because it's brittle and I'm risking my life? (**The Pawnbroker** *shakes her head.*) Are you even allowed to sell things that have been pawned?

The Pawnbroker   No. But the general disorder makes us think that we can get away with it.

The Black Knight (*exiting*)   Think well of me, dear woman.

The grey ravine

Seven graves, some being used as seats. A boxing ring has been made out of ropes and stakes. **The Second Guest** *is holding a white horse, which is formed by the other two guests. On the other side* **The Bartender** *is holding a black horse by its bridle, which is formed by* **The Proprietor** *and* **The First Waiter**. *A* **Photographer** *and a* **Reporter**, **The Boatsman** *as* **Umpire** *and a few* **Spectators**. *Next to the black horse stands* **Sylvia**, *doing her hair. Next to the white horse stands* **The Guest Maschner** *in knight's armour, nervously smoking a cigarette. Each of them is holding their watch in their hand.*

The Reporter   For the evening papers we simply must know the identity of the gentleman who in such selfless fashion is standing up for the beleaguered innocent.

Sylvia   I don't know myself. It was all completely unexpected. Write that I am very happy.

The Reporter   Then it's probably best that we sing: 'Who Could The Black Knight Be?'

The Photographer   Hopefully he'll actually turn up. I simply must get him on film, otherwise they'll say it's a hoax again. I had terrible trouble with my editorial department when I didn't get Lindbergh on film at Lindbergh's landing.

The Reporter   Yes, when is he likely to come? It's high time already. And who could it be? Do you think it's Adolf Hitler?

Sylvia   Or Hans Albers?

The Reporter   Gentlemen, please! (*He conducts.*)

All (*sing*)
Beleaguered innocent suffers shame.
Black Knight stands up for her name.
When will he hear her plea?
Who could he be?

The Bartender   He's coming. The boatsman just telephoned.

The Black Knight *enters with the lance.*

The Black Knight (*hurried*)   The cock hasn't crowed yet, has it?

The Umpire   Why would the cock crow in the middle of the night?

The Black Knight   This is very embarrassing. I tell you, once I've done him in, the cock must crow. Everything must be observed to the letter.

The Umpire   Good that you're here. We'll begin. Gentlemen, mount your horses.

The fighters mount their horses.

The Photographer   Your name, sir?

The Black Knight   I do not wish to be named.

The Cook (*behind* **The Black Knight**)   Oh, there's Mr Joppe too! You see, Miss Schmitt, your fiancé insists on standing up for you himself. Give him a wave!

Sylvia *waves to him. He looks away.*

Sylvia He's looking away. He wants nothing to do with me. You've driven him away from me.

The Black Knight When we're done here, Miss Sylvia, I will hand him the lance. Reckon he'll take it? He's simply waiting to be asked. I'll just break the horse in for him. (*He rides in a circle, greeted by everyone.*)

The Proprietor (*looking sideways out of the horse*) When you're done, come into my office. It's a scandal how you're loitering around.

The Black Knight *kicks his spurs into his horse's flank, making it rear up.*

The Black Knight (*roars*) One more word and I'll finish you! You think that you can bully me for 20 Marks a week?

The Umpire At the strike of the gong, you're off!

The Black Knight There you are, Mr Joppe, you have been called as you requested. Here, Mr Joppe, take the lance and stand up for Miss Schmitt, since you're her closest companion.

Mr Joppe Why should I do that? I just wanted her to cast less doubt on the gentlemen's chivalry. I'll risk losing my job!

The Black Knight What, you're hesitating? The girl you love needs you and you talk of your job? Has anyone ever heard the like? Surely any man would gladly give up his worldly goods in order to protect the woman he loves! Even I do it, and I do not love. Yes, Miss Sylvia, I am going into battle for you, I, the second waiter, whom you have never seen, but who is there for you now. Will you please take note! Take your place!

The gong sounds. The first round consists of a single charge, but the lances do not clash. Then the gong sounds again. The fighters are seated on chairs, and handkerchiefs are wafted in their faces.

The Guest Maschner (*to his second, the* **Second Guest**) Inform my old man. I suspect I shall not emerge from this battle alive. The worthy cause will be victorious, it is too strong. Waiter, a whisky soda! (**The Black Knight** *brings him a whisky soda.*)

The Cook Do you see how he refreshes his opponent with a drink before he strikes him down? That is true sportsmanship!

The Umpire For the second round, the duel management has determined to incorporate a business discussion. Would the gentlemen please be seated.

The knights dismount and sit opposite one another on plain chairs. They're given cigars. They smoke.

The Guest Maschner   So what have you used for armour? Your income surely can't be that good?

The Black Knight   I don't really think I owe you an answer to that, you know.

The Guest Maschner   I trust you can produce the receipts, though?

The Black Knight   What on earth has that got to do with anything?

The Guest Maschner   It is after all possible that the inn might be purchased by the yacht club.

The Black Knight   Then first of all there would have to be offers. Binding ones.

The Guest Maschner   Half would be offered, at the most.

The Black Knight   No chance. We wouldn't take less than double.

The Guest Maschner   But that's a pipe dream.

The Black Knight   As you like. You can provide assurances, I presume?

The Guest Maschner   As long as the armour is included, of course. I await your answer.

The Black Knight *says nothing.*

The Guest Maschner   So you're feeling uneasy? I request that the round is decided in my favour. (*He stands up.*)

The knights return to their corners and receive refreshment.

The Cook   A terrible blow. Now everything's hanging in the balance.

The Umpire   Gentlemen, the third round.

The knights mount their horses again. The gong sounds. This time **The Black Knight***'s lance meets its mark, but breaks off.*

The Bartender   For God's sake! The lance has broken!

The Cook   I told you, didn't I, that you should buy the more expensive one. The good one is more expensive, but lasts longer.

The Black Knight *thrusts his iron fist towards* **The Guest Maschner**. *They begin to tussle. At the same time the horses underneath them begin to talk.*

The Proprietor (*imploring*)   My apologies, gentlemen! The man will of course be dismissed. My staff are obliged to show the greatest reserve towards our guests.

The Guests   You can wave bye-bye to the yacht club.

The First Waiter   And if all is lost, if our inn isn't good enough for you, then get out! Oh summer 27!

The Black Knight *has knocked* **The Guest Maschner** *off his horse with a terrible blow. General movement. The gong sounds after* **The Umpire** *has counted him out.* **The Bartender** *and* **The Umpire** *drag the fallen man to the side and bind him with a rope to the black horse's tail.*

The Black Knight (*from his horse, motions for silence, and listens*)   No cock crowing! This is dreadful!

The Cook   Calm yourself, he's not done in yet.

The Guest Maschner   I am done for! I see now that I should never have laid hands on Miss Sylvia. It will be a lesson to me!

The Black Knight *shakes his head sorrowfully and rides the laps of honour, dragging the defeated man behind him. He rides faster and faster.*

The Spectators   He's dragging him to death! He shows no mercy! Poor, frivolous, young man! Though he is a handsome boy.

The Proprietor (*looks out of the horse again*)   Don't push it! We live off our guests, after all.

Sylvia *throws herself in the path of* **The Black Knight**, *arms outstretched.*

Sylvia   Stop! No further! Give him his young life!

The Black Knight (*stopping*)   Miss Sylvia, I shall follow your wishes entirely. If you wish for his death, it's yours! If you wish for his life, it's yours! There is just one thing I demand if you choose the latter course: he must atone for the disgrace done to you, by marrying you.

The Cook   Mr Maschner, the decision is now yours.

The Guest Maschner   Good. We'll draft the marriage contract.

The cock crows now. The gentlemen sit on the gravestones. They smoke cigars.

The Second Guest   Do you require separate estates?

The Black Knight   As you wish.

The Guest Maschner I need to know that my wife's position is secure.

The Black Knight One moment, Miss Sylvia! (*He takes her aside.*) Perhaps not tomorrow, in the first flush of happiness, but later, when your feelings for each other are weakening, your husband could criticize you for entering the marriage with nothing. Here, take this!

He hands her money. At this moment two men in top hats, who have just entered, place their hands on his shoulders.

The Men Follow us, and don't make a scene! You are arrested for shoplifting!

The Black Knight One moment, gentlemen!

He steps aside. **Sylvia** *and* **The Guest Maschner** *stand hand in hand.*

The Guest Maschner (*smiling*) Did you not notice, Sylvia, that I merely wished to test you? When you told me so proudly that you would stand for nothing more today, then I knew, it's her or no one!

Sylvia Perhaps I did not notice it, but the black knight did. Surely that's why he did not stop you last Saturday?

The Black Knight I just have a small account to close with these gentlemen. Off you two go, and be happy! Don't turn around! No shadow shall fall on your young love. Don't worry about me, the one who brought you together, whatever will be will be!

The pair exit, hand in hand. Others exit too.

Sylvia (*turning around*) And even if nobody here knows who you are, I know!

The Proprietor I can give you only the best reference.

The Cook But she actually wanted to marry Mr Joppe.

At this moment the man leading **Sylvia** *away begins to limp.* **The Black Knight** *points to him.*

The Black Knight He *is* Mr Joppe. Yes, Mrs Lange, you've underestimated me once again. And now to you, gentlemen! (*He draws a short dagger.*)

The Black Knight Miserable shopkeepers! You hustle for the sake of vile Mammon, but the black knight won't fall into your dirty hands. Never! Never! Never! (*He thrusts the dagger through his breast plate and collapses.*)

The Black Knight (*dying*)   Evening draws in. Weep not for me. I go from you as I came, with visor down. Hold me, I wish to face him upright! (*They set him upright.*) Thank you, friends!

Both Gentlemen   Dead! Do you know who he is?

The Cook (*opens the visor*)   I don't think I'm committing an indiscretion in doing this. It is Trotalong!

Change of lighting. The music stops abruptly. A telephone rings.

The restaurant appears. The waiter **Trotalong** *is leaning at the window again.* **The Bartender** *enters.*

The Bartender   That Joppe is on the phone.

Trotalong   Yes, that's right! Tell him I'm very busy and can't come to the telephone. But that everything is fine.

The Bartender (*on his way out*)   So everything is fine.

The Proprietor (*walks slowly and sadly through the bar*)   Are you daydreaming again, Trotalong? By the way, I hear that the washing-up girl is hanging around with the guests again. I don't want her to do that. Go in and tell her she must return to her work immediately. And if the guests have anything against that, throw them out.

Act Two

The Cook, **The Bartender**, *the* **Washing-Up Girl** *and* **Mr Joppe** *sit around a table. Jacob* **Trotalong** *sits on his own at a separate table, which is laid.*

The Bartender   Since Trotalong became head waiter in *The Black Knight*, he's been acting like a black knight himself. He paid 50 Marks deposit. Franz was clever. He resigned as soon as the sailing-club bubble burst.

Sylvia   He insists on being called 'Sir'.

Laughter.

The Bartender   Yesterday he picked up the menu and said: 'From now on, I expect the menu to be written properly, whether we have guests or not.'

Laughter.

Sylvia   And he told George off because his jacket collar was stained.

The Bartender   He wants me to shave every day.

Laughter.

Mr Joppe   And you know what he said to Sylvia? He said, 'If I don't keep my people in line … '

Raucous laughter.

Mrs Lange   Don't wind him up now. Otherwise how am I going to get my evening off later? And my daughter and her husband hardly ever come into town. When my son-in-law is there, who is after all a civil servant, I can't say I haven't got any time off. It's embarrassing.

Mr Joppe   And I could get you all free tickets for the cinema at the Admiral Palace. Just close the place up, nobody will come anyway.

Sylvia   And it's about to start raining too.

Mr Joppe   Yes, it's going to rain. It won't be at all easy to wangle the free tickets. Isn't that strange – rain is bad for an inn, but for a cinema it's good! So what would you call the rain?

The Bartender   Wet.

They laugh.

Sylvia   He's not reacting at all.

Mr Joppe (*loudly*)   Just say that you want the evening off, Mrs Lange!

Trotalong *taps his knife on a glass.* **The Bartender** *stands up sullenly and goes to* **Trotalong***'s table.* **Trotalong** *points sternly at a gap among the condiments.* **The Bartender** *turns lazily around and fetches a jar of mustard, grumbling.*

The Bartender   Trotalong, our Lange wants an evening off.

Trotalong   And what if someone comes?

Mr Joppe (*stands up*)   And who is going to come, Mr Trotalong?

Trotalong   Mr Joppe, it is our duty to be here. It's always possible that someone will come.

Mr Joppe   Ah, when you say 'someone' you mean the proprietor! You're afraid that the proprietor will come?

Trotalong   I am afraid of nothing. (*Furious.*) Mr Joppe, I have been watching you. You sit there and stir up the staff against me. And you're neither guest nor staff member, but an element that is completely unrelated to the business.

Mrs Lange   But no, Mr Trotalong, Mr Joppe just wanted to help me see my daughter. (*She cries.*)

Trotalong   But you knew yourself that you didn't have any time off this evening. I suppose you think you can do whatever you like, now that Franz has gone? Then let me tell you: as long as I am here, there will be order, even if heads must roll. I am in charge.

Mr Joppe   In short: the man refuses your request for time off.

Mrs Lange (*sobbing*)   Mr Franz would never have spoken to me like that.

The Bartender   Our Franz could afford to treat the staff decently. But a poor fellow like Trotalong trembles at the mere thought of the proprietor.

Change of lighting. Music begins, lending a sense of unreality to the scene. The following words are projected onto a screen:

THIRD DREAM OF JACOB TROTALONG: JACOB TROTALONG ATTEMPTS THE IMPOSSIBLE

Joppe, **The Bartender** *and the* **Washing-Up Girl** *are fussing around* **Mrs Lange**, *who is slumped in a chair, unconscious, with a cold compress on her head.* **Trotalong** *behind them at the window.*

Sylvia Don't you feel better yet, Mrs Lange? You must not misunderstand Mr Trotalong. He is very strict.

The Bartender But fair. If he considers it appropriate to give you time off, then nothing will stand in his way, even if the proprietor's wife herself has to cook. He yells at us occasionally, but he yells at the proprietor too, if it's in the inn's interests. He knows that he can't be dismissed. He is too irreplaceable.

Sylvia Mr Trotalong would give you time off without a second thought, if you asked him properly and not in a demanding tone, Mrs Lange. Anyhow, merely having time off is not going to help you at all this time, I'm afraid. You need so much more, something entirely impossible! You've kept quiet about the fact that for years you've let your daughter, who lives in Paris, believe that you are a rich woman and move in the loftiest circles. And you've just received the news that your daughter and her aristocratic fiancé are on their way to visit you. The young couple wish to see you for just one day, indeed just two hours. So the task that awaits you, Mrs Lange, is to maintain the wonderful illusion or to come clean, which would without doubt destroy your child's happiness. You confessed to me that you have corresponded with your daughter on stationery purloined from the luxury Hotel Astoria. If your daughter asks after you there tonight, she will be told: we know nothing of a woman by this name. And they won't even permit her to enter the foyer, they won't allow her even to wait, which would at least give you the opportunity to admit everything to your daughter. In a situation like that even the president of the United States could hardly help you, yes even the great Jacques-Trolong himself would probably be powerless. Although he is accustomed to helping the helpless, he vanished two months ago, sighted the last time in Philadelphia, and nobody knows where he is. Mrs Lange, by any measure you are lost.

Trotalong (*saunters over to the telephone and dials*) Is Franz there? Please note: grand excursion. With provisions and musical instruments. Meeting point Astoria. And take particular note: Jacques would like corn for supper tonight.

Mr Joppe Ah, Mrs Lange, your sorry situation shows us what happens when the boundary between high and low is breached. High and low are like water and fire. An implacable natural law dictates that they may never come together. If water comes to the fire, the fire is extinguished. If fire comes to the water, the water evaporates. You belong to the lower beings of this earth, Mrs Lange, simple as that, and so you'll never be able to get away with behaving as if you belong amongst the higher beings. You won't even get a night off.

Trotalong (*steps forward*) In view of your difficult situation, Mrs Lange, I permit you the evening off requested by yourself in respectable fashion.

Mrs Lange I thank you from the bottom of my heart, Mr Trotalong, but I'm probably not going to be able to make much use of it. I can't let my daughter see me in this outfit.

Enter a brutal-looking man wearing a top hat, with a cauliflower ear, several packages under his arm.

The Cauliflower Is there a Mrs Lange here, who lives in the Waldorf Astoria Hotel?

Mrs Lange My name is Lange, but I don't live in the Waldorf Astoria.

The Cauliflower Never mind. This is for you.

Mrs Lange But it must be a mistake, I haven't ordered anything.

The Cauliflower I told you that it's for you. (*He opens the package.*) First some lingerie.

Mrs Lange That's for me?

The Cauliflower Why not?

Mrs Lange Well, I don't wear silk underwear.

The Cauliflower Why not? I do. Secondly a pair of stockings. Thirdly a corset, fourthly shoes, damn, they won't fit. Never mind, you'll have to squeeze into them. Fifth a large evening dress. Sixth a fur coat. Please sign here. And put it all on, we're in a hurry!

Mrs Lange But what am I putting it on for?

Trotalong I advise you to sign and get changed. You have the evening off, after all.

Sylvia Couldn't it be from your daughter?

Mrs Lange But how could my daughter know … (*She sighs, excitedly.*) But my hair isn't done! (*Enter a* **Hairdresser**.)

The Hairdresser (*laying out her instruments, to* **The Cauliflower**) Is this the lady?

The Cauliflower Give her a vigorous pedicure, perhaps the shoes will fit her then.

Sylvia I'll help you. The only thing really missing now is jewellery.

Enter a **Short Man** *with a stack of jewellery cases.*

The Short Man The jewellery. These are worth 70,000 dollars, cash. But these two men (*enter* **Two Large Men** *with arms crossed, who remain standing next to the door, heads bowed in a reflective pose, their right hands resting on the butts of their revolvers in their armpits*) will keep an eye on them. You needn't worry. (*He opens a few cases and takes out several pounds of jewels.*)

Mr Joppe (*opening another case*) Well this is rather strange jewellery. It's an ammunition belt.

The Short Man (*shocked*) That isn't ammunition. And it isn't for you. It must be a mistake.

Trotalong (*furious, takes the belt and throws it into the corner of the room*) A nice mistake! I like that.

The Short Man *begins to tremble terribly, clumsily places the cases in* **Mrs Lange**'s *lap and goes out, devastated.*

Mrs Lange *is now seated, having a pedicure and a perm.*

The Cauliflower Get a move on! We must get to the Astoria. The steamer arrives at 10 o'clock.

Mrs Lange What, I'm supposed to go to the Astoria? They surely won't let me into the Astoria!

Trotalong Perhaps they will.

He and **The Cauliflower** *smile at each other.*

The Cauliflower If you know how to speak their language, they'll understand you immediately.

Mrs Lange I don't believe that, Mr Trotalong, surely there'll be a terrible scene.

The Cauliflower If there is to be a terrible scene, Mrs Lange, then certainly not without our music.

Enter four athletic figures with violin cases.

One of the men Is the concert to be held here?

The Cauliflower No, in the Waldorf Astoria.

Trotalong (*muffled*) You've clearly gone mad! I say: a grand excursion and you come with violins. And for once, I need your cellos. I like that.

The Four (*very upset*)   No offence, boss. We'll get the other instruments right away and come straight to the Astoria. (*All four exit.*)

Mr Joppe   Why are they off again?

The Cauliflower   They thought it was all going to be too easy.

Mrs Lange   But can we really all just leave? Someone might still come.

Mr Joppe   Oh, Mrs Lange, unless Prosperity returns, there's no more business here.

The sound of a car horn. **Trotalong** *goes to the window.* **Sylvia** *runs out and returns immediately.*

Sylvia   Guests. I think it's the whole sailing club. Car after car. They say that today at 5 o'clock the brain trust discovered the reason for the world crisis, which was then immediately resolved by a presidential decree. So Prosperity is back. It'll soon be the talk of the town. We must set the tables right away.

Mrs Lange   Well, I knew that nothing would come of the Astoria. But who will welcome my daughter now, while I'm stuck in the kitchen?

Trotalong (*indicates that all should be calm, goes to the door and locks it*)   Ye of little faith! Why should it bother us if guests come? Isn't your daughter sailing up the Hudson as we speak? Then let them fry their own beef steaks or eat their toenails. We've waited for them long enough, and now they arrive just as we wish to leave. But they don't know us well. Keep quiet, and then they'll think that the inn has already closed.

Everyone moves very quietly, while from outside calls of 'Open up!' 'Waiter!' are heard, and fists hammer against the door. But **The Proprietor** *has come in from the wings and is observing his staff.*

The Proprietor   Have you all gone mad? Might you perhaps open up when there are guests? Is it your birthday, Mrs Lange? (*Shouting.*) Open the inn immediately, Trotalong! What exactly are you waiting for?

Trotalong (*to* **The Cauliflower**, *very calmly*)   Billy, take Sylvia and George with you and get to the Astoria on time. Silence, Friedrich, until you are spoken to.

While **The Proprietor** *gasps for air and the* **two Philosophers** *plant themselves in front of him,* **The Cauliflower** *departs with* **The Bartender** *and* **Sylvia**.

The Proprietor   I shall speak to you afterwards.

He runs to the back and locks the side door. **Trotalong** *gives both* **the Philosophers** *a sign that they should leave him to deal with it, while* **Mrs Lange**, *with her head in the hood-dryer, can neither hear nor see. The guests flood in.*

The Proprietor   Gentlemen, please bear with us just a moment. My staff will be on hand immediately.

The Guests   Everybody help yourselves! There are chairs and tables over there!

They turn the tables and chairs the right way up and throng together into groups. **The Proprietor** *runs back to* **Trotalong**.

The Proprietor   Are you going to work or not?

Trotalong   Not.

The Proprietor   That is the absolute limit!

Trotalong   Calm down, Friedrich. How exactly are you planning to pay back your bank debts? Ah, you've obviously not given that any thought, have you? Always providing unlimited hospitality, and never knowing where it comes from, huh, dear Friedrich?

The Proprietor   What have my bank debts got to do with you?

Trotalong   You're lucky that I bought up all the notes!

He pulls a handful of notes out of his pocket.

The Guests (*to the beat*)
Waiter! Service!
Beef steak, beer!
Calf's liver! Chop-chop!
Waiter, whisky!
Chop-chop! Menu! Us first!

The Proprietor   You – have – my – promissory notes?

Trotalong   Indeed, my son. And now be a good boy and do what is asked of you. We're now closing my inn for a few hours and you will accompany Mrs Lange to the Astoria as her husband, where we intend to welcome Mrs Lange's daughter, since we're just short of a good-looking fifty-something.

The Proprietor   What, you want me to accompany my cook to the Astoria?

Trotalong   Certainly.

The Proprietor   And the guests?

Trotalong   They wait.

The Proprietor   I yield only to violence.

Trotalong   Rightly so. Mrs Lange (*the dryer is removed from her*), we must go to the Astoria right away.

Mrs Lange (*has stood up and sees* **The Proprietor**)   Mr Friedrich!

Trotalong   Our Mr Friedrich will play the role of your husband, Colonel W.G. Frederick, in front of your daughter. Get a move on, Friedrich! You shall call him William.

The large evening dress is thrown over **Mrs Lange**. **Trotalong** *leads her and* **The Proprietor** *to the door at the back.* **The Hairdresser** *and the two* **Philosophers** *follow them.*

Trotalong   And in the meantime we'll lock the guests in, so that they don't run away from us! Service to the customer. We must revive our business, Friedrich!

The six go out of the door. The key is turned from the outside.

Guests (*clamour*)

[*typescript breaks off here*]

The final scene

[B2]

At the monument to **Jacob Trotalong:**

A Father (*to his* **Son**)   Here, Robert, you see the monument to a man who, during his life, appeared to many to be a thoroughly insignificant person. Only after his death did the world recognize what they had lost in him: an unbelievably strong intellect, a heart that beat for all that is honourable, in short, a fighter. May this monument stand as a reminder to you, that in your future you should never be dazzled by external appearances. Some of the so-called great men, whom you read about in newspapers or even in books, are in reality absolutely nothing, while such an apparently ordinary man, burdened with so much, had what it takes to serve as an example to us all. Follow this example!

The alternative first scene

[*BBA* 527/78–83]

3 p.m. The staff are arriving at The Two Knights, an inn. **Jacob Trotalong**, *the second waiter, arrives first. He exchanges his jacket for a white waiter's jacket, clamps a cloth napkin under his arm and greets each of those who enter with a bow – sometimes deep, sometimes less so.*

Jacob Trotalong (*to* **The First Waiter** *as he arrives*) Good day to you, Friedrich, you didn't need to come quite so early, although it is Saturday. You know that before 4 o'clock we can't expect any business, I'd happily have covered for you until then.

The First Waiter I see.

Jacob Trotalong It's not because of the tips, as you might be thinking. I'd have settled up with you afterwards, it's just that …

The First Waiter *ignores him, changes his jacket and greets* **The Cashier** *with a loud 'Hello'.*

Jacob Trotalong Does he have to make me feel my lower status every time, just because he's the first waiter and I'm only the second? I'm sure he didn't talk to me because he saw the cashier coming. They both act as if I'm a complete nobody.

While speaking, he lifts down the chairs stacked on the tables and pushes them into the dining room.

And yet I can't look at them without feeling pity. These poor devils feel content in their own skin. It's enough for them to be first waiter or cashier. They make do with the position bestowed on them by risible happenstance. But I feel differently: there is more to me than meets the eye. I sense powers that should not lie fallow. Often I get sick of serving cutlets and coffee to the guests, who in reality are inferior to me, of having a measly tip tossed in my direction, and I know: this is not the truth!

He greets the cleaning lady offhandedly as she comes out of the dining room.

Jacob Trotalong Well, Mrs Krüger, got up late today, did we?

Mrs Krüger Oh Lordy, Mr Trotalong, a poor cleaning lady like me is only human too, you know. I'm plagued by gout and I'm not the youngest any more.

Jacob Trotalong (*nods condescendingly*)   I understand! (*Watching after her.*) The poor dear! Somebody should give her a hand!

The cleaning lady drops her bag and her belongings fall out. She bends over awkwardly and, groaning, gathers everything together. **Jacob Trotalong** *watches, deep in thought.*

Jacob Trotalong
In times like these it seems as if
I'm not at all that familiar oaf
But, as if I were some higher being
Like those of whom I'm always reading
No trot-along, but a real man
I don't just dream, but I actually can.
The day seems to follow its normal course
While I am filled with a mysterious force
My secret power grows and forms
My little room bursts at the seams
I step into the world: vengeance to wreak!
I confound the mighty! I succour the meek!
All those who are weak and trampled on
Look up and greet their champion
The air is filled with their grateful sighs
For I am the man who will change their lives.
And so: as well as my life of chores
I've a second life, where I settle the scores.

He has become increasingly emotional. The night **Porter**, *who has just entered, laughs as he points him out to the others.*

The Porter   He's dreaming again! Hey, Jacob!

Jacob Trotalong (*comes to with a start*)   Yes?

The First Waiter   Are there matches on all the tables? Have you checked?

Jacob Trotalong   Yes, that is to say, no, right away.

He bumps into **Sylvia** *the washing-up girl and her* **Boyfriend** *as they enter.*

The First Waiter   Our washing-up girl! What's up, Sylvia, can't you manage all those little plates by yourself any more? Decided to bring a strong man with you this time?

The Boyfriend Permit me to make the brief but apparently necessary remark that to you, and to every single one of you, my fiancée is called Miss Capp.

The First Waiter Well, well, well!

The porter Leave him to me, Friedrich! This is the Porter's business! (*Looks at Sylvia's* **Boyfriend**.) Who laid the cuckoo's egg in our nest?

The Boyfriend You are the porter? I would like to speak to the manager.

The Porter Anything else?

The Boyfriend Are you going to tell him I'm here, or not?

The Porter The manager is waiting in the back room for you, he's been there since the day before yesterday.

The Boyfriend I can do without your rotten jokes, tell the manager I'm here, immediately!

The Manager (*enters*) Good evening. So, you absolutely must speak to the manager? And what might this be about?

Sylvia Oh, Klaus, that's him!

The Boyfriend My name is Hat, Klaus Hat. Last Saturday my fiancée, Miss Sylvia Capp, was ordered by you to undertake a dishonourable deed. Obliged by her subordinate position to follow your orders, my fiancée asked both you and the staff at least to protect her from the worst. Nobody helped her. I demand your word of honour that in future my fiancée will be shielded from unreasonable demands of this nature, or I shall be forced to enter legal proceedings against your hotel, even if this means that the reputation of my fiancée, whom I have forgiven, since she was forced to act as she did, is on everyone's lips.

The Manager Sir, what precisely do you want from me?

The Boyfriend Don't try to shout me down! (*Suddenly to* **Sylvia**.) You see, I trust you completely, I know that you have been wholly truthful with me!

The Manager Quite so! What has the little miss been whispering in your ear? I assume that you have evidence to back up your ridiculous accusations, Mr …

The Boyfriend Hat, Klaus Hat.

The Manager Mr Hat. So what is the problem?

The Boyfriend Sylvia!

Sylvia (*to* **The Manager**) Sir ...

The Boyfriend Sylvia, tell him what happened, just as you told me half an hour ago, don't leave anything out and don't embellish, just tell the whole truth!

Sylvia   *tells the story*

The Boyfriend That's enough, I think. You have not respected the honour of one of your employees, on the contrary, you lacked the necessary chivalry to protect a defenceless girl from the very worst. If that happens one more –

The Manager Steady on, steady on young man! Why has your fiancée only just come out with this now?

The Boyfriend Sylvia!

Sylvia I was too ashamed to say anything, but I feared that the young men would come back today, so I spoke up.

The Manager And you're sure that you haven't just cooked up a pretty little fairy tale?

The Boyfriend Sylvia!

Sylvia (*firmly*) Sir, you must remember ordering me to go into the red salon?

The Manager A ridiculous suggestion! On the contrary, I have always strictly forbidden you – as I have all my staff – to enter the dining room if you are not needed there.

Sylvia But the bellboy can bear witness! Leopold, you remember, right, giving me the manager's order?

The Manager I haven't given you the right to interrogate the staff, and certainly not at the very moment that I'm expecting guests. But so that your fiancé can see how ridiculous your accusations are, go ahead: ask! But please, make it short and to the point! I'm sure that *my* staff will give the right answer!

Sylvia Leopold, you remember, right?

Leopold Me? I can't remember a thing, I never have anything to do with you, Miss Sylvia. I work in the lobby, not in the kitchen.

Sylvia Leopold! (*She looks around for help, then turns to* **The Cook**.) Frieda, you must remember, because when I asked you for a coffee, strong and black, you said ...

The Cook If, dear Sylvia, I had to remember what I said every time I poured a cup of coffee, I'd have run out of time to make coffee long ago. And in any case I don't make coffee for the staff, just for the guests.

Sylvia Oh, Frieda!

The Boyfriend (*starts to doubt*) Sylvia, what's this all about?

Sylvia You have to believe me, Klaus. They're afraid because the manager is right there, and so they're not telling the truth.

The First Waiter Feel free to ask me for the truth, Miss Capp.

Sylvia So, Mr Friedrich, are you prepared to admit that I clung on to you and Mr Trotalong, as they carried me to the car?

The First Waiter Of course I remember you getting into that lovely car and I remember precisely that I said: 'Sylvia, Sylvia, what if this goes wrong! You know that the management demands the strictest reserve in dealings with our guests!'

Sylvia You should be ashamed of yourself, Mr Friedrich. You are a bad person. But you, Mr Trotalong, you must help me, tell the truth!

Jacob Trotalong It is not done to accuse a lady of lying, Miss Sylvia, but listen: the truth is that I can't remember a thing about last Saturday, just think how busy it was, it was the first sunny weekend of the year.

The Boyfriend I would never have expected this of you, Sylvia! Farewell! (**Sylvia** *stands stock still.*)

The Boyfriend (*turns to* **Trotalong**) Listen, dear sir, I really must attend one of these gatherings of the society of young men. If this society – and it does sound like such a thing did meet here – comes back tonight, you absolutely must call me. I shall then come back and see how Miss Capp behaves and whether she is forced into anything. Will you promise to phone me? My whole happiness may depend upon it.

Jacob Trotalong Why don't you just stay here?

The Boyfriend This gathering is very important to me. Can't you just give me your word, so that I can be reassured?

Jacob Trotalong Fine, I promise!

The Boyfriend I can be here right away, it's very close by! Many thanks!

He rushes off and in the doorway bumps into a young gentleman. Oh, I beg your pardon! *Raises his hat and rushes out.* **Sylvia** *cries out softly and tries to leave, but the* **Young Man** *has already seen her.*

The Young Man   Greetings, Sylvia! Now don't run off!

Everyone has returned to their places.

The Manager (*to the* **Young Man**)   Good day, sir. I am delighted that you have returned. What can I get for you?

The Young Man   Reserve the red salon, and when my friends come, tell them …

Music. A large cloth falls from the middle of the stage, on it a larger-than-life image of **Trotalong**, *leaning against a wall with a cloth napkin under his arm.*

Underneath: 1st Dream of Jacob Trotalong

Jacob Trotalong   Just tell them that this man is a miscreant who must take immediate responsibility for his deeds.

The Manager   But Jacob!

Jacob Trotalong   Silence! You have lost the right to take part in this discussion. Young man, I ask you to tell me the whole truth: what did you do with Miss Sylvia Capp?

Sylvia   Oh, I knew it! Innocence finds its protector, injustice is chased away, wherever Jacob Trotalong shows his face.

The Young Man (*still trying to lie to* **Jacob Trotalong**)   I don't understand!

Jacob Trotalong   Then I'll ask you in a way that will *make* you understand: did

[*typescript breaks off here*]

Sylvia's description of the rape, handwritten by Margarete Steffin

[*BBA* 527/84–5]

4 young gentlemen came into the cellar. They wanted to have their way with me, but I wasn't having any of it. Half an hour later Leopold, the apprentice (*she points to him*), came into the kitchen and gave me a message from the director: I was to go immediately to the red salon. There

I found the same young men. They were laughing and were already drunk. They poured me some wine mixed with liqueur und forced me to drink it. I had to drink several glasses, which made me feel sick. I went into the kitchen and got the cook (*she points to her*) to give me some strong black coffee. That helped. The director ordered me to go back into the red salon. One of the young men took me firmly in his arms and said he wanted to show me his sailing boat. I cried and screamed, because I didn't want to go with him. I asked for help, nobody helped me. They carried me into the car, drove to the sailing boat and there, oh Franz! (*She cries loudly.*)

The Boyfriend That's enough, I think! Since you paid no heed to the honour of one of your employees, please note that I expect as much chivalry from you, my bride in the future

Director And why is the little miss only coming out with this eight days later?

Sylvia I was ashamed to say it. But I feared that the gentlemen would return today!

Director And you're sure that you

Additional outlines and notes

[A2]

EVERYDAY LIFE OF THE PETTY BOURGEOIS
Struggle with the employer
Struggle with the colleagues
Love or own home

[A3]

THE TRUE LIFE OF JACOB TROTALONG OR DREAMS OF A DIME-A-DOZEN MAN
a
Jacob Trotalong as a waiter. He has to participate in all the firm's dirty practices.

b
Jacob Trotalong as a spouse. He has barely any influence on his wife. He is dead tired during the day. She works.

c
Jacob Trotalong as a father. Instead of the boy's leader, educator, protector he is his tempter, torturer, exploiter and despised by the boy.

d
Jacob Trotalong as a political element. In the union he is the subject, in life the object of politics.

[A1]

1
Maurice   Sylvia
Chevalier. And the washing-up girl.
The unknown owner

2
Robinson, the gangster chief, and the broken blossom, now ageing flower seller, 'Lady for a Day'. He marries her pro forma for the old parents, then the parson was genuine.

The secret gang leader.
3
        Harald   May
Harald Lloyd, the avenger, and the vamp (May West)
The disguised detective.
May realizes, 'Jacob would have been the right one', but it's too late!

Suggestions for songs

[A10]

SUGGESTIONS FOR SONGS – TROTALONG

After the curtain rises, the song of the good old days, the time before the crisis. That was the golden age, when anyone who'd been given the boot could find another job straight away, or at least the promise of one. So few people bedded down under the arches, it was barely worth mentioning them.

But what a crowd today (the dark sides of the good old days will have to be brought out, while praising them). Instead of coming at the beginning of the play, this song could perhaps be sung later by Franz.

A song before the first dream: 'Something has been asked of you.' This song must articulate the philosophy of submission: the one who submits is shown to be in the right, because anyone who answers questions truthfully brings about their own destruction.

For page 9 the song about the man with a paunch. Praise for inner merits, which thoroughly overshadow the physical misshapenness.

Possibly the song Everything is Fine, at the end of the first Act the choral song, in which it is asserted that the chaos is in fact all perfectly fine.

Songs

[B3]

Song from *The True Story of Jacob Trotalong*

Buy one get one free, we're two a penny
Always one, at least, too many
We stand here grousing, touching forelocks, shining shoes
All for hire
Make a bid, we need a buyer
We have to live, we haven't much to lose.

Oh no sir, all those luxury oddities
They were sold out long ago
We're the bargain basement commodities
Don't expect too much, oh no.
We're cut-price fathers, knockdown offers
Our own kids see that we don't fit
And if they show they're frightened of us
Then we box their ears a bit.

We're husbands from the sale bucket
No returns, no money back
By Saturday we'll all be wed or chucked
We're the absolute remnant rack.
Dear me, the tender souls amongst us
Quickly end up on the rubbish heap.
We're the last ones hanging on the shelves now
Damaged goods and going cheap.

[B5]

That great man Ford was not great from the start
And when he was so great, he still had woes,
His capital, how did he make a start?
How did he take control, what deals did he close?

And some they said then: No, that just can't be,
Nothing comes of nothing. How did he make a dime?
That money was borrowed – y'all must surely see!
He was in the right place, it was the right time.

And some they said: but it's an impossible task!
Nothing comes of nothing. – How did he make a dime?
Whatever he did, y'all know, it was the right ask!
He was in the right place, it was the right time.

They say: in every soup there is a hair,
You see it there, it floats, you fish it out;
Or you don't see it but you taste it, there,
And spit it out again dead quick, without a doubt.

Wherever you look the conclusion is clear,
We live together just like cattle, cow to cow;
Something must change, it must, y'all hear:
It's easily done, for sure. But how?

Outlines of the second act

[A6]

Difficulties leaving the inn. The sailing club arrive (Meyerhold). Prosperity since 5 o'clock. (Man, haven't you heard, this afternoon the brain trust discovered the reason for the crisis, which was then immediately resolved by a presidential decree. So Prosperity reigns once again, it's already the talk of the town.)

The proprietor has to play Mrs Lange's husband.

Chorus of the demanding guests, who have already given their orders. The staff lock them in and go to the Astoria.

2
Seizing a table, since the Astoria is overcrowded. Eight dead. The duke is compelled to dance with Mrs Lange. The check. News: the military is deployed and there is fog over the Hudson.

3
Nerves. Time is short. Normandy is blown up. Jacques-Trolong has to get going and leaves the Astoria as a duke.

[*BBA* 527/58]

II, 1
When an old cook faces an emergency, the waiter Trotalong appears as a clandestine great ruler.

The band of gangsters dresses the old cook.

Since prosperity suddenly breaks out, the inn is full of guests. But oddly, the waiter Trotalong sticks to his intention to accompany the cook to the luxury hotel Astoria.

The proprietor arrives but even he cannot prevent this, since his waiter reveals himself as the clandestine owner of the inn. The proprietor is forced to play Frau Lange's husband.

crisis talks. Mr Giaguera is invited.

II, 2

Notes on the plot

[A5]

He has to keep his people under pressure (to squeeze surplus value out of them).

He can't associate with them (he insists on being served, on being called 'Sir', he arrives early and leaves late, considers himself to be above the inn, has a sense of honour, does not complain when his wages are late, does extra work, is available even during his time off).

He is mocked because he keeps his collar clean and starves.

He is a teetotaller. He plays the lottery.

Heads must roll. Mr Joppe the outsider. The considerate Mrs Lange. Mr Friedrich, who regrettably has no sympathy for his most loyal assistants, and who would do better to pay attention to Mrs Lange's emotional wellbeing, because then she would happily do without wages (which she is not keen to do currently).

He takes on the responsibility. Considering the bigger picture.

'Do you see now, Mrs Lange, why I had to cancel your day off?'

[A7]
[*BBA* 527/71]

THE REAL LIFE OF JACOB TROTALONG

Arc of decline. The competitor, ready to pounce. Various restaurants. Perhaps various ages?

He wants to be able to treat the guests badly. The night-shelter. He can do so here.

The poorly dressed guest. Who turns into a second Trotalong. And is served well. Shortly beforehand he is put on tips.

Restaurant near the docks. A ship owner who has left his office. The owners of a ship in trouble at sea don't want to pay for the rescue. Jacob Trotalong badgers the owner and convinces him. He has previously seen a couple. The young man was a sailor.

The landlady. She refuses to let prostitutes stay. Jacob Trotalong sees her as a prostitute and shames her.

His fiancée is pregnant. He marries her. But he also takes another girl to the altar, because she is pregnant too.

[*BBA* 527/62]

The First Waiter Our second waiter often dreams with his eyes open. If he didn't work like a machine while dreaming, I'd have to put the screws on him. But really, when he dreams he does the work of two men. He works away all the work that I give him, including my own.

The First Waiter Don't just stare into space, Jacob! It's creepy for our guests.

Jacob I beg you to forgive my staring into space.

The First Waiter Now just make sure you don't look creepy, otherwise we won't be able to keep you on here.

Sylvia, The Washing-Up Girl You're about to hear what really happened that night. Then you'll see that I told you the truth and everything will be alright between us again, just as you promised me.

[A9]

7

DEATH AND POSTHUMOUS REPUTATION

In an accident while performing bold, self-sacrificing deed. Despair at the deserted surroundings. Reward of those who have recognized him as a higher being, or honoured him despite his low position. Punishment to all others. Father and son at his memorial. The female street sweepers.

The Judith of Shimoda

Based on a play by Yamamoto Yūzō
In collaboration with Hella Wuolijoki

Reconstruction of the play script by Hans Peter Neureuter
Translated and introduced by Markus Wessendorf

Introduction

The textual genesis of *The Judith of Shimoda* (German: *Die Judith von Shimoda*) published here is complex: It is the first English translation of Hans Peter Neureuter's German-language reconstruction (2006) of Bertolt Brecht and Hella Wuolijoki's respective adaptation(s) into German and Finnish (1940) of Glenn W. Shaw's English rendering (1935) of Yamamoto Yūzō's 1929 play *The Sad Tale of a Woman, The Story of Chink Okichi (Nyonin Aishi, Tōjin Okichi Monogatari)*.[1] Different from Brecht's other dramatic fragments included in this volume, the English version of *The Judith of Shimoda* closely follows Neureuter's reconstruction of the full play script without further editorial changes by the translator.[2] Even though scholars had already been aware of the fragment in the 1970s, it was Neureuter's 2006 publication that first established *The Judith of Shimoda* (similar to *The Bread Store*) as one of Brecht's nearly complete fragments. Günter Glaeser, the editor of the original publication of the dramatic fragment in 1997, had merely juxtaposed Brecht's adaptation of several of Yamamoto's scenes, the two different versions of his added framing action, and his various other notes and outlines with no attempt at integrating them into a coherent play.[3] Even though Glaeser, in his annotations, referred to Wuolijoki's Finnish stage version of the adaptation that had resulted from her collaboration with Brecht, he did not consult it for a possible German-language reconstruction of the full script.[4]

The Story of Chink Okichi is one of the last plays completed by Yamamoto before he began to write novels. It draws upon historical events that occurred after Commodore Perry compelled Japan to open to the West in 1854 and covers the period from 1857 to the early years of the Meiji period (1868–1912). Townsend Harris, the first American general consul on Japanese soil, has threatened to bomb the city of Shimoda if the magistrates' promise to get the young geisha Okichi to serve him is not fulfilled. Initially reluctant because of her relationship with the carpenter Tsurumatsu, Okichi ultimately submits to the consul's demand, so as to prevent the bombardment of her home town. As a result of her personal and sexual sacrifice, however, Okichi's life is ruined: samurai spit at her in public, people call her a 'foreigner's wife', she becomes an alcoholic, her marriage to Tsurumatsu breaks up, and she dies impoverished in a hovel.

Unlike the ending of Yamamoto's play, the historical Okichi drowned herself at the age of forty-nine. A restaurant that she ran for two years, a temple that includes her grave, and a museum dedicated to her are still major tourist attractions of Shimoda today. The first two acts of *The Story of Chink Okichi* were staged in January 1933 at Tokyo's Meiji Theatre, followed in May of the same year by the performance of Acts Three and Four at the Shin-Kabuki Theatre in the Shinjuku district of Tokyo. Yamamoto wrote his play during a major resurgence of public interest in Okichi's story. Other 'Okichi plays' produced at the time include Seika Mayama's *Chink Okichi* (1929) and *Chink Okichi and Joigun* (1931) as well as Karyo Kawamura's *The Maiden Time of Chink Okichi* (1931).[5] There were also several Japanese film adaptations of the story in the 1930s, and in 1958 John Huston directed a Hollywood version with the title *The Barbarian and the Geisha* (with John Wayne as Townsend Harris and Eiko Ando as Okichi). Even Brecht, in a short note to *The Judith of Shimoda*, considered a film treatment of the material.

Whereas Yamamoto's play tells a largely linear story that combines realistic dialogue with occasional surrealist imagery, Brecht's adaptation adds a framework plot. In his version the Japanese politician and newspaper mogul Akimura (possibly intended as a counterpart to the nationalist German magnate Alfred Hugenberg)[6] has hired a troupe of actors to perform Okichi's story for his guests as an example of Japanese patriotism. Since the guests include the British Orientalist Clive (perhaps alluding to the first British colonial administrator of Bengal, Robert Clive, 1725–74), the American journalist Ray, the Japanese poet Kito (potentially pointing to the famous haiku author, Takai Kito, 1741–89), and the unnamed director of Yamamoto's play, these meta-dramatic scenes allow Brecht to interrupt Yamamoto's plot with socio-political commentary on its recurring themes (patriotism, nationalism, imperialism, heroism, militarism, etc.) from varying points of view.

The Judith of Shimoda is one of several projects that Brecht and the Estonian-born Finnish playwright Wuolijoki worked on during his stay on Wuolijoki's country estate at Marlebäck from early July to early October 1940. Brecht, his family, Margarete Steffin, and (for a short while) Ruth Berlau all stayed at Marlebäck while waiting for visas to enter the United States. This was already the third project on which Wuolijoki and Brecht had collaborated, following discussions to create a play about the Finnish statesman Johan Vilhelm Snellman and Brecht's adaptation of Wuolijoki's *The Sawdust Princess* into his *Puntila and His Man Matti*. Brecht and Wuolijoki worked on *The Judith of Shimoda* for only a short time, between Brecht's completion of the first version of his *Puntila* on 19 September and the beginning of his work on *Conversations in Exile* on 1 October. On 25 September, Brecht wrote in his journal: 'h.w. gives me CHINK OKICHI by YAMAMOTO YUZO, a good play for which she holds the rights. i quickly sketch a framing action and a few stage moves on the basis of the (bad) english translation.'[7] Wuolijoki had already considered translating *Chink Okichi* in 1937 when a group that she belonged to had proposed a

Finnish production of the play to Yamamoto. Despite Yamamoto's positive response and the offer of a Japanese theatre company to provide support, the production never materialized. The divergent aesthetic preferences of Brecht and Wuolijoki, which had already surfaced in their collaboration on the *Puntila* material, also emerged in their assessment of Yamamoto's work:

> h.w. thinks CHINK OKICHI is too epic, and that the second half consequently tapers off. the fact is that her heroic deed takes place in the 3rd act, but her decline continues for nine more scenes. in addition to which her heroic deed is depicted with such restraint that it will be forgotten as soon as it has been told, except where it forms part of a national legend. it would be the same if i wrote a WILLIAM TELL and let him live for 20 years after murdering gessler.[8]

Glenn W. Shaw, an American academic, writer, and translator who lived in Osaka in the 1920s and 1930s, translated *The Story of Chink Okichi* and included it with his translations of two other plays by Yamamoto in the volume *Three Plays*.[9] As he states in the introduction to this volume, he had aimed for a 'sentence-for-sentence translation' and considered the plays a 'trilogy depicting feudal, transition and modern Japan'.[10] As the second play in the volume, *The Story of Chink Okichi* represents the transitional period and is bookended by *Sakazaki, Lord Dewa* (1921), about the thwarted love of a feudal lord for the shogun's daughter whose life he has saved during the early years of the Tokugawa shogunate (1603–1867), and *The Crown of Life* (1920), which portrays a shrimp canner's plight against the backdrop of a modern Japan integrated into the world economy.

Whereas *The Story of Chink Okichi* consists of four acts with a total of twelve scenes (Act One: three scenes; Act Two: two scenes; Act Three: four scenes; Act Four: three scenes), Neureuter's reconstructed version of Brecht and Wuolijoki's adaptation features a prologue, eleven scenes that alternate with ten interludes, and an epilogue. As he states in the afterword to his reconstruction, Brecht worked on the framing action for *The Judith of Shimoda* in two stages: The first resulted in a prelude and a short dialogue segment, both featuring Yamamoto himself as a character; the second led to a series of drafts and sketches that were not further developed as well as a complete set of the framing scenes without Yamamoto as a character.[11] For his reconstruction, Neureuter used all scenes finished by Brecht (i.e. his treatments of Yamamoto's first four scenes, a newly written tenth scene, and the complete framing action of the second conceptual stage) and translated the missing scenes (Scenes Five to Nine and Eleven) from Wuolijoki's full Finnish script of the adaptation, which he had discovered in the early 1980s with the help of her daughter, Vappu Tuomioja. As an outline for his reconstruction,

Neureuter used both Brecht's second provisional scene breakdown of the play (*BBA* 518/57–62) as well as Wuolijoki's completed stage version.[12]

Brecht and Wuolijoki's adaptation is much tighter than the original source and condenses, rearranges, and omits many of its elements. By switching the second and third scene of Yamamoto's play, for example, Brecht emphasizes Okichi's agency. Whereas in Yamamoto's version Tsurumatsu persuades Okichi to go to the authorities to volunteer to serve the American consul, in Brecht's version she surprises her fiancé with that decision after having already visited them. Isa Shinjirō, the authority figure to whom Okichi reports, is just a superintendent of constables in Yamamoto's play, but in Brecht's adaptation he has been upgraded to a lord, which heightens the class differences between the two characters as well as the gravity of Okichi's decision. Different from *The Story of Chink Okichi*, the primary reason for Harris's threat of bombardment in *The Judith of Shimoda* is not Okichi's initial refusal to serve him but the Japanese prevarications over the ratification of a trade deal. Yamamoto's fourth scene starts with Okichi organizing cow's milk for the sick consul before the sound of cannons announces the arrival of an American merchant ship, whereas Brecht rearranges this sequence into a dynamic 'parallel montage' and turns the ship into a warship, thereby clarifying and intensifying the political stakes: out of gratitude to Okichi for having healed him by procuring milk, Harris now revokes his earlier threat and decides to stay one day longer for a meeting with Lord Isa that will prepare for direct trade negotiations with the shogun. (In Wuolijoki's adaptation of Scene Five, minor characters declare these negotiations a historical event and mention that the general consul and the lord are on their way to the shogun.) Brecht cuts Yamamoto's sixth scene (Act Three: Scene One), which is now summarized by the director at the end of the fifth interlude. Also, Brecht replaces Yamamoto's tenth scene (Act Four: Scene Two), a nightmarish sequence in which the ghostlike appearances of the other dramatis personae torment Okichi, with a new scene in which an audience attacks a drunk and unrecognized Okichi for disrupting a singer performing a ballad of her heroic deeds. This added scene emphasizes the radical disconnect between patriotic rhetoric and nationalist ideology on the one hand and the social reality of the 'little heroes' who have sacrificed themselves for their country on the other. Wuolijoki also makes significant edits: By omitting the beginning of Yamamoto's final scene, when Okichi is visited by her adopted daughter Osen and her lover Densaburō, Wuolijoki emphasizes Okichi's ultimate isolation even further.

Even though *The Judith of Shimoda* appears to attack nineteenth-century Japanese nationalism and American imperialism, its actual target was the German war machine at the beginning of the Second World War: Shortly before Brecht and Wuolijoki started working on the adaptation, German troops had overrun France in less than three weeks. Brecht's interest in the biblical Judith legend and the trope of the woman who sacrifices herself by sleeping with the enemy to save her nation or community can be dated back to his very first play from 1913, *The Bible*. This play inverts the Judith motif by featuring as protagonist the virgin daughter of the mayor of a Dutch protestant town under siege by Catholic forces, who is prevented from saving her town by sleeping with the Catholic general because of the intervention of her deeply religious grandfather. The short outline of one of Brecht's unrealized film projects contrasts starkly with *The Judith of Shimoda* by providing a happy outcome for the protagonist more in line with the biblical legend. *The Judith of Saint Denis* (1937) is set at the beginning of the First World War and is about a French wife and her German husband living in northern France when the German troops conquer their town. The husband, who was originally expelled from Germany because of his pacifism, escapes to Paris. After all the remaining men in town have been rounded up, the wife manages to postpone their transport behind German frontlines for forced labour by seducing the officer in charge and spending one night with him. The French start their counter-offensive the next morning and retake the town. The husband, who has returned from Paris, accepts his wife's sacrifice and leaves the town with her on the very day on which the residents celebrate their 'Judith of Saint Denis' in full awareness of her heroic deed and fall. In *The Judith of Shimoda*, by contrast, Okichi's heroic deed – that is her sexual self-sacrifice to save her town – is linked to the biblical Judith, whereas her fall – that is her having had sexual relations with a foreigner – leads to her public 'burning' by her own community, figuratively evoking the fate of Joan of Arc. As the poet Kito states in the prelude to the play, 'If you like, you can also interpret the girl as a kind of Saint Joan, since she will be, in a certain sense, burned. Actually, by her fellow citizens.' Brecht had already used the Joan of Arc story for *Saint Joan of the Stockyards* (1932), and he would later return to it in *The Visions of Simone Machard* (1943) and his adaptation of Anna Seghers's radio play *The Trial of Joan of Arc at Rouen 1431* (1952).

Neureuter notes that Scenes Five to Nine and Eleven of Wuolijoki's adaptation closely follow Shaw's English translation of Yamamoto's play, while at the same time trimming its verbal and dramaturgical digressions. For his reconstruction of the full play script of *The Judith of Shimoda*, Neureuter approached Wuolijoki's version similarly by aiming for a close German translation without omissions, except in those cases where Wuolijoki had ignored the 'gestic' consistency of the material.[13] Neureuter corrected obvious syntactical and idiomatic errors in Brecht's extant scenes but did not try to improve upon the writing's rawness, which still included regional or naturalistic expressions probably deriving from Margarete Steffin or Wuolijoki, and which had not seen a final edit or authorization by Brecht himself.[14] According to Neureuter, Brecht never intended a full recreation of *The Story of Chink Okichi* (as he did with Wuolijoki's *Puntila* comedy) but respected the quality of Yamamoto's source material enough to aim only for a cautious adaptation.[15] Since Brecht's comment on Shaw's '(bad) english translation' referred less to a lack of fidelity to the original material (which Brecht wouldn't have been in any position to assess) than to its inadequacy as dramatic dialogue, the current translation consulted Shaw only when necessary. The sole passages from Shaw's version that appear unaltered in the present text are the few lines of English dialogue by the non-Japanese characters Heusken and Harris that Brecht had incorporated into his adaptation, and which were already included in Yamamoto's original play. This translation has only corrected one typographical error: Brecht's (and Neureuter's) rendering of the Japanese name 'Nakamura' as 'Makamura'.

An earlier version of the translation included in this volume was produced at the University of Hawaii's Kennedy Theatre in Honolulu in April 2010 (director: Paul T. Mitri) and at La MaMa in New York in May 2012 (director: Zishan Ugurlu, with students of Eugene Lang College). Stephen Brockmann, in his review of the Honolulu production, stated that 'Mitri has demonstrated that it is possible ... to stage a dramatically effective, gripping production' of *The Judith of Shimoda*.[16] He also argued that this 'play is of interest primarily for four reasons: as an instantiation of Brechtian ideas about theatrical estrangement, as a variation on the problem of heroism in Brecht's plays, as an intercultural experiment in literary and theatrical translation ... and as an attempt to come to terms with the history of American imperialism in an Asian country'.[17]

MARKUS WESSENDORF

Notes

1. Glenn W. Shaw translated 'tojin' ('Tang person': a Chinese foreigner in Japan) with 'chink', i.e. the English slang word for 'Chinese'.
2. Bertolt Brecht, *Die Judith von Shimoda. Nach einem Stück von Yamamoto Yuzo in Zusammenarbeit mit Hella Wuolijoki. Rekonstruktion einer Spielfassung von Hans Peter Neureuter* (Frankfurt am Main: Suhrkamp, 2006).
3. See Bertolt Brecht, *Die Judith von Shimoda*, BFA 10.2, 832–77.
4. Brecht, *Die Judith von Shimoda*, 1230.
5. Marumoto Takashi, 'From *The Story of Chink Okichi* to *Die Judith von Shimoda*', in Reinhart Meyer and Sven Schmalfuß (eds), *Chink Okishi/ Die Judith von Shimoda: Text, Materialien und Kommentar* (Regensburg: Selbstverlag des Studententheaters, 2009), 171.

6 Takashi, 'From *The Story of Chink Okichi* to *Die Judith von Shimoda*', 146.
7 Bertolt Brecht, *Journals 1934-1955*, ed. John Willett and trans. Hugh Rorrison (New York: Routledge, 1993), 102.
8 Brecht, *Journals 1934-1955*, 102.
9 Yamamoto Yūzō, *Three Plays*, trans. Glenn W. Shaw (Tokyo: Hokuseido Press, 1935).
10 Yūzō, *Three Plays*, v.
11 See Brecht, *Die Judith von Shimoda* (2006), 140.
12 Ibid., 124–5.
13 Ibid., 154.
14 Ibid., 155.
15 Ibid., 156.
16 Stephen Brockmann, '*The Judith of Shimoda* (Hawaii)', *Communications from the International Brecht Society* 39 (2010), 81.
17 Brockmann, '*The Judith of Shimoda* (Hawaii)', 77.

Note on *The Judith of Shimoda*

[A4]

The play *The Judith of Shimoda* is an adaptation of the play *The Sad Tale of a Woman, The Story of Chink Okichi* by Yamamoto Yūzō. Yamamoto's play is about a historical figure whose sacrificial act has become famous. The author focuses on the life of his heroine after her heroic deed. Most European audiences simply interpret the play biographically without understanding its main point. They don't readily see that the life story depicted in the play is similar to that of William Tell or the biblical Judith after their heroic deeds. We have therefore created a framing action for our current adaptation. The first five scenes, which deal with the heroic deed itself, have been condensed; these are followed, more or less intermittently and as requested, by some further episodes from the later life of the heroine. The rearrangements and revisions of the first five scenes are meant to emphasize more clearly Okichi's decision to do a service to her nation and to make this decision appear less dependent on coincidence. Her initial resistance to the demands of the authorities, however, has been retained.

The dialogues of the framing action should not be considered fixed. They can be altered and expanded according to circumstance. The attitudes and views expressed in these dialogues, however, need to be maintained.

Characters

Characters appearing in the interludes

Akimura, *Japanese newspaper mogul and politician*
Clive, *British Orientalist*
Ray, *American journalist*
Kito, *Japanese poet*
The director of the play
Silent servants

Characters appearing in the scenes

Townsend Harris, *General Consul of the United States*
Henry Heusken, *his translator and private secretary*
Ah Lo, *his servant*

Inoue Shinano-no-Kami, *member of the city council of Shimoda*
Nakamura Deba-no-Kami, *member of the city council of Shimoda*

Wakana Miosaburo, *police officer*
Matsumura Chushiro, *police officer*

A civil servant

Saito, *police officer, later Excellency*
Lord Isa

Okichi
Omoto, *her sister*
Tsurumatsu, *her fiancé, later husband*
Ofuku, *her girlfriend*
Litter-bearers and samurai guards
A crowd of people
Ferryman
Two samurai
An old teahouse owner

Oshimo, *one of Okichi's customers*
Osai, *Tsurumatsu's lover*
A messenger boy
A fish seller

Two council members and additional members of the city council of Shimoda
Takagi Kamekichi, *remote relative of Okichi*
Waitresses and waiters, geishas
A street singer and passers-by
A sailor

[B3]
Prelude

*Small hall in a mansion in the Japanese capital. The master of the house, the politician and newspaper owner **Akimura**, talks to his guests the British Orientalist **Clive**, the American journalist **Ray**, and the Japanese poet **Kito**, while the sparse decoration for the first scene of 'The Foreigner Okichi' is set up quickly and gracefully.*

Ray But we could just as well have gone to the theatre, Mr Akimura. How complicated and expensive to invite the actors to your mansion for this purpose.

Akimura You will feel more comfortable here. The air is better and the seats are softer, and that is important because the play is a tragedy.

Kito It also includes a heroic act, and someone sitting uncomfortably might take offence, Miss Ray. You have to sit comfortably when you observe heroes at work.

Clive Anyhow, I deeply regret that you have felt challenged to counter my minor objections by resorting to such an extravagant argument as a theatre performance.

Akimura I can't leave you under the delusion that patriotism in this country is only a matter for the upper classes.

Kito Mister Clive could argue, however, that a myth such as the O-Kichi myth doesn't prove very much. Myth is myth, you know.

Akimura I don't agree with you, Kito. Myths provide evidence. Recent myths in particular. Any nationalism that generates myths is undoubtedly a popular nationalism, don't you agree, Mister Clive? The O-Kichi myth isn't yet fifty years old. And something else: the scenes I have arranged to be performed for you are from a modern play. It was written by Mister Yamamoto, one of our youngest and more radical dramatists, with whose opinions I don't agree at all. A realist.

Kito That's right. You won't get to see an idealized representation.

Ray I am so anxious to see your Japanese Judith!

Kito You will see her in the lion's den.

Clive The lion, that is your fellow-countryman.

Ray I know. The first American consul on Japanese soil, right?

Kito And the new Holoferneses threaten less with fire and sword than with trade agreements.

Ray Oh, those are said to be no less destructive.

Kito If you like, you can also interpret the girl as a kind of Saint Joan, since she will be, in a certain sense, burned. Actually, by her fellow citizens.

Ray Oh, Clive, you have to translate every sentence for me.

Akimura I think the actors are ready. (*He claps his hands.*) Please, sit down.

Small folding screens have been set up in front of the stage. **The Director** *appears in front of them.*

The Director Ladies and Gentlemen, the first scene you are going to see is set in the city hall of Shimoda, a historical encounter between the American consul and Japanese politicians. The year is 1856.

Servants move the folding screens to the sides. The play begins.

[B1]
Scene One

The great hall of the city hall of Shimoda. The space is empty, but noises and heated words in English can be heard from an adjacent room. Suddenly, the sound of an object smashing against a wall. The paper-covered sliding doors are pushed open and **Townsend Harris**, *an old man and General Consul of the United States, enters screaming.* **Inoue Shinano-no-Kami** *and* **Nakamura Deba-no-Kami**, *members of the city council of Shimoda, enter behind him.* **Wakana Miosaburo**, *a police officer, tries frantically to restrain his colleague* **Matsumura Chushiro** *who, sword in hand, is trying to attack* **Harris**. **Henry Heusken**, *Harris's translator and private secretary, enters last.*

Harris Lies! Lies! Nothing but lies from beginning to end! With a pack of rascals such as this, how can I continue negotiations? I have finished with you. There is only one thing to be done!

Heusken Be careful, Sir! (*To the others.*) Are you crazy? You are attacking the General Consul of the United States of America!

Harris (*suddenly notices the sword in* **Matsumura**'*s hand*) So you would kill me, would you? Very well, kill away! Of course you are all aware of the consequences?

The council members and **Wakana** *manage to calm down the enraged* **Matsumura**.

Inoue (*to* **Heusken**)   Please ask the General Consul to come back and to continue the conference.

Heusken (*to* **Harris**)   They ask you, Sir, to return and to continue the conference.

Harris   No, why should I return? How can I negotiate with people like these, liars from habit, born liars as they are? No! Let the guns speak: then perhaps we shall have an answer. Come, Mister Heusken, we will return to our quarters.

Harris *knocks over a chair and walks away.* **Heusken** *wants to follow him, but* **Wakana** *rushes after him to hold him back.*

Wakana   Mister Heusken, please wait a minute!

Heusken   What for?

Wakana   What on earth has offended the consul so much that he is raging like this?

Heusken   You know exactly why.

Wakana   Don't take that tone of voice with us! Try to translate the sentences of the consul as precisely as possible, so that we can clearly understand them. We don't understand a single word.

Heusken   You are lying! You are lying! That's what the General Consul says. Everything that you have said, from beginning to end – lies. What you said yesterday and what you are saying today don't have anything to do with each other. We are seriously trying to negotiate with you, but we will never come to an agreement this way. It is fully understandable that the General Consul has lost his patience.

Matsumura (*angry*)   Fully understandable? To throw an ashtray at a council member, fully understandable? Is that common in your country?

Heusken   It's your own fault. He cannot stand those lies anymore.

Matsumura   What was a lie? Which promise has been broken?

Heusken   Oh, you want to see proof? Take the case of Okiri, for example!

Wakana   Okichi, you mean. As I have explained to you in detail, the girl has not given her consent.

Heusken Lie! Of course, she hasn't given her consent because you are not serious about this! We are treated like lepers in this country, that's it. For weeks we have been unable to get servants – new names every day, but no servants. And that's only to be expected: if your laws still bar anyone from entering the service of a foreigner, there is, of course, no chance of recruiting personnel.

Wakana But no, one of the two girls most recently mentioned to you will come! And regarding Okichi, we won't leave it at that. We have told you that we will send another girl instead of her.

Heusken No, that is not possible. We insist on Okiri. Especially on Okiri.

Wakana Her name is Okichi. How can you be so stubborn when I am trying to explain to you …

Heusken We are not stubborn. Okiri here, Okiri there, or Okichi, if you insist, it is a matter of principle. Not to mention the fact that we have already paid a deposit of twenty-five Reyo. And regarding the consul's travels and the exchange rate of the dollar, you've been trying the same tricks on us. Here, too, you twist and turn; here, too, you draw everything out. When, finally, is the reception at the Shogun going to happen? Tomorrow, you have told us for weeks. In short: it will never happen. No one here wants it to happen.

Inoue Mister Heusken, His Excellency Lord Isa considers it a matter of great honour to arrange that visit. Most of the difficulties have already been ironed out. The lord expects at the latest by the end of the coming week …

Heusken … another postponement for two months, eh? Dear Gentlemen, let me be discourteous enough to repeat to you the words that the General Consul uttered just a moment ago before leaving you; they are of major importance. Please listen carefully – this is what the General Consul said: He considers himself no longer in a position to continue negotiations with a bunch of born liars. From now on he will let the cannons speak.

Nakamura The cannons!

Heusken Yes, Your Excellency, the cannons!

Wakana Did the consul really say that?

Heusken I gave you a word-for-word translation.

Inoue (*trying to regain composure*) But that would not only be against Japanese interests but also those of the United States. Sir translator, is there no other way to appease the consul?

Heusken I am sorry, Excellency, but I don't know of any other way. When the consul makes a serious pronouncement like this, I have to assume that he has made up his mind.

Inoue But when matters come to a head like this –

Heusken You're right, you're right. I would find it regrettable if that were indeed the end. Which is not what the consul wants. But if Japan doesn't want war, it will have to demonstrate more honesty. In my opinion, the General Consul is a remarkably amiable man. And a consul, after all, is only a consul and not the captain of a battleship. If the negotiations move ahead, I cannot imagine that he would turn to the cannons. I will try everything to appease him. But sincerity is absolutely necessary.

Heusken *takes a bow and exits.*

Inoue (*dejected*) This is a fine mess, isn't it?

Nakamura We are definitely dealing with a tough customer here. And if we show the slightest weakness, we will have to pay for that.

Matsumura May I voice my opinion? It seems to me that our entire approach to the negotiation process is somewhat indecisive. These people see through us. They talk of cannons, but not a single American ship is here. What, then, should we be afraid of? Wouldn't it be best to answer them with a firm 'No!'?

Inoue No! Even if there isn't any ship here yet, that could easily change. Of course, they will not immediately start a war, but we would be in a serious situation if the negotiations were to be discontinued. (*Suddenly.*) By the way, who will report the incident to the lord?

Nakamura Not me.

Matsumura He wouldn't even receive me.

Wakana It is completely out of the question to report this to the lord.

Inoue I know for a fact that Lord Isa, in his negotiations with the Shogun, has finally achieved that the court will receive the General Consul. The negotiations must not be discontinued at this point. The lord would be furious.

Pause.

Wakana The best political solution would be first and foremost to send that Okichi lady to him. That would at least weaken the accusation that we don't stick to our promises. These foreigners will calm down when they no longer have to live completely without women. And the various issues that we are still negotiating about will be easier to take care of.

Inoue That's why we have agreed to turn a blind eye, as far as women are concerned. But if this Okichi, who has become so highly important, doesn't want to go, what can we do?

Nakamura There is no point in wasting too many words on this matter. But it was somewhat careless to make a promise without having asked for her consent.

Wakana I am sorry about that, but she is a geisha after all, and it wouldn't have befitted the reputation of our administration to consult with her about every detail.

Nakamura That may also be true. Anyhow: it would be a fundamental mistake to let a woman selfishly decide if she wants to go or not.

Inoue Couldn't we just give her a nice present?

Wakana Hardly. According to the report of police officer Saito, Okichi is sexually dependent on a ship carpenter, who she is afraid to lose if she follows the official order – which is why neither an offer nor a threat will be effective with her.

Inoue That complicates the situation. Has someone negotiated with the man?

Wakana Yes. He is difficult.

Inoue We no longer seem in control of the situation.

A Civil Servant (*announces*) His Excellency, Lord Isa.

All stand apprehensively.

Wakana He has already been informed.

[B6]

Interlude One

Clive You take our petrol or we light up your houses. Volatile traveling salesmen, these new Holoferneses!

Ray Were the Japanese really that dishonest?

Kito Terribly. That was an essential aspect of their backwardness. Honesty as a business trick is an accomplishment of modern times. Your Rothschilds were the first ones to skin the public with unadorned honesty. The moment of surprise, of course, played a major role in that. But then honesty and openness became common and the businessmen lost their initially superstitious fear of sincerity once they realized that honesty is completely harmless and doesn't get in the way of making big profits.

Clive The most honest language, of course, is the language of cannons. There is nothing crooked about cannons.

Ray Don't be so cynical. You, Clive, have always been against cannons. Why do you immediately get cynical the moment someone talks about them? Cynicism doesn't help against cannons, on the contrary, it helps the cannons.

Clive There is something to what you're saying. The language of cannons and the language of facts should both be taken seriously. But, oddly enough, this requires a real effort of will. 'The naked truth!' Strange cult of nakedness! Who does not reject nudity, if it is ugly?

Ray I have never heard anyone talk about cannons other than in the tone of those famous gentlemen's clubs. You only know dirty jokes about them. – But to speak about the play, I appreciate that it shows how this Judith refuses at first.

Akimura That is the truth.

Ray Our textbook heroes crowd around as if at a sell-off following their heroic deeds. Okichi, on the other hand, seems to display proper restraint.

Akimura I am glad that you comment on that. It is not in our interest as nationalists to represent heroic acts as self-evident. The more recent as well as the most ancient psychology allows the hero to be afraid of death. – But the play continues.

The Director (*steps forward*)   Second scene. At the command of Lord Isa, the old statesman, the geisha Okichi has been brought to city hall, where he talks to her.

The servants move the folding screens to the side. The play continues.

Scene Two

[B1]

Same location, half an hour later. **Saito** *and* **Okichi** *are waiting.*

Saito The city council is very, very angry with you, Okichi. Someone has suggested to send your head in a basket to the consul. The rumour of your stubbornness and stupidity has even reached His Excellency, Lord Isa. He just went inside.

Okichi I am not a servant but a singer. I will send my girl.

Saito Don't be impertinent. They are asking for you.

Okichi I won't go to the foreigners. Why, I could not let myself be seen in any teahouse afterwards. (*She speaks up.*) You yourselves are impertinent to even demand something like this. Why, then, have the authorities announced everywhere that we are neither supposed to have anything to do with the foreigners nor to accept anything from them – we are not even allowed to let them into the teahouse. And now they order me to go there to wait on them. As a geisha I am just an object to you, a woman that you can boss around as you please, but I don't like the words 'just an object'. Aren't women human, too? How come that I have to go to these dirty white devils, who, as everyone knows, have such repulsive habits?

Saito You will go to them, because the city council tells you to.

Okichi You cannot tell me to do anything, it is against the law and inhuman. I know Hikita, the judge, and he will give you a piece of his mind. I know what I am going to do. I will ask Kazama to compose a ballad that deals with all of this, and I will sing it every night. I am warning you.

The sound of a door opening.

Saito Keep your mouth shut!

The council members come out. They seem very depressed. When they see **Okichi***, they take deep bows and walk away quickly.* **Inoue** *addresses her politely in passing.*

Inoue Miss Okichi? Would you be so kind and wait for one more moment? The Lord wishes to talk to you in person.

Exits with a bow.

Okichi (*laughing*) I don't think that they look very sinister. More crestfallen, don't they? Perhaps they've read up on the law in the meantime.

Saito (*irritated*) I don't understand anything anymore. I hope you didn't misunderstand me right now. What I said, I said in your own interest, Okichi.

Okichi That's Miss Okichi to you.

Two litter-bearers enter and lower their palanquin. **Lord Isa**, *a very old man, enters through the door to the big hall, supported by an equally old servant. He ascends the palanquin and turns to* **Saito**.

Isa Is that her?

Saito Yes, your Excellency.

Isa Does she look intelligent?

Saito Very much so, Excellency.

Isa Is she a singer, a geisha?

Saito Yes, Excellency.

Isa Successful in her profession?

Saito She enjoys a certain reputation throughout Shimoda, Your Excellency.

Isa What has she been told about the matter?

Saito That she should report to the American consul.

Isa What explanation was given her to justify this request?

Saito The explanation that it would be necessary for the land of her ancestors.

Isa Has someone told her what that is, the land of her ancestors?

Saito Your Excellency!

Isa She has refused?

Saito Yes, your Excellency, incomprehensibly so.

Isa No, comprehensibly. What is incomprehensible, though, is your treatment of people that you expect to serve you.

Okichi *laughs out loud.*

Saito Your Excellency, she has been told that the administration regards it as absolutely necessary for her to join the staff of the American consul.

Isa Has someone told her that battleships are on their way to bomb Shimoda if the consul is not placated?

Saito Not to my knowledge, Excellency. If I may say so, the administration did not consider that a useful approach.

Isa Fools.

Okichi But they can't just shell the city.

Isa *doesn't respond.*

Okichi But all the people! The houses! The children!

Isa *remains silent.*

Okichi Why?

Isa Tell her that they will bomb any place that they can't have business dealings with. Tell her that they regard our island as a house that they want to enter to do business. If we don't invite them in, they will step over us to break into the house. Because their law is: The borders that cannot be crossed by goods will be crossed by armies.

Okichi (*excited*) But what can I do? I am nobody.

Isa (*to* **Saito**) How does she look?

Saito (*confused*) I don't know what you mean, Excellency. I think she would be considered attractive.

Isa (*impatient*) You seem to be an idiot. (*To* **Okichi**.) Step into the light. (**Okichi** *steps forward.* **Isa** *studies her for a moment.*) You look like an honest person. I will tell you what you can do. You can be honest and kind to these people. That is more than the city council is capable of. This bunch can only lie, and not even that very well.

Okichi But I can't do that, your Excellency. I have heard that they carry black pipes around their legs and a white pipe around their neck, and, even worse, they have the rosy skin of pigs. When they make love, they bite into each other's lips, and during meals they attack large slabs of meat with knives.

Isa One has to get used to it. I, myself, am not used to talking to someone like you. But it is not impossible. (*Slowly.*) You must understand, I have to sign a contract with them. Japan needs that. But stupidity and backwardness work against this plan. With dull lies and tricks, they try to frighten the people before I have had enough time to talk to the Shogun. They almost seem to hope that the Americans will lose their nerve and bomb Shimoda. Demonstrate to them that it will be worthwhile to trade with us.

Okichi But how could I? I never went to school.

Isa (*leaning back, tired*) I don't know if you can do it. I also don't know what I can do. I have tried for sixty years to do even the smallest service to this country, with little chance of success, so what do I know. How should I know what you are capable of?

Okichi *remains silent.*

Saito Answer His Excellency!

Isa But not too fast, that would be of no use. I actually doubt that you will be able to achieve much where so much has already failed. Indeed, only very few people are so favoured by fortune that they can be of service to their country during their short lives, consider that.

Okichi (*quietly*) Your Excellency, it is also because of my fiancé Tsurumatsu. We want to get married.

Isa *makes a sign to the litter-bearers. They lift the palanquin up and carry him out.*

Saito You shouldn't have mentioned your private affairs to him.

Okichi He is so old. I think I will do it.

[B6]

Interlude Two

Clive A veritable call-up for war service!

Kito Modern democracies don't work that much better, you know.

Ray Here, you have always had wise old men. Where I am from, you wouldn't see anything like that, not even on the stage.

The Director (*stepping forward*) In Okichi's house.

[B1]

Scene Three

Okichi's *home. A rainy afternoon.* **Okichi** *walks around nervously, stroking the shamisen. Her sister* **Omoto** *is preparing tea.*

Omoto Why are you so nervous, Okichi?

Okichi (*sits down and starts to sing*) Where are you going, Otsuru?
To the war, to the war!
The armies are marching.
The Emperor demands it.
Who will till your field?
What do I know? What do I know?
The armies are marching.
The fields are parched.
Who did you bring along, folks?
Your husband, your husband!
The armies are marching.
Soldiers are killed.
Omoto, I have told them that I will go to the foreigners. But I don't know how to tell it to Tsuru San. He will be angry.

Omoto Why did you agree, then?

Okichi The deal has to be closed. If not, Shimoda will be bombed by seven battleships.

Omoto But what will Tsurumatsu say?

Okichi (*sings*)
What do I know, what do I know?
The armies are marching.
The Emperor demands it.
But Tsuru San will be mad.

The ship carpenter **Tsurumatsu** *enters.*

Okichi Oh, Tsuru San, aren't you back early today? Did you take a day off?

Tsurumatsu No, not that, but …

Okichi In such weather! Where are you going, Omoto? You can stay, if you want to.

Omoto I'll be back soon. I'll buy cake. (*Off.*)

Okichi It has been raining and raining. It doesn't seem to let up.

Tsurumatsu Have you practised a new song?

Okichi No. Yes. No, nothing especially new. Tsuru San, what would you say if I ... You seem rather different today, no? With your long kimono. Have you been somewhere?

Tsurumatsu Me? No. Is the tea ready?

Okichi Yes, here. It's quite refreshing in this weather.

Tsurumatsu Yes, quite refreshing. Warm. (*Pause.*) Your hair is different.

Okichi A little bit.

Tsurumatsu More elegant.

Okichi You think?

Tsurumatsu You haven't asked me yet if I like it.

Okichi I'm sorry. I only changed it because the hairdresser no longer wants to do it if it's always the same. (*She laughs.*) She said: a new hairstyle and I almost picture you as a new client. I feel sorry for the hairdressers, I don't know why.

Tsurumatsu Did you give her too much again?

Okichi I only let her do my hair in a new style today. Have you heard, battleships are said to be on their way here. Shimoda is to be bombed. Won't that be terrible? The wharves are right on the front line. You shouldn't go to work tomorrow.

Tsurumatsu Yes, they talk of nothing else in the city. But why should they bomb? Anyhow, who knows what that's about.

Okichi No. (*Pause.*) So were you in the city?

Tsurumatsu (*slowly*) I was at a strange place today.

Okichi Where?

Tsurumatsu I was brought before the city council.

Okichi Before the city council? You? W-w-why?

Tsurumatsu I really didn't know what I was supposed to do. I have never been in so much trouble before as today.

Okichi Have they got something against you?

Tsurumatsu Nonsense. What should they hold against me? They talked about stupid things, I couldn't stand it. Half an hour of just standing there and grinning (*he imitates the grinning for her*) is appalling enough.

Okichi What in the world was it all about?

Tsurumatsu They questioned me for what seemed like an eternity about my relationship to you. I was in a cold sweat.

Okichi I would like to know where they get that kind of information.

Tsurumatsu Listen to me. There is a civil servant, his name is Saito, a detective, he knows everything, he finds out about all these kinds of things before you can say 'moo'.

Okichi If he wants to. That doesn't concern us.

Tsurumatsu (*unconvincing*) You are right.

Okichi (*suspicious*) Why don't you ask about my dealings with the city council?

Tsurumatsu Why? Is there anything new? (*Slowly*.) They were very friendly. They said that it would be for the country, that is why they want you there. Of course, when they talk, everything sounds reasonable, but what about us, I ask. Am I right?

Okichi What did you reply to them?

Tsurumatsu They say, Ofuku agreed immediately.

Okichi She is a coward, that's why. She probably caved in after seeing the money.

Tsurumatsu A lot of money, eh? And they wanted to give you even more. One hundred and twenty Ryos per year. Why, that is more than a civil servant makes under the Shogun. The dancing girls of the Shogun don't make that much.

Okichi What the devil are you talking about?

Tsurumatsu They throw their money around like dirt. You just stand there and say no, and they just add another ten until you break into a sweat.

Okichi They added another ten for what?

Tsurumatsu (*confused*) To tell the truth, damn it, I made a promise to them.

Okichi W-w-what?

Tsurumatsu   The entire city council supports it. How could I put up a fight, then? So I just promised it. Why are you giving me that strange look?

Okichi   I said no.

Tsurumatsu   Yes, you did indeed. No reason to rub it in. I am a sleazebag, is that what you mean? You stand in front of them and insist that you won't go because of me, and I cave in because they have promised me a job as a foreman at the Shogun's wharf, including the permission to carry a sword. And, of course, because it is for the country, in the public interest. You can't deny that. Or should I go hungry for the rest of my life? To be a ship carpenter means nothing. There are as many of them as yellow dogs. Why shouldn't I save something for a rainy day? To have your own shop in these times is not to be scoffed at. Okichi, do it, do it for me, go at least for a week, you'll be able to take it. Why don't you say anything?

Okichi   What am I supposed to say?

Tsurumatsu   Don't take that tone of voice with me, Okichi. If you don't want to go, you don't have to. We are not married, I cannot force you. I will go and tell them: she doesn't want to, and they can't do anything about it. Whatever the national emergency, she won't do it.

Okichi   Once I have returned from that house of pestilence, what will the people say when they see us in the street? Have you thought about that?

Tsurumatsu   We would have the money and could go somewhere else, Okichi, if that's the problem. They would also give me a different position, I assure you of that.

Okichi   I understand. (*She stands up.*) Tsuru San, I was at city hall at noon today, and there I made the decision to go to the foreigners. But not because of you. Not so that you can get a family name and be allowed to carry a sword. The food won't taste better because you have a family name. Okichi is an acceptable name and Tsurumatsu not a bad one. And what, for all in the world, is a sword worth? What do you want to do with it? Whenever they called for me, men of the highest rank told me all kinds of things, but I never cared for their swords. I fell in love with a chisel. Your chisel was enough for me, Tsuru San. If I go to the foreigners, I go so that Shimoda, my hometown, won't get bombed, and so that the old man gets his contract. I don't know what he needs it for, but he knows.

Tsurumatsu (*grouchy*)   Why didn't you tell me right away that you have already decided to go?

Okichi Because I was afraid that it might hurt you.

Tsurumatsu In that case I wouldn't have had to mention the promise I made to them. It doesn't change anything, you know. If you go anyway, what difference does it make?

Okichi *remains silent.*

Tsurumatsu I know what you think. Are you very angry?

Okichi No, not any longer.

Tsurumatsu (*gets up, tense*) I should leave now.

Okichi Yes.

Tsurumatsu When will you go there?

Okichi Tomorrow.

Tsurumatsu In that case I will come again tonight.

Okichi Yes.

Tsurumatsu We still have this evening. And the night, yes? I will come early. Will you be at home for sure?

Okichi Certainly.

Tsurumatsu Then I will come.

He leaves. She looks after him, silently. **Omoto** *enters.*

Omoto Has he left already? Was he very angry?

Okichi No.

Omoto Why are you sad, then? You were sad earlier because you thought that he would be angry, and now you are sad because he wasn't angry.

Okichi Yes. (*Pause.*) Why have you come in?

Omoto The litter is waiting outside.

Okichi Already? Fetch me the mirror, quickly!

Omoto *hurries to get the mirror for her.*

Okichi When Tsuru San comes back this evening, tell him that I went to the house of the foreigners. I didn't want to let him know that it is already this evening.

Interlude Three

Drinks and tobacco are served.

Clive   In any case, she's not losing much with this guy.

Ray   She just loses everything she had. Since she doesn't have much, she loses everything, but not much.

Clive   He seems a little corrupt, that's all.

Kito   Yes, that's what they say. He has been bribed, therefore he was corrupt. Since he was corrupt, not much is lost when he is bribed. You could say as well: X is vulnerable. Since he is vulnerable, not much is lost when he is wounded. After which one can proceed to the order of business.

Ray   Someone bought her lover, that sounds quite simple, as if he was standing in a store with a price tag around his neck. As if such a purchase were not a hunt where a wounded animal gets shot!

Clive   This, perhaps, is yet another one of your sentimental notions, Ray. Mister Yamamoto wishes merely to demonstrate that the patriotic act of his heroine is not motivated by financial expectations. And that is a good thing. Since where in the world do patriotic actions originate in financial considerations? People who are patriotic for financial reasons mostly choose others to perform their patriotic acts, and these chosen ones don't get anything for their actions – generally speaking.

Akimura   No, they don't get anything for their actions, except perhaps some collective glory. But people don't just do whatever they do because they expect something in return. Lifeguards don't jump into the river to get medals; mothers don't tend the beds of their sick children to get paid. Patriotism that's worth talking about is not driven by self-interest, of course.

Kito   Certainly not. Since otherwise, as you say, it wouldn't be worth talking about. Patriotism is not profitable – for patriots. It is profitable for other people. I could imagine countries where patriotism would also be profitable for patriots. It might even be pleasant to imagine such countries.

Akimura   Could I point out to you that I consider Mister Kito's ideas highly amusing but not representative of Japanese opinion?

Ray If an American had articulated them, no one in the United States would have considered them typically American either, I am afraid. But we're holding up the actors.

The Director (*has stepped forward*) We meet Okichi again, who is now in the service of the American consul. The consulate has been temporarily established in an old temple in the town of Kakizaki, which is close to Shimoda.

[B1]

Scene Four

Bedroom of **Mr Harris** *and antechamber in the village temple of Kakizaki, the provisional American consulate. Before dawn.* **Okichi** *watches over the sick consul.*

Harris No, I can't sleep. O-kichi San!

Okichi (*wipes the sweat off his forehead*) Wo-tah?

Harris No. Not water. It's not water I want. I am very sick. Very, very sick.

Okichi Not water? Not Wo-tah?

Harris No. If you must know, it's ships. It's ships I want. But they don't come. Never. Okichi, I am dying! Heusken! Where is Heusken? What has happened to Heusken?

Okichi Do you want Mister Heusken? Is that it? Shall I fetch him?

Harris No. Not Heusken. Let him sleep! What could he do? Stay! I want milk. That's what I want. Milk.

Okichi Mill?

Harris Milk! Yes.

Okichi (*considers*) Mill. (*She gets up and enters the antechamber in front of* **Heusken**'s *bedroom door. She softly shouts inside.*) Hiu-suké San! (*No answer.*) Ofuku San! One moment, Ofuku San!

Ofuku (*comes out, half asleep*) What's up?

Okichi He is very sick. He wants 'mill.' Ask Mister Heusken what 'mill' is, will you?

Ofuku He is asleep.

Okichi Tell him that the consul wants 'mill'. Quickly!

Ofuku (*goes inside and comes quickly out again*) It is cow's milk. Hiu-suké San thinks that he has a sick stomach from smoking too much.

Okichi But he cannot possibly drink that kind of stuff. Cows' milk! It is forbidden.

Ofuku Sure, it is cows' milk. Hiu-suké San said already yesterday that he wants cows' milk. They drink it in their country. Everyday.

Okichi Why didn't you tell me?

Ofuku What for? If it's forbidden.

Okichi But he needs it. I will get some.

Ofuku Are you mad, Okichi? To get cows' milk! You will be punished and you won't find any anyway.

Okichi I will find some. I know where.

Harris (*shouts*) Okichi-San! Where are you? Are you gone?

Okichi I am coming, Danna Sama. (*To* **Ofuku**.) Get me some of Hiu-suké San's sake! I need a sip before I take off. Hurry.

Ofuku (*gets the whisky*) You shouldn't drink this, Okichi. You will lose your voice. Really. It is poison for your voice.

Okichi (*drinks*) I no longer need my voice. Not here.

Ofuku (*walking back drowsily*) There is nothing you can do. Even Hiu-suké San is saying that.

Harris O-kichi San!

Okichi (*with him*) You mustn't be impatient, Danna Sama! This 'mill', cows' milk, I will get some, day is already breaking. I will get it somewhere. Try to sleep for a minute. (*She indicates to him through gestures that he should try to fall asleep.*)

Harris I cannot sleep. What's the matter with milk?

Okichi Mill! (*She nods her head, indicates to him that she will try to get some.*)

Harris But you can't. It's against the law. You can't get milk in this goddam country. But, of course, you could try. Why not? Yes, try to get milk.

Okichi Mill!

She knocks something down and walks quickly off. Pause. **Harris** *tosses and turns around restlessly. It is getting brighter. Then voices can be heard and* **Omoto**, **Okichi***'s sister, and the Chinese servant* **Ah Lo** *enter the antechamber.*

Ah Lo   I tell you, she has left. And you can't talk to Ofuku. She is with mister Hiu-suké San.

Omoto   In here? (*Pushes him back.*) Ofuku San! Ofuku San! (*To* **Ah Lo**.) It is really urgent! Something terrible has happened. Ofuku San!

Ofuku (*from inside*)   What is it this time? Uh, it's you, Omoto! What are you doing here?

Omoto   Where is Okichi? Oh, Ofuku San, how terrible! The battleships are sailing into the bay!

Ofuku   The battleships!

Omoto   Everyone in the city is awake. Word is they will bomb us. People are already packing their belongings onto carts. Okichi has to talk to the consul at once. At once!

The sound of a cannon shot in the distance.

Ofuku   Cannons!

Omoto   They have already started!

Harris *rises quickly and rings.* **Heusken** *comes out of his room, drowsily.*

Heusken   What's the matter? Wasn't that …

Ofuku   O Hiu-suké San! (*She clings to him.*) The battleships!

Harris   Heusken!

Heusken   Yes, Excellency!

Harris   Mister Heusken, I think, a ship has come into port. Get your telescope!

Heusken *runs into his bedroom and returns with a telescope, which he sets up in front of a window to search the ocean.*

Heusken   It's a warship, Excellency. She is flying a flag, but I can't see it clearly. Oh, it's all right. I can see her flag now; our thrice-blessed Stars and Stripes floats from the stern. (*He runs into* **Harris***'s room.*)

Harris   At last! The Stars and Stripes! Commodore Armstrong! Get our bags packed! But I can't travel. I am too sick.

Heusken (*returns to the antechamber and claps his hands*)   Go on! Start packing! The consul will travel! Ah Lo, wake the staff!

Ah Lo *runs off perplexed, with* **Omoto** *in tow, but almost instantly returns alone.*

Ah Lo   Mister Hiu-suké San, a high-ranking member of the city council would like to visit the consul. Inoue Shinano-no-Kami. It's very urgent.

Inoue *enters. Mutual bows.*

Heusken   I will let the consul know. (*Goes in to* **Harris**.) Excellency, Inoue wants to see you.

Harris   I won't see him. None of them. That's over now. And I am glad. But I cannot rise. I am really too sick. It's the stomach. It is like hell. I am poisoned. That's what I am. Poisoned. They have poisoned me, I know it. That's the reason, why they are coming. They want to know. Devils. Oh my stomach!

Heusken   It can't be that, Excellency. Please be patient some minutes only. They must have a surgeon on board, to be sure. (*Leaves*.) Mister Inoue, the consul cannot receive you. (*To the servants, who are busy with packing.*) Go on!

Inoue   But it is of tremendous importance. You know, the meeting with the Shogun has already been arranged. Lord Isa is merely negotiating some final formalities. And after rushing here to tell you this, I see that you are making arrangements for your departure!

Heusken   Ah, the reason for your coming here, in the middle of the night, is news from the Shogun?

Inoue   Certainly. And isn't that good news?

Heusken   And it is not, perhaps, the ship that made you come, eh? You probably haven't even seen the ship yet, eh?

Inoue   The arrival of the American ship will accelerate everything, without a doubt. It increases the forcefulness of the lord's demands.

Heusken   Be assured, Mister Inoue, that your assertion of a forthcoming meeting with the Shogun will not keep His Excellency from taking off. Not any longer.

Inoue   There is something else, then, that prevents His Excellency's departure?

Heusken I will tell you what is holding up his departure, only to convince you that your ridiculous, improvised and, by the way, umpteenth pronouncement in this matter isn't the reason: his health doesn't allow him to go aboard today. But he will be able to do it tomorrow.

Inoue (*sighing with relief*) Ah! (*Quickly.*) Don't think that I am not aggrieved to hear about His Excellency's illness, Mister Heusken. I will run to get doctors. Anyhow, this one-day delay caused by a deplorable indisposition will give the lord some hope. (*He wants to leave.*)

Okichi (*returns, hiding something under her long sleeve*) Oh, Hiu-suké San, is it true that the black ships have returned? Why is everyone packing?

Heusken Come inside quickly to see Mister Harris, Okichi. He is very sick.

Okichi I have medicine for him.

Heusken *pushes her inside.*

Harris (*lies moaning*) Heusken! Where are you?

Okichi I am coming, Danna Sama! (*She retrieves a huge bottle from under her sleeve and, with her face turned away to evade smelling it, carries it to the consul's bed.*) Mill, your Excellency, medicine!

Harris Oh, milk! Really, it's milk! (*He grabs the sake bottle out of her hands and begins to drink from it.*)

Okichi (*restraining him*) Oh Lord, to gulp it down like that! One moment, I will at least pour it into a cup! (*Covering her nose with her sleeve, she pours the milk into a cup and passes it to* **Harris**.)

Harris Oh, it's good to see and taste milk again. Ah! (*He drinks like someone dying of thirst.*)

Okichi Oh Lord, how he drinks it! As if it were a beverage, this foul-smelling stuff from a cow's belly! (*She watches him with astonishment.*)

Harris (*embraces* **Okichi** *once he has drunken the milk*) Darling! You angel! There are no words to thank you with. Really, I feel good again. (*He stands up.*) I must tell Heusken. (*He goes to the antechamber, where* **Inoue** *is still standing.*) Heusken! I am nearly all right. The little drop of milk she brought me has given me back my life. And there is the ship, too. Ah, you, Inoue! Well, I am leaving, you are the winner. But your Okichi is a wonderful woman. Mister Heusken, the ladies are invited to breakfast today. (*He exits.*)

Heusken Hurray, Okichi San! The consul invites you to his farewell breakfast. He says that you have given him back his life, Okichi. You are the only human being in this country who doesn't lie. Ah Lo, breakfast!

Ah Lo *exits with a grin.*

Heusken (*to* **Inoue**) The General Consul will leave Japan today at noon. (*Exits.*)

Inoue (*stiffly, to* **Okichi**) Tell His Excellency that the city council of Shimoda has received the news of his recovery with joy. (*Exits.*)

Ofuku Oh, Okichi San, that is bad. Because of you the consul has recovered and can now go aboard. You got the milk for him – and it is prohibited to milk a cow.

Okichi Yes, this looks bad. Even so, let's change our dresses and I will have some more of Hiu-suké's drink and then, at lunch, I will ask the consul to stay. Come! (*She exits, pulling* **Ofuku** *after her.*)

The stage remains empty for a few moments, then servants carry pieces of luggage into the antechamber. Finally **Omoto** *re-enters, pursued by* **Ah Lo**.

Omoto But I have to talk to Okichi San.

Ah Lo What for? The bombing won't happen. Okichi San has joined His Excellency for breakfast. (*While pushing her outside.*) If you want to, you can tell it to everyone that it is only thanks to Okichi San if we are not going to bomb the city of Shimoda.

Harris *and* **Heusken** *return.* **Harris** *smokes a big cigar.*

Harris It is very unfortunate, and I am sorry I cannot entertain the ladies today with the Commander coming. Will you please tell them so? Put it as politely as you can.

Heusken Very good, Sir.

Okichi *and* **Ofuku** *enter, carefully dressed.*

Ofuku Is that good?

Heusken Girls, I don't enjoy having to tell you this, but the consul won't be able to have breakfast with you today. He has asked me to respectfully tell you this.

Ofuku Oh, is it because the Commander is coming?

Heusken Yes. You have to understand. Please be so nice tonight and go back home.

Ofuku That's a bit much, isn't it? After saying only a minute ago that his life had been saved!

Heusken Please, try to restrain yourself and don't forget who you are talking to. Go home, calmly and decently. We will send you a beautiful gift. The General Consul is known as an honourable man of high moral standards. When his fellow countrymen arrive, you cannot be here.

Ofuku That's unbelievable.

Okichi (*holding her back*) Keep quiet, Ofuku San. Mister Hiu-suké San, I have to tell the General Consul something. (*She steps forward and speaks with great dignity.*) Danna Sama, we are not guests here, we are just paid girls and we will leave without a word. But half an hour ago you said that you couldn't get up to travel because you were very sick. I left to get milk for you. After that you could get up and smoke a cigar. And the city council will say that I am to blame if you can board that ship. Therefore, I implore you not to leave so soon as today. Could you translate this, please?

Heusken But that is ridiculous!

Harris What is she saying? Offended?

Heusken No, she is not offended. She states only that you couldn't leave without the milk, and asks you not to leave before tomorrow.

Harris (*laughs awkwardly*) Well, that's not much. We are not in a hurry, if it comes to that. She is really a good sport. Tell her I'll stay until tomorrow. But I cannot have breakfast with her, that I can't.

Heusken Okichi San, the General Consul regrets that he can't invite you for breakfast, but he has decided to postpone his departure until tomorrow.

Harris All right?

Okichi *takes a deep bow.*

[B6]

Interlude Four

Ray Do you know that almost nothing infuriates me as much as the randomness with which the masters of the world come to their decisions? We are going to bomb, but no, we probably should have lunch first!

Kito Nations have a hard time when their fortune continually depends on such things.

Akimura It doesn't depend on them, of course. They're just like the small discontinuities of major curves, which only come to light under the microscope. Of course, the rise of Japan did not depend on Okichi fetching a foreigner a jug of milk, on a day in May 1856. Although it is small acts like this one that make up the larger ones.

Ray There is something about this that I find particularly beautiful. Okichi carries out two revolutions. The first one: that she goes to the white people, disgusting creatures, with whom to consort is degrading and can only be endured under the influence of hard liquor. The second: that she fetches cow's milk. And the second revolution she makes out of simple kindness, out of mere compassion, and possibly because she goes the whole nine yards each time she sets out to do anything.

Kito Oh, you can't hold anything against Okichi, absolutely nothing.

The Director (*steps forward*) Lord Isa starts on a journey to the Shogun with the American General Consul. Okichi returns to Shimoda by ferry.

[Neureuter]

Scene Five

Landing stage of the Shimoda ferry at the Kakizaki-side of the Inozawa river. In the distance, beyond the river, the city of Shimoda can be seen. To the left a country road, to the right a teahouse. People have gathered at the landing stage and are looking towards the street on the left.

First Man There, she is coming, she is coming.

Second Man Really?

Third Man Yes, that's her, this time I am sure.

Fourth Man (*shouts towards the back of the teahouse*) Hey, hurry up, the Yankee Okichi is coming!

Voices from the back: They say, the Yank Okichi is coming. The foreigners' whore, etc. *More and more people come along.* **Okichi** *is carried in a beautiful, large palanquin that belongs to* **Harris**. *Through an open sliding door,* **Okichi** *can be seen reading.* **Ofuku**'*s palanquin follows behind. A samurai guard accompanies the palanquins. They stop at the landing stage.*

Guard (*to the ferryman*) Will the ferry take off soon?

Ferryman Yes. (*Pointing towards the river.*) It is just coming in, but we will send it back right away.

The crowd pushes towards **Okichi**'*s palanquin to get a better view of her.*

First Man Don't push, Mister!

Second Man Step off my feet!

Third Man I want to see her, too, after all.

Guard Out of the way! Move back, I say!

Okichi *and* **Ofuku** *slide their doors shut. Two samurai emerge from the crowd, savagely fling open the doors of both palanquins, and spit at the faces of* **Okichi** *and* **Ofuku**.

Guard Hey, what are you doing?

Samurai Nothing. We have only offered our modest congratulations to the ladies.

They leave, laughing. **Ofuku** *takes a paper tissue out of her kimono, wipes her face and starts to cry.* **Okichi** *wipes her face with the sleeve of her precious silk robe and steps quickly out of the palanquin. She takes off her robe, uses it again to wipe her face, then throws it into the street and walks over to the teahouse. The crowd shouts after her*: Okit San, your robe, take your robe!

Okichi I no longer need this rag.

A Man Really, you no longer want it?

Okichi Anyone who wants it can take it.

The crowd starts to fight for the robe.

Ferryman (*goes into the teahouse, to* **Okichi**) The ferry has come in. I am sorry that you had to wait.

Guard Miss Okichi, the ferry has arrived, what are you doing?

Okichi I have to clean myself up a bit. Inwardly. (*To the old teahouse owner.*) A bottle of sake!

Guard Wouldn't it be better to go home than to drink sake at such a place? So many people are passing by here, and an unpleasant incident like the one a moment ago could easily happen again.

Okichi It wasn't the first time. It would be best for you to go back. I don't want you to accompany us home.

Guard But I am under orders –

Okichi Don't worry about leaving us here. I don't appreciate being carried home in fancy litters that cause a stir everywhere. Just do as I say. Ofuku San, come inside.

Ofuku *steps out of the palanquin and goes into the teahouse.*

Guard Well, as you wish. (*Winks at the carriers and leaves with them.*)

The Old Man *brings sake.*

Ofuku Oh, it is disgusting. I am so sick of it, so sick!

Okichi Talking like this won't help. Not any longer. Here, drink this. (*Offers* **Ofuku** *a bowl, then pours sake for herself and gulps it down. Then she turns to the still-gawking crowd.*) Why do you stand there and stare? If you want to see us, why not come closer, don't be ashamed. (*Prepares for opening her kimono.*) I can show you a great deal, and quite closely. – They have left. Don't be afraid, Ofuku, they are gone, everything is fine.

Ofuku I didn't just mean them.

Okichi Of course not.

Ofuku The Americans are even worse, if you consider how they behaved today.

Okichi All men are mean, Japanese men as well as foreigners. (*To the* **Old Man**.) Old man, another bottle, please.

The Old Man (*brings the bottle*) Here, it's well warmed, but not too hot.

Okichi Heat up another one right away.

Ofuku Aren't you drinking too much, Okichi?

Okichi I can't bear it, without drinking.

Ofuku Lucky you.

Okichi Then drink with me, Ofuku.

Ofuku I can't. (*Chuckles.*) You really are a sake bowl.

Okichi What do you mean?

Ofuku Because you always have to be full.

Okichi A sake bowl, that's right. I am a sake bowl. Make sure that the bowl is never empty! (*Empties the bowl and offers it to* **Ofuku**.) Here, take it.

Ofuku But I don't want to drink.

Okichi Catch it. (*She throws the bowl to* **Ofuku**, *who catches it*.) We are both sake bowls. One man tosses us to the next one, and everyone presses us against their lips, whether we find that repulsive or not.

Ofuku Oh, Okit San.

Okichi These creatures who call themselves 'men' pass each other the bowls – 'I want one', 'There you have one' – and some even flatter themselves for having a whole range of bowls on their tray. Men are disgusting.

Ferryman (*shouts*)   The ferry is taking off!

Okichi Yes, sake bowls or ferries. They are both moved back and forth by men. You know, Ofuku San, you'll find women like us anywhere. Even the girls that marry into wealthy families or become the wives of samurai – look at their lives, they are like us, nothing more than sake bowls. One raises them to one's lips as long as they give sake.

Cannon shots can be heard in the distance. People are running away.

The Crowd The ships are shooting! Cannons! Let's get away from here!

First Man The foreign devils are bombing the town.

Okichi (*coming to the door of the teahouse*)   Don't worry, they are just shots of salutation.

Ofuku Okichi, let's make off.

The shouts of litter-bearers can be heard on the street: Make room for Lord Isa! Clear the path for His Excellency, the General Consul! *Council member* **Inoue** *and another* **Man** *enter and converse with each other while staying near the door.*

A Man (*explaining*)   The Lord and the General Consul are on their way to the Shogun. The big contract will finally be drawn up. Here, the city council is arriving as well.

The officials of the city council approach.

Nakamura This is an event of historic significance for our entire nation.

Inoue Finally the consul and the Lord have come to an agreement about this journey. I most certainly prefer salvos of salutation by the American ships to their bombardment of us! Listen!

From the left the palanquins first of the consul, then of **Lord Isa** *pass by.* **Okichi** *bows deeply without, however, being noticed by any of the two notables. She retreats into the teahouse.* **Saito** *appears behind the carriers running quickly; he stops at the ferryman.*

Saito Has Okichi's litter already crossed the river?

Ferryman The one of Okit San?

Saito Yes. When did she cross?

Ferryman Okit San is over there, in the teahouse.

Saito (*enters the teahouse, addresses* **Okichi** *brusquely*)   There you are at last, Okichi.

Okichi Isn't this gentleman Mister Saito? And so out of breath, what's the matter? How are you feeling today?

Saito Don't be so duplicitous, this is about you. You have committed a serious offence, Okichi. You have broken the laws, and you have to justify yourself before the authorities.

Okichi You don't say! Do I hear you right?

Saito Why did you do it?

Okichi I don't know what you are talking about, Mister Saito. Please don't be so indignant and nervous.

Saito Don't pretend that you are innocent! You know very well what you have done.

Okichi Ah, you are talking about the milk? I gave milk to the consul because he was sick and because he ceaselessly asked for it.

Saito Idiotic fool that you are! You know very well that no one in this country would milk a four-legged animal, and just when we were finally able to convince the foreigners that we could not fulfil their wishes in this regard you have to bring up this sore point again with your unwelcome deed.

Okichi (*calmly drinking her sake*)   Oh yes?

Saito Just now, as we were starting our shift, the person in charge of foreign affairs called us in unexpectedly. He held the stinking milk bottle under my nose and asked me for an explanation.

Okichi Are you implying that it was wrong of me to get milk for the consul?

Saito I am not talking about wrong, it was a crime, even worse, a scandal. We completely lost face. It was absolutely unnecessary.

Okichi But Mister Saito, now you are contradicting yourself. When I went to the consul I was ordered to serve him in any way possible. I did my best and endured everything and fulfilled all of his wishes under the assumption that that was part of my service. And when I fetched the milk for the consul, I believed that you would be grateful for it. I am really surprised at your accusations, Mister Saito.

Saito It is as I said: you are the most stupid bitch on earth.

Okichi Well, Mister Saito, if that is what you think, why did you send such a silly woman to the consul? I didn't want to go to him, isn't that so? Don't you remember how all of you more or less forced me to do it? I was harassed and pressured, and now you call me a fool, but I can't do anything about that. I tell you, I hate those Americans like the plague. But once I had gone over to them to serve them I had to serve them honestly, foreigners or not. I am a woman, and when he tells me that he is sick, I'll sit by him for the entire night, that is my nature. And if he wants to drink cow's milk, I won't rest until I have organized cow's milk from somewhere. If you sent such a stupid bitch like me, the mistake lies with you, and your yelling around is of no use whatsoever.

Saito You defy and deride the authorities?

Okichi No. But it was right to give milk to the consul. No one in this country will be harmed by the milking of a cow. But since you always make a fuss over such trifles and behave in such a petty fashion, you annoy the consul, and your negotiations lead to nothing.

Saito Don't be impertinent, Okichi. You don't know anything about it.

Okichi I won't interfere with your affairs. I am only trying to explain how I fulfilled my task. But even though I tried my best, I cannot go into the street without someone spitting at me or yelling 'Yankee Okichi' or something worse. Mister Saito, I ask you, to whom do I owe this? And you of all people come here and call me a fool. Obviously, only someone lucky enough to be born a man would dare such a thing.

Saito What is that supposed to mean?

Okichi I am not only referring to you, Mister Saito.

The **Ferryman** *enters.*

Ferryman (*to* **Saito**) Sir, the boat is leaving.

Saito I am coming. – Listen, Okichi, I won't let the matter rest. I won't let you get away with this crime. (*Exits.*)

Okichi Please do whatever you want.

Ofuku Okit San! You shouldn't talk to an official in this way.

Okichi Nonsense! (*She gets up and walks over to a birdcage at the window. Salvos of salutation in the distance.*) Listen, Ofuku, how they fire a salute for me. What a pretty bird, old man – a yellow bunting?

The Old Man Yes.

Okichi How long have you kept it in a cage?

The Old Man I would say, two years. It is very tame. It even sings when people are nearby.

Okichi It's doing it right now. A beautiful song. (*She contemplates the bird for a while, then suddenly opens the cage, and the bird flies away.*)

The Old Man (*startled*) What are you doing there, girl? I don't care how much you've had to drink!

Okichi Sell me the old bird, father.

The Old Man What is left to buy, daughter, the bird is gone, up in the clouds, no longer to be seen. (*He looks sadly up to the sky.*)

Okichi That doesn't matter, it's fine. Don't be angry, old man. Here is all I have, it belongs to you. (*She pulls her purse out of her kimono and throws it down before the old man. Both girls stand and gaze after the bird. In the distance cannon shots can still be heard.*)

[B6]

Interlude Five

Akimura (*rising*) The end.

Ray Oh.

Akimura Aren't you satisfied?

Ray Doesn't it continue?

The small group has stood up and applauds. The actors step forward and take a bow.

Akimura (*while he is clapping*) But you have seen everything. Judith has gone to the camp of the enemy, and she brings back his head to Lord Isa. What more should there be to see?

Ray But I have always wanted to know what happened to Judith later on, after her heroic deed! What became of her? Did she have Holofernes' child? How do the neighbours receive her? Are monuments built to honour her while she is still alive?

Akimura Some of this has already been indicated, I believe.

Ray Truly, Mister Akimura, what became of Okichi?

Akimura Is that really of interest to you? She just disappears in the crowd from which she has risen. Her great days are over. She has had the great privilege of doing her duty; she has done that and returns to her earlier life. What else?

Ray But I seriously would like to know more about her. Didn't you say, the play was biographical? In that case it can't be over yet.

Akimura (*hesitant*) The play isn't over yet. (*He raises his hand to stop the applause and turns to the actors.*) Could you please hold off on removing your makeup for a few minutes? It seems that a small change in our program is desired. (*The actors take their bows and retreat behind the stage.*) Indeed, there are additional scenes that deal with the later fate of Okichi. I have to admit that I didn't expect you to be interested in that. I also don't know if the performers are well enough prepared to play those scenes. I only wanted to show you an action that sprang from the heart of the Japanese people and helped to turn their country into what it is today.

Clive Indeed, it would be extremely interesting to hear just once what the Bible conceals: the further life of Judith!

Ray Please, please! The private life of the Unknown Soldier! What about Okichi's wedding, for example? Yamamoto's play certainly deals with that! Just show us one more scene! This additional one!

Akimura (*smiling*) If that is what you wish, I will consult with the actors if they can add one or two more scenes. In the meantime, would you like a snack in the hall?

Long pause.

The group returns and takes their former seats.

Ray   Most of all, what happens to their love, Mister Akimura? Has she really lost her Tsurumatsu?

Akimura (*smiling*)   You will see. I hope that you won't be disappointed. The lives of most people are not that dramatic. Life doesn't know about Yes – No, White – Black, All or Nothing.

Ray   So, they meet again?

The Director (*steps forward*)   It was early in the evening when Okichi and Tsurumatsu met again at the pier of Yokohama. Ballads tell how Okichi, as a street singer with her shamisen and her braided hat, strolls along the walls of a shipyard. The moon is shining and the faint roar of a ship's siren comes from the ocean. She notices that someone, a worker, is trailing her. It is Tsurumatsu. Oh, is it you, Tsuru San? – Yes, and I am ashamed, I am ashamed. – How did you recognize me in these clothes? – Oh, by your gait and your voice. By your gait and your voice. – So, you haven't forgotten me after all? – No, I didn't forget. They walk away together. We will play the scene where they enter Tsurumatsu's house in the Shimoda quarter of Motomachi, Yokohama.

The screens are moved to the side.

[Neureuter]

Scene Six

Tsurumatsu's *house in Yokohama, rather squalid.* **Tsurumatsu** *enters hesitantly, pulled in by* **Okichi**.

Okichi   Is this your house?

Tsurumatsu   I didn't really want you to see this poverty.

Okichi   Nonsense. Look at my hair. *She takes off her hat and nestles her plainly dressed hair against his cheek.*

Tsurumatsu   Your hair is beautiful.

Okichi   You don't understand anything. Look, how plainly it is dressed. I am poor, too. I fit well into such a house.

Tsurumatsu   You're just trying to console me.

Okichi   Why didn't you call for me?

Tsurumatsu I am ashamed, I can't explain it. I couldn't write you because – everything turned out differently from what they had told me. I came to the workshop of Itani Sama in Edo and thought, now I will advance to foreman. But after the Shogun fell from power, everything turned upside down; our workshop was shut down and the gentlemen from Shimoda, Wakana and Lord Isa – everyone – had suddenly disappeared, leaving me behind. No one ever gave me a family name or a sword. On the contrary, I soon sank to the level of the lowest day labourer, with nothing else to wear than this worn smock. That's why I'm ashamed and why I can't look you in the face.

Okichi You mustn't be ashamed in front of your wife. I didn't have it easy myself. The people yelled 'Yankee Okichi' after me and called me a 'foreigners' slut'. When I returned from the consul and didn't hear from you, I thought that you despised me like all the others. I then gave up on myself and began to drink. It was a terrible life. To let other people know how little I valued them, I blew my nose into their banknotes. Bit by bit, I lost all the money that I had from the Americans and from our government. At the end I could no longer stay in Shimoda. So I went to Kyoto, but my story always travelled with me, and the government hasn't done anything for me. How often have I thought about ending my life!

Tsurumatsu Forgive me. It's my fault.

Okichi When I left the house of the consul I hated all men, and not only those hairy Americans but also Saito and Lord Isa and even you, Tsuru San.

Tsurumatsu I understand.

Okichi But finally it became clear to me that I could not forget you. It is cruel for a woman to be alone. I was unhappy while roaming through strange cities, and I always kept my eye out for you. Whenever I saw a man in a smock, I followed him. I didn't know that you were here in Yokohama, but I thought, a new harbour town with shipyards, you might have found work here. I had some kind of inkling, an inner voice.

Tsurumatsu So, you don't hate me anymore?

Okichi What are you saying? I have always only belonged to you. But you yourself – do you have – anybody – ?

Tsurumatsu What do you mean?

Okichi Is that so difficult to understand – are you with another woman?

Tsurumatsu (*laughs*) And you believe that?

Okichi Seriously: If you have another one, I won't stay with you.

Tsurumatsu I don't have anyone.

Okichi Is that really true? (*Suddenly pulls open a wardrobe door.*)

Tsurumatsu What's that supposed to mean? Do you think I hide my wife in the closet?

Okichi I think, some rags from another woman could hang in there.

Tsurumatsu Nonsense. And please don't look too closely.

Okichi (*pulls out dirty laundry*) What's that?

Tsurumatsu Don't look at it. Put it back!

Okichi Dirty laundry! I will wash it for you.

Tsurumatsu You can wash laundry?

Okichi Of course. How is it that men are such helpless creatures? Where is your wash tub?

Tsurumatsu What would I do with that – you have changed, Okichi.

Okichi It is much more miraculous that you haven't changed at all and are still living alone.

Tsurumatsu Of course. Because of you.

Okichi I am glad, my dear. It is good after all that I didn't kill myself.

Tsurumatsu I wouldn't have endured that. I was a fool.

Okichi Let's no longer speak of the past. Let's start from scratch. What's money, after all? Something you get for working. Let us work together. I will help you with all my strength.

Tsurumatsu Of course, I want to work, but in the long run it doesn't lead to anything – this job at the shipyard.

Okichi Don't lose heart. I will make enough additional money for us to get by. But I will no longer work as a geisha nor perform as a singer. Once we have our own home I will no longer carry this around with me. (*She nudges her shamisen.*) I made a living as a performer until today because I couldn't see any other option. But now I will show you that I have changed from the bottom of my heart. I want to work honestly, even if I have to do people's hair – the main thing is to do something respectable. And I will stop drinking sake.

Tsurumatsu Will you be able to do that?

Okichi Yes. I will do it for you. I only drank because I was without hope.

Tsurumatsu You – love ...

Okichi No need to cry. Did you have dinner already?

Tsurumatsu Yes, I've had some – and you?

Okichi To be honest, I haven't eaten anything all day.

Tsurumatsu That is bad.

Okichi I see a stove over there. Where is your rice chest?

Tsurumatsu I don't have one.

Okichi Where do you keep your rice, then?

Tsurumatsu In the fruit crate over there, but ...

Okichi (*looks into the crate*)   It's empty! Wait, I will go shopping for you.

Tsurumatsu I feel awkward asking this – but do you have any money?

Okichi What?

Tsurumatsu You haven't either. I feel ashamed, but please be patient a little longer. Tomorrow I will find money somehow.

Okichi Calm down! (*She lifts her shamisen.*) I will pawn this, which should get us enough rice.

Tsurumatsu But – don't you have to play it again tomorrow to make money?

Okichi But no, of course not! Didn't I just tell you that that is all over now? As long as I carry this thing around with me, I cannot lead a decent life.

Tsurumatsu (*grabs* **Okichi***'s hands*)   Okit San, you are ...

Okichi Don't squash my shamisen. Wait for me, I'll be back soon.

[B6]

Interlude Six

Clive So, love triumphs over everything! Isn't that somewhat banal?

Kito As you will see, love cannot prevail. But that, too, is somewhat banal. Don't forget that we are now following the curve on its downward trajectory. The hero has been dismissed. Judith takes up her household chores again.

The Director   Seven years later.

[Neureuter]

Scene Seven

Tsurumatsu's *house in Shimoda to the left. In the centre an alley that leads to a river in the back. To the right a shed that serves as* **Tsurumatsu**'s *carpentry shop.* **Tsurumatsu** *is smoothing boards in front of his shed. It is early in the evening.* **Oshimo** *arrives.*

Oshimo   You are working late.

Tsurumatsu   I have to finish this order.

Oshimo   Is Okichi at home then?

Tsurumatsu   Okichi? I am sorry. Today the Tobayas are having a major celebration. She has been there all day. They asked her to help doing their hair and also to serve food.

Oshimo   I see. I only came to ask her to get my hair back into shape.

Tsurumatsu   I am very sorry. Are you in a hurry?

Oshimo   Not at all. But anyone lucky enough to have had her hair styled once by Okichi cannot possibly go to someone else later. Also, she learned so many new techniques in the capital, she has become a true master. Her hairstyles are so flamboyant. How she has changed – as if she were a new person.

Tsurumatsu   Yes. Thanks to all those who supported her.

Oshimo   Who would have thought that Okichi would become such a skilful and hardworking person one day. I really shouldn't talk about this, not to you: but only seven years ago she was just awful.

Tsurumatsu   Yes, that's what they say.

Oshimo   It is truly marvellous how she has shed all of her flaws since marrying you.

Tsurumatsu   She had seen quite a bit of the world.

Oshimo   Anyhow, now that you are both working, you must manage quite well?

Tsurumatsu   Yes, thank you.

Oshimo   Then just continue with your work.

Exits.

Osai (*comes running*)   How terrible, how dreadful!

Tsurumatsu   What is the matter?

Osai   Your wife, Okichi!

Tsurumatsu   Has something happened to her?

Osai   Come quickly, quickly!

Okichi (*enters drunk and surrounded by a large crowd*)   Give me another glass.

First Man   No more.

Okichi   When you're celebrating a wedding it is only proper that I get something to drink, as much as I want. You cheapskates.

Tsurumatsu (*pushes forward to* **Okichi**)   Okichi!

Okichi   Who are you? You have to call me 'Mrs Okichi'!

Tsurumatsu   Please don't shout like that. You are ruining our reputation. – I sincerely regret the incident and apologize to all concerned parties for the disturbance.

First Woman   Listen, Tsurumatsu, Okit San asked us for wine and we gave her as much as she wanted.

Second Woman   She is pretty drunk. We only wanted to accompany her home.

Tsurumatsu   That is very kind of you. Again, my apologies. I will take care of her.

Okichi   Why kowtow to them? No need to apologize. First they let me sing until my throat began to hurt, then they kicked me out. That's how they treat me these days. I once used to be the well-known singer 'Shinnai Okichi', a star!

Second Man   Don't talk rubbish. You are the Yankee Okichi, that's who you are. (*Everyone is laughing.*)

Okichi   What did you say?

All   It's true, it's true, the Yank Okichi!

Okichi Which son of a bitch said that? Say it again! (*She attacks the crowd.*)

Tsurumatsu Okichi, what are you doing! Let's get away from here.

Okichi You are dogs, if you say such things!

Tsurumatsu It's all right, Okichi! Come! – She doesn't know what she is doing. I ask everyone to leave. She will apologize to you tomorrow. I am sorry that we have inconvenienced you.

The crowd leaves, and **Osai** *with them.*

Okichi (*sits down on the ground*) Get me some water!

Tsurumatsu Stand up and come with me. (*Pulls her forcefully towards the entrance of the house, where she tumbles down.*)

Okichi Give me water. Wo-tah. Wo-tah!

Tsurumatsu (*drags her*) Come inside!

Okichi Leave me alone.

Tsurumatsu What did you do?

Okichi I drank. Until I was full.

Tsurumatsu Didn't you swear to me that you would stop drinking?

Okichi I did. But they were all holding their sake bowls under my nose and offered them to me in celebration of the day. I told them that I had sworn to never have a drink again. I stood my ground because I thought of you.

Tsurumatsu But what made you drink after all?

Okichi Then they asked me to sing. I refused to do that, too. I told them that I hadn't held a shamisen in a long time. But they didn't let up because this was a wedding party after all. And because they had already heard me sing seven years ago, or so they claimed. I no longer resisted. I sang a song. Then they applauded and asked for more. And at that point I suddenly felt like singing, and I sang and I sang, and then they all thanked and applauded me and offered me their sake bowls again. I told them that I shouldn't drink, but they put a bowl into my hand, and then they all gathered around me, and I had to take a sip from everyone's bowl.

Tsurumatsu What a shame to find yourself in a situation like this. If you had only taken a 'sip' – but you have to get drunk and make a scene and pick a fight with people. I feel embarrassed to go out into the street tomorrow morning. You, too, should think of your work. Who would still ask you to do their hair?

Okichi What's that supposed to mean? You want to lord it over me now? I am not half-witted. Why do you boss me around then? I have never taken orders from men like you.

Tsurumatsu I don't give orders, I am just telling you the truth. Oshimo was here just now and praised you. We both have work, we are doing well. Have you already forgotten the hard times we had in Yokohama?

Okichi Shut your mouth! You beast! What are you talking about! (*She pushes* **Tsurumatsu** *aside.*) Leave me alone! (*She gets up with difficulty and steps outside.*)

Tsurumatsu Where are you going?

Okichi That's my business.

Tsurumatsu You can't even stand on your feet. Be careful …

Okichi Stay out of my affairs. Even if you are my husband, you're welcome, as often as you like, but today I can't take it. (*She falls down again.*)

Tsurumatsu Didn't I know it – please come inside, Okichi.

Okichi Don't patronize me, you – . What have you achieved in your life? Where are your great accomplishments, your family name, your sword? What were you thinking at the time when you 'sacrificed me to the land of our ancestors'? You were an imbecile and you believed everything the officials were telling you when they were only using you for their own purposes. You are a fool. – What happened to the good times? Helter-skelter, they vanished and left us high and dry. (**Tsurumatsu** *is speechless.*) – Give me 'Wo-tah'!

Tsurumatsu Stop this American gibberish!

Okichi Who sent me to the Americans, after all? Who of all people sent his own wife there!

Tsurumatsu Okichi, how can you say such things?

Okichi Why not? Just when I thought that I had finally forgotten everything, the old wound is ripped open again and I am again the 'Yankee Okichi.'

Tsurumatsu They only yelled that because you were drunk.

Okichi And whose fault is that?

Tsurumatsu How often have I told you that I feel sorry – for everything that has happened!

Okichi Is this supposed to be a plea for forgiveness? If you want to properly beg for my pardon, you have to touch the floor with your forehead and address your plea to the ground. Come on, apologize!

Tsurumatsu Don't to talk to me like that. I can't do it – here, in the middle of the street.

Okichi People spit at me in the middle of the street. It is nothing, by comparison, to ask your own wife for forgiveness. Come here and do it! Over here, won't you! (*She tries to push* **Tsurumatsu***'s head to the ground.*)

Tsurumatsu (*shaking her off*) What are you doing? That's enough. (*He grabs her from behind and drags her forcefully into the house.*) Go inside! You go inside now!

Okichi (*inside the house*) You cruel beast, you're hurting me!

Tsurumatsu Don't shout! It's disgraceful! Lie down here, like this, and don't move!

Okichi Get me some water.

Tsurumatsu I will get you some water, but you have to stay where you are! (**Tsurumatsu** *exits weeping and collects his tools.*)

Osai (*enters*) Excuse me.

Tsurumatsu Ah, it's you, Osai San. Thanks for your help earlier.

Osai I am only bringing you Okichi's hairdressing tools.

Tsurumatsu Thank you very much.

Osai They were scattered across the street.

Tsurumatsu Thanks for your kindness. Sadly, we've become a burden to everyone.

Osai No, not at all. – I cried, too. I feel so sorry for you. I know how you feel.

Tsurumatsu Did you hear what just happened?

Osai No. (*She turns her face away.*)

Interlude Seven [B6]

Kito (*quotes, while smoking*) 'Even blood spilled legitimately will leave stains.' 'Wounds make you worthy of veneration, scars make you ugly.' 'Those who escape the war will fall in peace time.' 'The swift heroic action will be repented for a long time.'

Clive   Yes, for the great hero it may be pleasant to have survived his heroic deed, but for the small hero it is terrifying. When the victors come home all hearts beat for them, but the day of triumph is usually the last one on which they're seen gladly. People everywhere try to forget the war, and the victors belong to the war. Not every Unknown Soldier manages to hole up under the triumphal arch. In only a few weeks the surviving victors turn into blind beggars, clumsy cripples, and monsters without noses. They are no longer regarded as heroes but as wretches, and wretches soon become annoying. You have to admit that we expect much of heroes. Not only do they have to excel in battle, they also have to be able to stand at street corners, crippled, in the rain, among people that impatiently push them aside. Truly, they have to be as insensitive as the marble statues that are erected for the few!

Akimura   That may well be. But why would it matter? I had no plans to show you Okichi's entire life story, but there is also no reason for me to withhold it from you. In my eyes it can only increase the veneration for this woman. But do you really want to see more?

Ray   Yes. All of it.

Akimura *claps his hands.*

[Neureuter]
Scene Eight

In **Okichi***'s and* **Tsurumatsu***'s house. At the centre is the entrance hall, to the right the living room, to the left the room that* **Okichi** *uses as her hair salon. To the far left the kitchen where* **Okichi** *is preparing food. Outside, in front of the window, a sake seller drives by and announces his goods ('White sake!').* **Okichi** *puts the food onto a tray and carries it over into the living room, where* **Tsurumatsu** *is lying in bed.*

Okichi   How are you feeling today?

Tsurumatsu   Quite well. I was just going to get up.

Okichi   Please don't. You could have a relapse.

Tsurumatsu *sits up.*

Okichi You want to sit up? Very well, but only to have some food. I'll get you some water. (*Fetches a bowl with water.* **Tsurumatsu** *washes his face.*)

Tsurumatsu That is refreshing.

Okichi But you have to eat a lot now, so that you can regain your strength.

Tsurumatsu I am feeling great already.

The door opens, a messenger **Boy** *enters.*

Boy Good morning. The Nishikawaya family sent me, they ask Mrs Okichi to come straight away.

Okichi Thanks, I'll be there.

Boy Please, don't let them wait!

Okichi All right. Thank you very much! (*The* **Boy** *exits.*)

Tsurumatsu Don't let me keep you, you should go.

Okichi But you are sick.

Tsurumatsu I will manage. You have already cooked the rice.

Okichi Well then. I will do the dishes when I come back. Should I get you some other medicine?

Tsurumatsu I don't need anything.

Okichi (*packs her hairdressing equipment*) But please stay in bed today and get some rest.

Okichi *exits.* **Tsurumatsu** *eats his food. A voice can be heard from outside*: Can I come in?

Tsurumatsu Who is it?

Voice I would like to get my hair done.

Tsurumatsu I am sorry, but Okichi just left a moment ago.

The door opens quickly, and **Osai** *enters.*

Tsurumatsu Ah, it's you. (*Uneasy:*) You shouldn't have come.

Osai But I was worried. I was thinking of you all the time, if you were doing well.

Tsurumatsu I had a cold, I couldn't come.

Osai   But why didn't you let me know at least, I have been waiting and waiting.

Tsurumatsu   I couldn't. Okichi would have noticed right away. And I am amazed that you have the nerve to show up here.

Osai   I would like to get my hair done. What is so unusual about that? This is a hair salon, after all!

Tsurumatsu (*puts his bowl down*)   Please, you need to be cautious!

Osai   You are a coward.

Tsurumatsu   You can't stay here.

Osai   You are rude to a guest.

Tsurumatsu   There is nothing else for you here. Be a good girl and go home.

Osai   Since I am already here, I will stay until I get my hair done. That will look far less suspicious than to come running all this way only to turn around immediately.

Tsurumatsu   I don't know what to do with you.

Osai   That's astonishing! I am sitting next to you, completely calm and relaxed.

Tsurumatsu   You can't do that!

Osai   I don't even dare to prepare tea for you or to lend a helping hand with something else.

Tsurumatsu   Don't sit so close to me.

Osai   I can't move further away from you, I am already close to the wall. Perhaps it's you who should prepare tea for me, I am your guest, after all.

Tsurumatsu   I can't.

Osai   You are terrible.

Tsurumatsu   How could I offer you tea and start some kind of conversation – that's crazy, that's what it is.

Osai   Try me!

Tsurumatsu (*gets up to go outside*)   Excuse me, I have work to do.

Osai   But you are sick!

Tsurumatsu I am up and about again. When she comes back and finds us sitting next to each other like this, hell will break loose. (*He slips off his kimono and changes into his working clothes.*)

Osai As you say. (*She picks up his kimono and folds it.*)

Tsurumatsu (*seeing this*) Don't.

Osai What's the matter?

Tsurumatsu Stop doing that.

Osai Now I am no longer even allowed to touch your kimono?

Tsurumatsu I didn't mean it that way, but if you fold it so neatly she might get suspicious. (**Osai** *laughs.* **Tsurumatsu** *joins in.*) Do you understand now?

Osai Yes, Sir, certainly, Sir. (*She throws the kimono to the ground.*)

Tsurumatsu *kicks the kimono and the bedlinen into the corner, casts a penetrating look at* **Osai**, *and then walks out to his work shed. Pause. After a moment,* **Tsurumatsu**'s *and* **Okichi**'s *voices can be heard from outside.*

Okichi Why are you working again! Haven't I told you time and again to take it easy!

Tsurumatsu I am fine. I am fed up with lying around all day, and there is still so much work to be done.

Okichi Forget about work. And if you start feeling worse again, then what?

Tsurumatsu As I said, I am fine. In there, Osai San has been waiting for you for some time.

Okichi Oh. (*Goes inside.*) Good morning, I am sorry that you had to wait so long.

Osai No problem.

Okichi This space hasn't been tidied up yet. Well, let's start anyway. (**Okichi** *gives* **Osai** *a cushion to sit on and starts doing her hair.*) It is very nice of you to have come from so far away. There must be quite a few hairdressers in your own neighbourhood.

Osai But not a single one who is good enough. I had been planning to come here for a long time, but it is quite far indeed.

Okichi Yes, it's not that easy to get across the river. How would you like your hair?

Osai In the Ginkgo style, as before.

Okichi Very well.

Osai I have heard that many women come to you, which is why I thought that a young thing like myself dropping in out of the blue would have to wait for a long time.

Okichi Please don't worry about that, Osai San. I'll gladly schedule your next appointment at a time more convenient to you, since you come from so far away. You can come at whatever time you want.

Osai That is very kind of you. Apart from you there is no one in the entire city who can do the hair in the Tokyo style.

Okichi I don't know if I am doing it properly. – Last fall I must have caused you great trouble. My husband told me about it, but I was too embarrassed to thank you in person.

Osai Let's not talk about it anymore.

Okichi Whenever I've had a drink of sake, I behave quite inappropriately. I hope you can forgive me. I am a bit embarrassed to talk about these things, but you were so kind to come to me to get your hair done.

Osai Please don't talk about it anymore. I would prefer you to tell me something interesting about Yokohama, since you have been there.

Okichi It wasn't that interesting (*partly to herself*) to me. I had a bad time there.

Osai But Yokohama is a nice city, isn't it?

Okichi To some people. I prefer my old hometown to any other place.

Osai I see! (*Pause.*) What nice beautiful dolls you have!

Okichi Oh no, very few really beautiful ones are left.

Pause. Even though the two of them are trying to be friendly to each other, their conversation is running dry.

Osai The weather is so beautiful today.

Okichi Yes, you're right.

Osai The Doll Festival season, that is always the most beautiful time of spring.

Okichi Most women would probably agree. (*Pause.* **Ofuku** *enters.*)

Ofuku Good morning.

Okichi Ah, Ofuku San! I am glad that you are here.

Ofuku Yes, I finally made it.

Okichi Belated congratulations!

Ofuku Quit joking around, I am not so sure that you have much reason to congratulate me.

Okichi What could be a better reason than that you got finally married.

Ofuku But since then there has been so much to do and so much running around that I no longer know if I am working for my marriage or for a company.

Okichi In that case I will do your hair in the high Shimoda style, so that you can feel like a genuine young bride.

Ofuku Please don't, I really don't want that.

Okichi Which style would you like?

Ofuku A quite ordinary, more roundish housewife style.

Okichi Ah, you insist on being in a bad mood. (*She finishes* **Osai***'s hair, telling her:*) That took quite a while. The first time you may not even like your hair.

Osai No, it turned out beautiful. Thank you. (*She pays and gets up.*)

Okichi (*lighting her pipe*) I thank you.

Osai (*to* **Ofuku**) I am sorry, but I am in a hurry now.

Ofuku Good luck! (**Osai** *exits.*) Well, you have rather unusual customers today.

Okichi Do you mean the one who just left?

Ofuku Yes.

Okichi It feels good, of course, if someone comes such a long way just to see you.

Ofuku Are you looking for new customers, then?

Okichi Not exactly. Should we start? (*Puts her pipe away.* **Ofuku** *positions herself in front of her.*) Wasn't that quite – daring, to marry a farmer?

Ofuku Not at all. – Anyway, I have a small favour to ask of you.

Okichi Which is?

Ofuku To be honest, that's the real reason for my coming here. Tomorrow we will have our housewarming and I'd like you to come to our party and sing.

Okichi It is very kind of you to invite me, but I can't.

Ofuku Why not?

Okichi I have decided once and for all to no longer go to such events.

Ofuku Only this one time!

Okichi I am sorry, but I won't go to any place where sake is served. I get so dizzy that I no longer know what I am doing nor what I am saying. And afterwards I am so embarrassed that I no longer have the courage to show my face.

Ofuku In that case, just don't drink as much.

Okichi That won't work. I have been trying since last fall, without success. When I go to such parties, I always drink too much. And afterwards I always have to apologize, even if only to my own husband. I have sworn to myself to never touch sake again.

Ofuku You don't even want to come to sing?

Okichi No.

Ofuku But many people will be there who would like to hear you.

Okichi Don't try to win me over with flattery.

Ofuku
'Oh, do you still remember the time,
Oh, do you still know how it sounded,
When down by the pond,
The lovely Okichi sang … '
There is already a popular song about your beautiful voice.

Okichi Ofuku, I am no longer a geisha –

Ofuku Too bad.

Okichi – but a hairdresser. Honest work is still better and more reliable than anything else.

Ofuku You may be right. It's nice to see that you are so enthusiastic about your new line of work. And that you even do her hair for the slut that's stealing your husband from you!

Okichi What do you mean?

Ofuku I just doubt that it pays off to work so conscientiously and – so gullibly.

Okichi Ofuku San, what are you talking about?

Ofuku Nothing really.

Okichi Don't beat around the bush, speak plainly.

Ofuku I don't know anything.

Okichi Tell me. Come on, tell me at once. Or else …

Ofuku Don't pull my hair.

Okichi I will pull, if you don't talk. Why these vague insinuations, if you are my friend!

Ofuku But you will be angry with me if I tell you.

Okichi No.

Ofuku I feel so sorry for you, I have asked myself many times if I should tell you, but that could also be completely wrong …

Okichi Start talking.

Ofuku But – (*The sound of* **Tsurumatsu** *smoothing wood can be heard from outside.*)

Okichi He can't hear us, go on.

Ofuku (*quietly*) Earlier, when you combed her hair, didn't you notice …

Okichi What?

Ofuku This woman, she was already married once, she is really dangerous. – You're hurting me, Okit San.

Okichi I am sorry. So I just did the hair of the woman who stole my husband? That is so funny, I could laugh my head off. I did her hair really well.

Ofuku She is shameless.

Okichi Thank you for letting me know. To tell you the truth, I have often wondered quietly if things were all right. But I wouldn't have suspected my husband, not him. But now I get it. (*Drops a comb.*)

Ofuku And now what?

Okichi First I need a smoke, just a few drags.

Ofuku But please finish my hair first!

Okichi Don't be so impatient.

Ofuku I was wrong to tell you after all. Of course, I can understand how you feel.

Okichi Stop talking for a moment! (*She lights her pipe. Pause.*)

Ofuku Now I am in deep water. I can't go anywhere with this half-done hairstyle. It wasn't my fault that this person and your husband – come on, Okichi, be reasonable.

Okichi (*lost in thought, suddenly throws her pipe away*) Turn your head towards me! (**Ofuku** *positions herself and* **Okichi** *resumes her work.*) It's not going that well today.

Ofuku Never mind, but I can't go into the street like this. (*Pause.*)

Okichi Tell me everything, if you are my friend.

Ofuku About this woman?

Okichi Yes. How long has this been going on?

Ofuku I don't know.

Okichi Did it start last fall?

Ofuku I think so. But I only heard about it recently. (*Pause.*) The woman is who she is; but Tsurumatsu also deserves some of the blame. (*Pause.*) You really can't rely on men. Heusken had many women too. (**Okichi** *remains silent.*) This woman is not an amateur. She has a child from a wandering musician who left her. (*Pause.*) Okit San, why don't you say anything?

Okichi (*finishes her work*) Done.

Ofuku Thank you. (**Okichi** *remains silent.*) And what do you say to my earlier request? Will you come to our housewarming party the day after tomorrow?

Okichi No. I no longer sing.

Ofuku It can't be helped then. (*Puts money on the table.*) Very well, goodbye Okichi. Please don't tell anyone what I have told you about Osai San.

Ofuku *exits. A temple clock strikes twelve.* **Tsurumatsu** *enters in a hurry.*

Tsurumatsu I am so hungry. Did you cook the rice? (**Okichi** *sits motionless.*) That was the noon bell, didn't you hear?

A **Fish Seller** *comes to the door.*

Fish Seller Would you like some salmon? It is particularly good today.

Tsurumatsu No, thanks. Some other time!

Fish Seller Well then, goodbye. (*Lifts up his fish basket again, prepares to leave.*)

Okichi Please wait. Give me half of this one here.

Fish Seller There you are.

Okichi Please cut off enough for one person.

Fetches a plate from the kitchen.

Fish Seller Here you go, it's fresh. (**Okichi** *pays, lets him keep the change.*) Thank you. Goodbye. (**Okichi** *prepares the raw fish with sauces and garnishes and puts the tray in front of* **Tsurumatsu**.)

Tsurumatsu This is a real feast. I usually don't eat that much, in the middle of the day.

Okichi Just eat.

Tsurumatsu When it comes to salmon, I don't hang around long.

Okichi I didn't have enough time this morning to take care of you, so I am doing it now. Pass me your bowl.

Tsurumatsu (*complies*) Indeed, a feast. What's the matter?

Okichi Nothing. Just eat.

Tsurumatsu Don't you want to eat with me? The fish is very good, really fresh.

Okichi I don't care for it.

Tsurumatsu But you had breakfast very early this morning!

Okichi I don't want to eat anything now.

Tsurumatsu   Just try this one piece. It literally melts on your tongue. (*Holds out a piece of fish to her with his chopsticks.*)

Okichi   I don't care for it.

Tsurumatsu   No? (*He eats it himself.*) It's delicious. Please pass me some more of the rice.

Okichi *gives him more rice. A female voice can be heard from outside*:

Voice   Could you please do my hair now?

Okichi   I am sorry, but I can't do it today.

Voice   Can I come back tomorrow morning?

Okichi   I am afraid it won't be possible at all in the next few days.

Voice   Ah, that's a pity. (*Leaves.*)

Tsurumatsu   Why can't you do her hair then?

Okichi   Because I don't want to.

Tsurumatsu   And why not?

Okichi   Would you like more rice?

Tsurumatsu   No, that's enough for today.

Okichi   Please take the rest. This is the last time that I'll serve you food.

Tsurumatsu   What? What are you saying?

Okichi   Tsuru San! It's over between us, for good.

Tsurumatsu   You are talking nonsense!

Okichi   I am leaving now. I have everything prepared for you. Some raw fish is left, and the boiled rice will last until tomorrow. After that the two of you can carry on as you please.

Tsurumatsu   This is crazy stuff …

Okichi   I am sober today, and I know what I am saying.

Tsurumatsu   You are imagining things. This is a misunderstanding.

Okichi   Perhaps I am a dimwit. But when I got to do your lover's hair, it dawned even on me. (**Tsurumatsu** *starts.*) This is not about jealousy. But since you got involved with this woman I have no other choice than to leave.

Tsurumatsu Are you speaking of this Osai, who was just here? Who is she? I assure you …

Okichi Hold on! Don't say another word! Once you start explaining and exculpating yourself, I will have to respond, and we will part in discord.

Tsurumatsu But …

Okichi You are not the only one to blame. Our marriage was already cracked a long time ago. Lord Isa once told me that a rift between nations can often be mended by a woman, not, however, the rift between a man and a woman. (*She notices her dolls on the chest of drawers and takes them in her arms.*) Look, the dolls know neither worries nor pain. They don't break up, either. Do you remember how we bought them in Yokohama, we had saved some money for our return trip to Shimoda. You didn't want to lug more stuff around, but I wanted to have them in place of the children that we didn't have. And I also liked how a man and a woman could sit so peacefully and happily next to each other. And I thought how beautiful it would be to be together like this for the rest of our lives, even if we had to sleep on the bare wooden floor. That's the life that I wished for myself, and that's why I learned to dress hair and why I tried as hard as I could to do a good job. When I look back now, all of this seems so childish.

Tsurumatsu Okichi, please stay with me.

Okichi That would lead nowhere.

Tsurumatsu That is not true. I will start a new life.

Okichi No. As I said, you are not the only one to blame. We both have failed. Even before we got married, there was a vast divide between us. We never bridged it. We are like a cracked shamisen. Whatever you try to fix the crack, the shamisen will never sound the same again. (**Tsurumatsu** *remains silent.*) Back then, in my misery, I turned to drink, and who knows when it will seize hold of me again, even though I have sworn to abstain from alcohol for the rest of my life. And now that you have found someone you like, this gap between us can only widen. Here is some tea for you. Let this be our farewell drink.

Tsurumatsu (*sad*) Okichi!

Okichi Don't be so sad! I would like to leave with a laugh. (*She sets the tea kettle on the burning coals, but the kettle is cracked and a cloud of steam sizzles up. She secretly wipes her tears away.*) Now look, my dear, even the kettle is cracked. You have to fix it. (*She exits through the door, crying.*)

Interlude Eight

[B6]

Akimura (*rising*) That's what became of Okichi's marriage. To a certain extent, though obscurely, it is the shadows of those days of May 1856 that have destroyed this life. Daily life, the passing years, the struggle to survive, all of this covers these events like a layer of dust. The marriage, rather than being thwarted by her 'war service' in Shimoda, actually comes about because of it, and that turns into the real tragedy. It is not the heroic act that leads to the downfall of the heroine, but that little addition, the foreigners' whisky. The husband turns out not to be the rogue that he seemed to be in the heroic light of the first few scenes, but a good and patient man. And this proves even more fateful. Well, I did not advise you to watch these additional scenes. (*He seems to expect that everyone is preparing to leave.*)

Ray (*remains seated*) But the State! Didn't the State take care of her?

Akimura Yes, of course. That Saito, whom you may still remember from the first half of the play, got on in the world and visited Shimoda again twelve years after the events at the American consulate. He also intended to get in touch again with Okichi. Unfortunately, the encounter between Okichi and the State was not particularly successful. I don't mind at all showing you this scene also. (*He claps his hands.*)

The Director Which additional scene would you like to see, Mister Akimura?

Akimura The encounter between Okichi and Saito, please.

The Director (*smiling*) You are very kind.

Scene Nine

[Neureuter]

A restaurant in Shimoda. It is evening, candles are lit on the tables. **Saito**, *with a full beard and in an elegant European frock coat, sits at the centre. He is surrounded by members of the city council of Shimoda as well as by* **Takagi Kamekichi**.

First Council Member The government constantly disadvantages our city in some way or other that one could justly call it a form of oppression. We would be extremely grateful for your help.

Saito I will take care of this matter. By the way, I was stationed here during the Shogunate. I am familiar with the conditions here and have always remembered Shimoda fondly. It will be an honour to support you to the best of my abilities.

All That's what we've been asking for, and thank you for that.

Waitress (*enters and takes a deep bow, her hands on the mat*) Dinner is ready, could I serve it now?

First Council Member Yes, please. Your Excellency, would you like to take off your coat and make yourself comfortable? (*He helps* **Saito** *out of his coat.*)

Saito Thank you.

A group of geishas bring in trays. At the same time the sound of voices and commotion can be heard from outside.

Second Council Member What's that noise?

A Geisha It's probably Okit San again.

First Council Member Okichi! That outrageous person!

Saito Did you just mention the name Okichi?

First Council Member Yes.

Saito Who is that?

First Council Member I regret offending your ears with that name. People here call her the 'Yankee Okichi'. She is a drunkard, a dishonourable woman.

Saito Ah, this Okichi is still around!

First Council Member So you know her?

Saito Yes, very well indeed. I heard that she had left for America.

First Council Member No, no. It is true that she once disappeared and moved somewhere else, but apparently she returned six or seven years ago as the wife of a certain Tsurumatsu, whom you might also know, then.

Saito Yes, I also know this Tsurumatsu. What is he doing now?

First Council Member He died a few years ago. He separated from Okichi and married another woman. But that night when Okichi became a geisha again, he passed away.

Saito How sad.

First Council Member If you would like to hear more details about Okichi, Mister Kamekichi here, a distant relative of hers, knows more than anyone else.

Kamekichi Ah, that's an exaggeration. I gave up on that woman a long time ago.

Saito Why?

Kamekichi I tried to take care of her in every imaginable way. I finally lost my patience since she couldn't let go of her drinking habit.

First Council Member Mister Kamekichi has done a lot for Okichi. He gave her money and established a fine brothel for her. But every morning, before she even put a toothbrush in her mouth, she was already filling up with sake.

Kamekichi That's not the whole story. If she had a customer who was just after some decent pleasure, she would yell at him: 'You are such a cheap bastard! Just pick a geisha and amuse yourself with her! It's on me!' That way it didn't take long before she had lost everything she owned. I can only imagine what this woman would have been able to accomplish. After that she started working again as a hairdresser as well as a dance and voice teacher. But when she is drunk, she doesn't know what she is doing, and so people have been avoiding her. Lately, she's gone on a rampage in the streets, demanding of every passer-by to buy her sake, and no one can tame her. The commotion outside sounds just like her.

Saito So, she has sunk that deep. But since she is already here, why don't we ask her in?

First Council Member In here – ?

Saito Yes, certainly. I am in the right mood to see her again after all these years.

Kamekichi But she is completely out of place in such company.

Saito I wouldn't invite her if she led a normal life. But since she has hit rock bottom, I would like to try to raise her morale somewhat.

Kamekichi Your Excellency certainly has the former Okichi in mind. Even though she was already a short-tempered and insolent person then, she is now in such bad shape that you wouldn't even want to touch her with a ten-foot pole. It would be best for you to not invite her.

Saito That doesn't frighten me. By all means, ask her in.

First Council Member Even though we are somewhat disconcerted by your Excellency's wish, it will be granted. (*To a* **Waitress**.) Please ask Okichi to come inside. (*The* **Waitress** *exits*.)

Saito I certainly don't intend to tell her directly, but Okichi did our government a great service. It would be wrong, in my view, to only see her drinking habit and to abandon her because of that.

Kamekichi You really think … ?

Saito A few years ago, when a crazed samurai killed the secretary of the American ambassador, a certain Heusken, all foreign ambassadors sent protest notes to our government and left Edo. Only the American ambassador himself, Harris, remarked that there were criminals in other places, too, and that things like that could happen in any civilized country. He wasn't just the only one to stay in Edo, he also didn't make unreasonable demands of compensation for the murder of his officer. It is generally said that this foreigner only held Japan in such high esteem because of Okichi.

First Council Member Really?

Okichi (*enters, dressed in rags and obviously drunk*) Who is it that wants to see me?

Waitress Oh, watch out, Okit San!

Okichi Don't worry, I won't fall.

Kamekichi (*goes to the entrance, to* **Okichi**) No yelling here. There is a high-ranking gentleman from Tokyo who wants to see you. Behave yourself!

Okichi What, you're here, too?

Kamekichi Take a bow before His Excellency.

Okichi *looks silently at* **Saito**.

Saito Okichi, you have changed a lot, but I have probably changed, too: Do you remember me? (**Okichi** *scrutinizes him silently*.) Don't you recognize me? I am Saito!

Okichi I don't know him.

Saito You no longer know me? But you must recognize me! Of course, my appearance has changed after all these years. But take a good look at me! You don't recognize me?

Okichi   No. I don't know this man.

Saito   You must be in a bad state if you can no longer recognize me! (**Okichi** *doesn't answer.*) Do you remember Lord Isa, at least?

Okichi   Yes, of course.

Saito   Once, a long time ago, you caused him a great deal of sorrow.

Okichi   Where is he now?

Saito   I don't know, but I have heard that he is still alive. He must be rather old. He was no longer able to keep up with the times and to adapt. He completely kept himself out of everything in our new state.

Okichi   Do you have some tobacco for me, Kamekichi?

Kamekichi   But not now – how can you smoke it, anyway, you don't even have a pipe.

Okichi   Yes, I do. I am just asking you for some tobacco.

Kamekichi   She is stubborn, that woman. Here you go.

Saito   Okichi, take this. (*He holds a banknote out to her.*)

Okichi   What is that?

Saito   A small token of my gratitude, for old times' sake. Buy yourself some tobacco.

Okichi   Very well then. Thanks a lot. (*She stuffs her pipe, takes the banknote, holds it to a candle, and lights her pipe with it.*)

Kamekichi   What are you doing? Are you mad! (*He snatches the burning banknote from her hand and tries to salvage it.*) You are reckless!

Okichi (*blowing rings into the air*)   Superb! You've probably never had a smoke as good as this. Here, take a drag.

Kamekichi   You're mad. To burn money!

Saito   She is already in a rather advanced stage. – Aren't you ashamed at all?

Okichi   Are you ashamed?

Saito   How dare you?

Okichi   What does that really mean: to be ashamed? Because of what? Have you completely forgotten how you all danced around me while I was being burned by you? But I should be ashamed of setting a banknote on fire?

First Council Member   Don't be so insolent to His Excellency.

Saito   Let it go. It doesn't matter. She is a pitiful creature. – You have joined the Cynics Club, haven't you?

Okichi   Oh no, how fine, how classy your words sound! Don't talk so big, you, who have only climbed the social ladder because he organized whores for the foreigners.

Kamekichi   Shut your mouth, Okichi!

Okichi   Hogwash, shut your own mouth.

Saito (*laughs*)   Ha, ha, ha. You do remember the old Saito! Back then I had my hands full with you and often had to take drastic measures. But the circumstances have changed, and I am no longer the same minor official.

Okichi (*sings*)
Yes, keep talking, talk until you sweat,
What doesn't one say for a handful of rice.

Saito   You are very angry with humankind, aren't you? And that is only too understandable. I have told everyone here of your merits. If you only weren't so stubborn. Be meek! Be compliant! Leave the past behind! I pity you, and I would like to do something to help you. Tell me in what way I could be of help to you.

Okichi   Just listen to him, before other people he talks as if he truly had a heart. With such a voice – as if stroking a cat. What's the point of pitying a woman that you yourself turned into what I am now! It's disgusting. I don't want your pity. Please be as vicious as you used to be, I would feel better.

Kamekichi   How dare you?

Okichi   What a monster that likes to treat women like toys. I am not the dimwit you take me for.

Saito   Well, she can't be helped any more. When someone no longer recognizes friendliness and only responds with ingratitude, that person is lost. It brings tears to my eyes to remember what a gorgeous geisha she once was, and in what a miserable state she is now. – What would Lord Isa think of you?

Okichi   When you wanted something from me, you showered me with adulation. The word was then that only I could save you, that I was the real remedy, that I was gold, and who knows what else. I was supposed to be a 'tokiwa' or one of those women from China who sacrifice themselves for the land of their ancestors. And, indeed, that's what I have become.

Saito   You just squander everything, you debauched person. Back then they granted you a sum that would have allowed you to live comfortably until the end of your days. And what did you do with it?

Okichi   Go to the devil. Should I have taken your stinking money and put it in my piggybank?

Saito   Why, then, didn't you kill yourself right away instead of falling so low? Weren't there samurai in your family? In which case you know the code of honour and how a samurai behaves in such a situation. If it was so bitter and humiliating to go to the Americans, why didn't you bravely stab yourself to death? Then you wouldn't need to endure such a rotten and dishonourable life now.

Okichi   But then I also wouldn't have 'needed' to save Shimoda! – I can't kill myself. I've thought of it, but that is over now. Now I want to *show* the world what has become of me, and who trampled me down. I am still alive, but only to serve as an example of how you treat women in this country.

Saito   She can't be helped.

Kamekichi   That's why I said it wouldn't do any good to invite her in. Now we have no other option than to throw her out again.

Okichi   You want to throw me out! How very nice of you! Go ahead and kick me so hard I fall to my death. (*She throws herself down in front of the door.*)

First Council Member (*calls for the* **Waiter**)   Please come here – and throw her out!

Waiter   Yes, Sir. – Okichi, you can't just lie there. Get up and leave. (*Shakes her.*)

Okichi   Back off! What do you want?

Kamekichi   Get out of here!

Okichi   Not of my own free will. Why did you invite me in in the first place?

Second Council Member   You're in the way here, get lost.

Okichi I am in the way? Come on, trample over me then. To you men, women are just dust and dirt, anyway. Well, kick me, punch me, don't hold back. Nothing was holding you back then, so why now. Go ahead and kick a woman when she's down. Hahaha – you're not afraid, are you?

Saito (*gets up and walks over to her*) All right, then, if that's what you want, here, you shameless bitch! (*Kicks her hard with his foot, so that she rolls down the staircase.*) Didn't want to see reason, that woman.

[B6]

Interlude Nine

Kito It is terrible how we mistreat our heroes. The abuse to which heroes are subjected is worse than the abuse of any other gifts from the gods. Someone should make an appeal against the abuse of heroes and start a club for their protection.

Ray Clive, you could achieve a lot with a letter to the *Times*: Dear Sir, may I turn our nation's attention towards the fact that so much is being done for our songbirds in winter, but almost nothing for our heroes in the wake of their heroic deeds.

Kito That's true for small heroes. The great ones are defiled in a different manner. Just consider how they are wronged through popular representations! Their obituaries are nothing else than diatribes. To give one example, I have studied with horror a biography of one of your greatest warriors, which portrays this man, who conquered half a continent by fire and sword, as the anaemic and timid student of a Sunday school. He didn't need laurels but cod liver oil.

Ray You are right, we deny Benjamin Franklin his glass of wine and force George Washington to give his brother a goodnight kiss every evening. We insist that the nation can only be saved by well-behaved men. Armies have to be led by honest simpletons, classical works must be written by harmless paragons of virtue. We are very demanding and rigorous in our treatment of people who achieve things.

Kito But we have to be strong and show some backbone if we don't want to be overrun by heroes. We have to prepare and print a list of all disqualifying traits. And we have to be stingy with financial rewards – or, at the very least, cautious.

Clive Well, at least the Saitos of this world obtain some profit from patriotic acts. Those who track down heroes get remunerated.

Ray Only the Okichis are forgotten.

Akimura But no! Her glory increases from year to year. She becomes a legendary figure. The people celebrate her in any number of songs. Japan is undergoing radical changes. But modern industry will not suppress the memory of Okichi's deed. (*He claps his hands and tells the director, who is stepping forward:*) The ballad, finally!

[B2]

Scene Ten

Harbour alley. Boys are passing by.

The Boys He went down there, to the shipyard!

A Woman (*holds one of them up by grabbing his arm*) Who? A thief?

The Boy Someone dressed like a foreigner! (*He breaks loose.*)

A Young Man (*who is showing a middle-aged man the city*) It seems we're lucky, uncle! Look, there is one of the office employees from the shipyard wearing a European suit.

The Uncle I thought, the shipyard was closed.

The Young Man Not the offices. Only the carpenters have stopped working. It's called a strike.

The Boys (*returning*) He is coming!

A young Japanese man with a European jacket comes down the alley. Everyone stops and looks after him.

A Boy Pants like a woman! And a tube around his neck!

Another Boy And what a hat! (*They follow the man in European attire.*)

The Woman Such foolishness! (*She moves along, shaking her head.*)

The Uncle Let's go! I can't really say I like that.

The Young Man Oh, no one likes it, but I have heard that more and more people in Tokyo are dressed like this. It's a new era. I still have to show you the new silos, come on! (*Both exit.*)

A Fat Man (*has stopped with another man*) Monkey business!

The Other Man But the French singer at the Clos de Paris is brilliant! She is already quite old, admittedly, but still very indecent.

The Fat Man I have heard that the people from the British branch office don't go there. Will you come to the bank with me, Kimura? (*Both exit.*)

A street **Singer** *has appeared.*

The Singer Stop and stay put, folks! Hear the new ballad about Okichi's fight against the battleships! Okichi, the heroine of Shimoda! The unforgettable one! She who vanquished the white devils! Who does not know her name? Who has not seen her pictures? Ladies and Gentlemen, please observe a minute of silence for the beautiful Okichi, the saviour of Shimoda!

An audience gathers, **Okichi** *among them.*

The Singer
The fishermen are mending old sails.
The women are tying straw around cherry trees.
The boys are diving for shells.
Oh peace! Oh golden noon!
Seven battleships are headed for Shimoda.

A Woman Stop pushing me. She keeps poking me in the ribs. If you're drunk, go home!

A Man (*to* **Okichi**) Come over here, old woman! From here you can see everything.

The Singer
The Shogun's jittery soldiers are grinding sabres.
The council members are hiding under tables.
The people are loading carts with pads and copper kettles.
Oh terror! Oh bloody battle!
From the house on the river Okichi emerges, radiant.

Okichi Did he say 'radiant'? That is good. (*She laughs.*)

The Woman Shut your mouth!

The Singer
The women warn Okichi: the white devils are coming!
A getaway boat is ready: get in, you apple of Shimoda's eye!

Okichi Apple of Shimoda's eye! For the foreigners' whore!

The Audience Shush!

The Singer
The council members beseech her: get yourself out of harm's way!

Oh, you joy of Shimoda! Where are you going, Okichi?
I am going to hold back the seven battleships!

A Young Girl   Can no one here get rid of this person? She is spoiling all my fun.

Okichi (*to the* **Friendly Man**)   What do you think of the song? I have heard many songs on the same subject, but this is the most stupid one. The council member's 'get yourself out of harm's way!' He turned her into a foreigner's whore. Every child knows that.

The Woman   You'd better watch out! Sake barrel! To say such things in front of young girls!

The Friendly Man   What do you have against Okichi? That she saved Shimoda is true, after all!

Okichi   Well, so what? Damn your dirty Shimoda!

The Singer   Ladies and Gentlemen, could you please lend me your ears?

Another Woman   Let him please finish his song, old woman. It's how he earns his daily bread.

Okichi   That's right. Well then, what more do you know? What else happened? But cut it short! Earn your bread quickly!

The Singer
How, folks, did Okichi beat the seven battleships?
Only with her small shamisen, folks!
Only with her cheerful songs, folks!
Only with her smile, folks!
Only with her beauty did Okichi beat the battleships!

Okichi (*applauds ironically and laughs*)   Ah, she smiled? And that's all she did? What modest battleships! Seven deeply moved battleships for young girls! Give me your shamisen, you bungler! (*She grabs at it.*) I will sing you a song, you oafs! (*Since she can't get hold of the shamisen, she tries to sing without it but barely produces a sound.*)
The bedspread is pulled back.
The foreigner is waiting.
Here is your sake, Okichi.
The Emperor demands it.

The Audience (*enraged*)   Shut her up! That is enough! Throw her out! Aren't there any men here? Away with her! She has no decency! Get the police!

They kick and push her away.

Okichi (*yelling loudly, while she gets dragged off*) You blockheads! You and your stinking manners! You liars! You drunkards!

The Woman Get on with your song, man!

The Singer
As long as fish swim in Shimoda's bay
As long as cherries blossom in Shimoda's gardens
As long as shells lie at the bottom of Shimoda's sea
Oh glory! Oh eternity!
Will the people of Shimoda sing of Okichi's deed!

Everyone applauds.

[B6]
Interlude Ten

Ray This is terrible! But her friends! Does she have no one?

Akimura Oh yes, she does. But do you really want to know the details of this unhappy fate right to its bitter end? I could not see by any stretch of the imagination why you would be interested in that. But, of course, we have nothing to conceal. No one has ever claimed that it would be particularly pleasant to perform great deeds. Anyhow, what about this person could still be of interest to you? She is simply a drunkard in her final stage, nothing else! (*He summons the director with a clap and tells him impassively:*) Play the final scene as well, please!

[Neureuter]
Scene Eleven

Okichi's *lodgings in a squalid shack. It is snowing outside.* **Okichi** *and* **Ofuku** *enter.* **Okichi** *falls to the ground and cries out in pain.*

Ofuku What's the matter? I'll help you.

Okichi (*speaks, with difficulty*) The wine bowl is broken.

Ofuku Come, I'll help you get into bed! (*She does it.*) And I'll get you a new kimono, this one is too thin, as cold as it is in here.

Okichi Thank you, Ofuku San, you are so good to me.

Ofuku   Don't mention it. The main point is that you take care of yourself, so that you can get back on your feet. I'll make some tea for you.

Okichi   Please pass me that thingy over there.

Ofuku   This notebook – with your handwriting?

Okichi   Yes. And those other ones, too!

Ofuku   The sake bottle and the glass? Here. What do you want to do with them?

Okichi   You have always been so good to me. I would like to give you a present. But I have sold and eaten up everything.

Ofuku   Don't beat yourself up over that.

Okichi   This is the notebook in which I penned all of my songs. I give it to you, and the bottle, and the photo. That's all that's left of my belongings.

Ofuku   But what are you talking about. You are not going to die yet.

Okichi   I will feel relieved once it's gone.

Ofuku (*wipes away her tears*)   You mustn't think of death.

Okichi (*caresses her hand*)   Never mind. I know the score.

Ofuku   Don't be so sad.

Okichi (*smiles*)   Good, in that case I won't die quite yet.

Kamekichi (*comes in, followed by a* **Sailor** *who carries a sack of rice on his shoulders*)   Excuse me for interrupting.

Ofuku   Ah, Sir, that is very kind. You come at the right time. I heard that Okichi had been sick for days, and came here to look after her.

Sailor   Where does this go?

Kamekichi   Over there, against the wall. Then you can go.

Sailor *exits*.

Kamekichi   Oh well, Okichi. You no longer have to worry. I brought you rice and I will take care of you. You can stay in bed and go to sleep.

Okichi   What?

Kamekichi   Once this sack is empty, I'll bring more. Don't you worry!

Okichi (*trying to sit up, with difficulty*)   What a nerve!

Ofuku Okit San, be calm and lie down. You are too weak.

Okichi But not so weak in the head that I would accept your food like cat and dog. Do you seriously believe I would allow you and your sort to feed me until I'm dead? Whatever you have brought along, take it back with you!

Kamekichi Don't talk nonsense! Is there a single person around the world who would resent it if someone offered her help in such a situation! I only want to make sure that you can recover at your own pace.

Okichi You are jabbering! (*She gets up, staggers to the table, takes a knife and walks over to the sack of rice.*)

Ofuku Don't do that. You'll catch your death.

Okichi As impoverished as I may be: I don't want to owe you and your kind a living until the end of my days. (*Slits the sack of rice open.*) Do you think I would take alms from you and your sort and actually eat that. (*Takes a handful of rice, opens the window, and throws it out.*) That is for the sparrows.

Kamekichi Heaven will punish you for such a sin.

Okichi Heaven has punished me for a long time. (*Throws more rice out of the window.*) Take it, you sparrows in heaven and finches on earth! Pick it off and eat your fill! Today Okichi is scattering golden seeds for you. And you, come too, my neighbour's hatchlings! Crows and magpies, ravens and jays, come, all of you! Even if I didn't have a single grain of rice left, and even if I were starving, I wouldn't accept alms from these people! Here, eat, pick it all off! (*She generously throws the rice out of the window. She finally stumbles and collapses. A gust of wind blows flurries of snow through the window.*)

[B6]
Epilogue

Everyone rises and applauds the actors.

Ray What a story! What a heroine! All that's been asked of her! All that's been accomplished! How much it takes until a heroic deed is fully paid off! And you only ever want to tell just half of the hero's story!

Garbe/Büsching

With Käthe Rülicke

Translated and edited by
Marc Silberman

4 Decorated 'worker activist' Hans Garbe (right) with members of his Socialist Workers Brigade at the Siemens-Plania Factory, September 1950.

Introduction

The 'Garbe' material constitutes Brecht's last and most extensive fragment play from his years in East Germany. Arriving in late 1948 in East Berlin, in the Soviet Occupied Zone, with the promise of a theatre of his own, he was considered one of the most prominent of the returning German exiles. From this position of strength, Brecht found himself one year later in the newly established German Democratic Republic (GDR), a state committed to the construction of a socialist society that would be characterized by central planning and the Soviet model of cultural production. With a theatre at his disposal and influence in cultural institutions arising from his international reputation, he saw himself in a position to leverage things, in his sense. In the course of the next seven years before his death in August 1956, Brecht worked on three other fragments: *The Salzburg Dance of Death*, a fragment like *Garbe/Büsching* consisting of several lists of scenes and half a dozen very brief monologues or dialogues that captured his attention intermittently between March 1949 and October 1951, a period when he was officially stateless and therefore trying to obtain an Austrian passport by cooperating with the Salzburg Festival; *Life and Death of Rosa Luxemburg*, consisting of eight very short fragmentary texts that were written between 1926 and 1944 but mentioned by Brecht still in 1948 as a project he wished to complete; and *Life of Einstein*, even briefer than the former with six very short fragments and envisioned in 1955 as a contemporary version of Galileo in the context of rehearsals for his *Life of Galileo* at the Berliner Ensemble. In short, the *Garbe/Büsching* fragment is one of several projects Brecht was considering for new play productions at his Berliner Ensemble but the only one – except for the prologue to the *Caucasian Chalk Circle* (1944) – that attempts to formulate the problems of a society transitioning to socialism.

The *Garbe/Büsching* fragment in the Bertolt Brecht Archive comprises twenty-six leaves in four folios, mainly typescripts with some handwritten corrections from between 1951 and 1954: nineteen leaves with lists of scenes or descriptions and notes, and seven leaves with four short, partial scenes, three of which are written in blank verse.[1] In view of the nature of the material, we have chosen a facing-page layout in what follows, with Brecht's texts on the left and the editorial commentary on the right. The twenty-three numbered texts in the *Berliner und Frankfurter Ausgabe* (*BFA* 10.2, 971–9) appear not in the order they were written but roughly according to the plot sequence. In addition, two of the folios contain over 200 leaves with background material: transcripts of conversations with Hans Garbe and his wife Erika, interviews with his co-workers, documents about Garbe, as well as technical explanations of furnace construction and

[A2 (1951)]

1
The liberation
2
Black market trafficking with the owner
The union
Grand and petty theft
The Socialist Unity Party
Büsching finds himself starving
Büsching is thrown out of the Socialist Unity Party
3
The owner is ousted
Büsching, traitor to the workers
4

[A4 (1951)]

1
Berlin, May 1945. Büsching hides from two SS officers because he thinks they want to hang him, because he has deserted. But they want his jacket because they want to desert.

[A6 (1951)]

Büsching's wife has a sister who was raped by a drunk Russian soldier. The sister of the apprentice Jacob is going out with an American for chocolate, drinks, and cigarettes. Later on Büsching erupts. The next day the Russian brought bread and meat.

[A7 (1951)]

Büsching is at the Lemke company, foodstuff. His family is starving. With his wife Büsching calculates that per year flour for 60,000 loaves of bread is being stolen. 'What's going to happen?'

[A5 (1951)]

First scene and more
His friend, a worker, helps him against the SS guy.
Then they become enemies.
On one occasion he points out to the cook the SS guy, sitting with the engineer ...
Can the SS guy be considered a worker? He'll hail the workers, and they will remember. But they will decide that he can't be changed back into a worker. Not so fast, not now.

relevant newspaper clippings. In the earliest drafts and lists, the project is consistently referred to as 'Büsching', the name as well of a character in the earlier *Fatzer* fragment, but by 1953 Brecht refers to it as 'Garbe' (*Journals*, 416), and the folio with most of the material is labelled 'Notes Hans Garbe I'.

> A2 Even the earliest notes from 1951 indicate Brecht's intention of including biographical details about the protagonist, here emphasizing Garbe's track record of acting on individual initiative without considering the broader context. Many of the notes from 1951 focus on the difference between Garbe's actions and his lack of thinking through the consequences.
>
> A4–A9 These notes touch on episodes planned for the first three scenes, both in the earliest sketch of 1951 (A2) and in the final outline of 1954 (A1). They depict the misery, confusion, and distrust among the workers as a consequence of experiences in the Third Reich, the ruins on which working-class solidarity and the new socialist state were to be constructed.

The protagonist of *Garbe/Büsching* is based on the bricklayer Hans Garbe, a 'worker hero' who was well-known to the contemporaneous public in the GDR. The Garbe 'legend' evolved around events that took place from late December 1949 to February 1950 when he repaired a thirty-six-chamber circle furnace (known as a Hoffmann kiln) at the Siemens-Plania factory in East Berlin without stopping production and consequently saved the company about half a million marks in half the projected time. To complete the repair, Garbe established the first 'workers brigade' at this major factory, which also marked the beginning of the 'socialist competition' for the reconstruction of industry in post-war East Germany. The deed drew a lot of press attention both to this 'worker hero' – a model worker introducing new efficiencies on his own initiative – and to pioneering ways for organizing labour to increase productivity in the planned economy. On 13 October 1950, Garbe was officially decorated as a 'worker hero' for his innovative plans. In some ways he reincarnated the Soviet Stakhanovite movement of the mid-1930s (when Alexey Stakhanov, a miner, emerged as a worker activist helping to industrialize the country). But unlike the Soviet archetype, Garbe was not 'constructed' by the party apparatus. He had developed his own 'worker's consciousness' outside political institutions; in fact, the party had expelled him as a dreamer, and even his fellow workers and the union steward refused to join him in his ground-breaking repair project. For Brecht, Garbe represented someone who saw work as a sport, taking calculated risks to win; he

[A8 (after August 1953)]
The functionary who kicks Garbe out of the party is a good functionary. He's given the difficult task of trying to hold together the members of the party cells. Garbe acted on his own against the owner, against his fellow workers.

[A9 (1951)]
Büsching begins to drink after he is kicked out of the party.
He curses the workers.
And he earns applause.
His curses get more radical.
And he looks around: surrounded by rabble.

[A11 (1951)]
With a piece of chalk he draws the plan for his furnace construction on the wall. They stand there and mock one of their own who pretends to be smarter than an engineer.
(One of the workers mimics him)

[A17 (1951)]
The workers brand Büsching as a traitor of the workers.
An old worker says that he's been standing at a machine at Siemens-Plania for the past 40 years, and no one has stabbed him in the back like this. Büsching proves that the worker is a scoundrel: the huge strike at Siemens-Plania was in 1910 and the old man a scab.

[A16 (1951)]
Foreman Z. opposes Büsching: first, he's not in the party, and second, he's unpopular among the workers.

[A15 (1951)]
Büsching suspects that foreman Z. rejects his recommendations only because he is in cahoots with the private company that wants the bid. He's found to be in the wrong, which jeopardizes his recommendations. When the culture centre is being built, it turns out that Büsching was right.

[A12 (1951)]
When he encountered many who rejected his plan, he did meet one who agreed. But this one he disliked because he was a crooked opportunist.

personified the contradictions of political transformation, someone who was historically 'necessary' for the construction of a socialist economy, but did not know why. For the party, he had made history with his new bricklaying procedure and was elevated post-factum into a monument.

> A10–A19 These notes, all addressing the central events around the planning and implementation of the furnace repair, direct attention to actions of Garbe or the workers, showing how the protagonist takes risks upon himself that can harm him (physically and materially) and that alienate and isolate him from his work colleagues. In the 1954 outline these actions are consolidated into Scenes Four and Five.
> The Kostytshev research referenced in A18 points to the agricultural scientist Pavel Andreievitch Kostytshev at the University of St. Petersburg prior to the Bolshevist revolution, who focused on sensible ways for human beings to harness the forces of nature. Brecht knew about this research through the Soviet science popularizer Mikhail Ilyin, whose book on man and nature translated into German (*Besiegte Natur*, 1951) mentions Kostytshev as well as the 'Saga of the Wanderer', which Brecht quotes almost literally in connection with the figure of Cidher in B1 and B2.

Brecht first took note of Garbe in spring 1950, met him for the first time probably in March, and then had his assistants begin collecting material (newspaper articles, photos, documents), which were later assembled into an album that he presented to Garbe's wife. By the autumn, he had decided this could become a play, and he met Garbe once again in early November after the celebratory presentation of the activist medal of honour. When Käthe Rülicke joined the Ensemble as one of Brecht's assistants in December 1950, he had her arrange several encounters. The Garbes attended the new staging of *The Mother* at the Berliner Ensemble in January 1951, and in February Brecht and Rülicke visited the Siemens-Plania factory. By April he was thinking about a scene with music by composer friend and collaborator Hanns Eisler, and he had Rülicke organize a series of three interviews with the Garbes that took place between May and June 1951.[2] In summer 1951 the multiple obstacles he faced with the Garbe material had become obvious. A discussion with students revealed that they were being trained to memorize ideas, not to think for themselves (*Journals*, 437). Meanwhile the anti-formalism debate had touched him directly when Paul Dessau's opera *The Trial of Lucullus* with a libretto by Brecht was put on ice under pressure from the party after a general rehearsal at the East Berlin Staatsoper in March (*Journals*, 433). Moreover, the party harshly

[A13 (1951)]
In desperation he goes one night to the partly destroyed factory yard and shouts his accusations against his class comrades into the winter night's storm. He curses them. No answer. He threatens to abandon everything. No answer.

[A18 (1951)]
In a desperate mood Büsching listens to an engineer who explains Kostytshev's agricultural research: you shouldn't say that weeds grow where there is good soil, instead there is good soil where weeds grow etc. You don't have the wind in your hand but soil etc.
He feels invigorated.

Engineer, future enemy?
Possible there, not here?
A young person as well?

[B1 (July 1951)]
Büsching learns about science

Watter
Science is
Like Cidher, the Wanderer.
Every five hundred years
He comes along the way.
Walking through the streets
Of a very old city
He asks someone: is this city old?
So old, he hears
That we no longer know
How long it exists.
And after five hundred years
He comes along the way again
And meets a farmer
Who mows the pasture at this place.
How was the city destroyed, he asks
Which once stood here
With towers and houses?
Never was there a city here, he learns.
After five hundred years
He comes along the way again
And he finds a sea
At the place where there was a field.

criticized his staging of *The Mother* for its avant-gardism. On the one hand, Brecht wanted to put a central GDR theme on the stage to show his support for the socialist values underpinning this part of divided Germany, but on the other, he didn't want to make concessions to ideological assumptions favoured by the party nor to conform to the shallow, mimetic realism that dominated other such topical undertakings in the cultural sphere.

For Brecht and his circle, 1951 was a discouraging year. Yet Garbe attracted their attention as an uneducated, non-ideological worker whose relationship to his labour, to the means of production, was vital and sensual. This was a figure who could demonstrate the new contradictions arising in a transitional society. If the context of his labour was still dominated by 'old habits', then Brecht's goal was to make 'the new' visible to the audience, even if the hero himself was blind. In other words, he was faced with the question: How can the play convey more to the audience than the protagonist himself understands? In addition, for the first time in his writing career Brecht was dealing with a dramatic figure based on a person whom he could actually get to know, and his contact with the Garbes was part of an extensive network of discussion partners he had begun to consult for his theatre projects in 1950, including audience members, farmers, construction and metallurgy workers, students, and so on. In this respect, the *Garbe/Büsching* project functions like a lens to focus attention on the model of theatre practice Brecht was developing in his last years of creative activity.

B1–B3 Brecht wrote these three sample scenes ('Probeszenen') during his summer vacation in July 1951 in Ahrenshoop on the Baltic Sea, according to Käthe Rülicke's summary (*BBA* 1375/01). In B1 the speaker Watter is a fictional figure (never mentioned in the transcripts of the Garbe conversations), and Cidher refers to the narrator in Friedrich Rückert's ballad 'Chidher' (1829), an eternally young wanderer. He also mentions the 'Cidher technique' in his 'Notes on *Katzgraben*' (*Brecht on Performance*, 271–2), that is, the idea of using the eternal wanderer on stage to evoke changes over a long period of time. In Watter's speech he is closely paraphrasing the German translation in Mikhail Ilyin's book (see previous note on A18). B2 and B3 introduce Jacob, the apprentice, and thematize the issue of risk, that is Büsching's willingness to take responsibility on his own, on the one hand, and the animosity between Büsching and his fellow workers who do not yet recognize their own advantage in the GDR, on the other.

And he asks a fisherman:
Since when has a sea been here?
And the fisherman tells him:
There has always been a sea here.

Büsching
Never was there a city here.
No houses, no towers!
Clean pasture! Clear water!

[B2 (July 1951)]

Cidher, returning

Büsching
Yesterday I remembered
Watter's story about science
That knows what has been
And recognizes how things change.
How the pasture grew and a field was there
And never could there have been a city
If you listened to the farmer, never a house
Never a tower and yet there was
Once a city and could be
Once again a city.

Jacob
                Great wisdom.
The factory can be built. Where something
Was, something can be again.

Büsching
                You have
Understood nothing. One thing can disappear.
But another cannot. Something good
You can make again, if you know how it is made
And the filth you can shovel away
And forever. Those then are two
Valuable ideas.

During his summer vacation on the Baltic Sea in July 1951 Brecht studied the transcripts Rülicke had made of the three long interviews with Garbe and came to the conclusion that it would have to be a historical play, using the kind of non-rhyming, irregular verse he had tested in the *Fatzer* fragment twenty years earlier. This explains his interest in compiling his own chronicle or source material, yielding the mass of notes in the Archive collected by his assistants. At this point Brecht conceived of a plot-line in which a worker comes into his own through his labour; the play was to examine what changed in him and for him if, instead of being shaped by history, he begins to shape history, not just through this one individual's deed but through its impact on the entire working class: 'What I envisage, formally, is: a fragment in huge, rough-hewn blocks' (*Journals*, 438).

Brecht returned to his notes and sketches in early 1952 with increasing doubts as to whether he could write a contemporary, topical play and he played with the idea of dialogues in iambs as a *Verfremdung* technique for both the actors and audience, that is, endowing the quotidian, banal events in the factory with historical grandeur. By March he reached the conclusion that the material was 'too epic', full of too many details that yielded no more than discrete moments but no scenes, as if the entire trajectory of the play could only end with the repair of the furnace.[3] At this point he interrupted his work on the Garbe material and turned his attention instead to other pressing projects: the large volume of photos and texts called *Theatre Work*, featuring the first productions of his Berliner Ensemble and meant to defend his approach against the dogmatism of the reigning cultural bureaucracy; the staging of Erwin Strittmatter's comedy *Katzgraben* about rural land reform and class struggle in the GDR (premiere on 23 May 1953); and a major conference on Stanislavsky scheduled for April 1953 where his theory and practice of epic theatre would be under attack.[4]

Meanwhile Hans Garbe the bricklayer was working on the showpiece construction projects along the Stalinallee in East Berlin, and he reported to Rülicke throughout the spring about the construction workers' complaints. After the events of 17 June 1953 – the workers' uprising that began in the Stalinallee and quickly spread to other GDR cities, leading to an intervention by the Soviet occupation army – Brecht also sought him out to gather first-hand information about the strike wave. It became clear to him that a different form was needed now for the Garbe material. If the history of the furnace repair would not yield a play, then Brecht decided to aim for a larger plot trajectory stretching from the end of the war until the uprising of 17 June. This kind of plot could represent the working class in its most depraved condition, emerging from its defeat under National Socialism to the point where it raised its fist, now against

[A10 (1951)]
When Büsching gathers his work brigade for repairing the furnace, he promises high wages. Some of the workers participate with obvious pangs of conscience because they see the activist project as a betrayal of the workers' interests.

[B4 (1951)]
Question
Why did the seven of you do it?

Büsching
Let's say because we wanted to earn one pound more of the butter.

Question
Not because you wanted to help the factory get back on its feet?

Büsching
Maybe the only new thing about it was that we helped the factory back on its feet because we earned one pound more of the butter.

[A19 (1951)]
The apprentice
He covers for a small mistake of the apprentice
He doesn't allow him to cover for his own, later.

[A14 (1951)]
For weeks the colleagues come to his furnace every morning and mock him. One morning they stop coming. He's discouraged and considers abandoning the project. Then he realizes why they are no longer coming: now they know that the furnace will be successful. He works with renewed zeal.

[B3 (July 1951)]
Büsching's Furnace. Lunch break.

Two workers walk by with an apprentice who is carrying bricks.

Worker
I have an idea. The stinking dogs
Must be stunk out. Close your eyes.

The apprentice closes his eyes, grinning; the worker takes several bricks and drops them into one of the ducts.

the socialist leaders governing in its name. From Brecht's dialectical perspective this rejection could not be seen simply as negative; instead it marked the first real evidence of a connection between workers' renewed self-consciousness and their political power, something that the defeat of 1945 had erased (*Journals*, 454–5; see A3). In October Brecht met with Hanns Eisler in Vienna and discussed with him his new ideas for

> B4 This brief conversation touches on a central motif of the *Garbe/Büsching* fragment, the causal connection between the 'naïve' motivation of the worker hero (more butter) and the social consequences of his actions. Individual material interests can change history (workers recognizing their collective self-interest).

the Garbe fragment, including a chorus in the style of the learning play *The Decision* or the agit-prop play *The Mother* through which a collective can make visible what the individual cannot perceive (*Journals*, 438). But the move to the new home for the Berliner Ensemble in the Theater am Schiffbauerdamm that opened in May 1954, rehearsals for new productions (e.g. *The Caucasian Chalk Circle*), and the Paris guest performances of the Berliner Ensemble in June 1954 apparently left no time for the Garbe project. Brecht's last note about it was the November 1954 sketch with a revised list of scenes, now expanded to eleven and including one about 17 June and another in which Garbe dies (A1). This outline embedded Garbe's heroic deed within a larger historical frame but still produced no coherent plot-line and contained several additional, vaguely designated scenes.

The clash of the old and the new, invoked consistently by Brecht after he arrived in East Berlin and always at the forefront of his questions about the appropriate form for the *Garbe/Büsching* project, emerged as his central concern for depicting the changes underway in the transition to socialism. What were the essential conflicts in a revolutionizing country whose people had not brought about their own revolution? In 1950, for example, he commented that 'embedded in the new conflicts brought about by politics and the economy there are still the older ones, and if they are ignored, the depiction of the new conflicts appears anaemic and schematic', and he continued: 'The old and the new do not simply split people into two groups, the old and the new ones; instead the new struggles with the old in every single person' (*BFA* 23, 128). For Brecht, this had practical consequences. The fundamental transformations of the time would bring about changes in the arts as well, he argued, so that poetic forms such as verse could not simply disappear from the stage, but rather a layering of the old and the new had to be the goal in plays treating contemporary issues (*BFA* 23, 139). Indeed, his experiments

If decency doesn't drive them out
Then maybe the gas will drive them out.

Second worker
That can cook them through.

First worker
Did someone see it?
I didn't. Not you and Jacob's
Eyes keep falling shut
Because he thinks of eating. Do you recall
Karl, how we tricked the canteen bacon
Out of Nierlinger, that Nazi pig
In forty-two?
Do you recall what I told you?
Not only do we have it
But they also don't have it.

Büsching (*stepping out from behind the column*)
That was right. I
Ate until I was sick.
When the bombs fell
I nailed shut the shop windows. I
Had everything, coffee, chocolate. What
Was in the shop windows was mine.

They watch as he begins to pull the bricks out of the duct. The two workers leave, glowering, the apprentice stays behind.

My brother in Pomerania
Used to smoke in the squire's stall. Today
He has his own stall and my sister-in-law
Would no longer let him smoke, if he
Even had tobacco. Hold the rod for me.
The apprentice puts the jug down and holds the iron rod for **Büsching**.

[A3 (1953)]

Garbe

A biologist explains that grafting fruit trees is a severe intervention.

Garbe erupts in anger. The resisting workers must be broken. Shame and retraction.

A colleague: He's just a bricklayer. (But will they let you lay bricks?)

with Strittmatter's *Katzgraben* comedy in 1953 demonstrated how verse can become a filter that removes the inessential (*Brecht on Theatre*, 258). Equally important was Brecht's assertion that the new plays being written during these early years of the GDR were not depicting social reality accurately. His advice to fellow writers and his work at the Berliner Ensemble insisted on the contradictions in dramatic conflicts, on making visible the destruction of the old and the rise of the new through leaps, ruptures, and setbacks, not in a continuous line of progress. In this respect the *Garbe/Büsching* project was aimed directly at what he considered to be the common weakness of many other attempts to depict Garbe, 'the worker hero'.[5] They tended to celebrate him as an allegorical hero, as the anticipatory realization of socialist society, based on a teleological view of the historical process that would end in the triumph of socialism. For Brecht, Garbe was 'the new', a prototype for the contemporary German working class whose members were motivated less by what the party was planning than by their personal, spontaneous needs, full of contradictions that could trigger a new level of consciousness about their ownership of the means of production.

> A3 The Egyptian Song cites Brecht's 1953 biblical poem 'Jakobs Söhne ziehen aus, im Ägyptenland Lebensmittel zu holen' (*BFA* 15, 272–3; 'Jacob's Sons Set Forth to the Land of Egypt to Fetch Food Supplies', set to music by Paul Dessau), which also dates this text, probably to August 1953, when Brecht returned to the *Garbe/Büsching* material. Its mention here relates to the West German practice of distributing packages of free food to East Germans who crossed over the sector boundary dividing East from West Berlin. The allusion to tree grafts restates the way the introduction of socialism in the GDR was grafted onto the Soviet experience, and the workers' resistance refers to the events of 17 June 1953.

Here we may identify the reason for Brecht's conceptual shift after the June 1953 uprising, preferring now the *Lehrstück* (learning play) form to that of the chronicle or history play and envisioning Garbe's death rather than the triumph of the new. If the history play follows in this case the plot-line of Garbe's life in which individual material need ('one pound more of butter' in B4) reveals how attitudes can change in response to changing social conditions, then it conforms to Brecht's epic theatre model that shows how these emerging attitudes estrange the present. The learning play model, on the other hand, suggests a pedagogical structure that confronts the viewer with a character who is limited in his knowledge about the context of his

On inequality. The Egyptian Song.
Of course, the functionaries, themselves proles. They speak for a decrease in wage rates but retain their own salary.

Are we for the Russians? Should we become Russians?
Russians are for socialism. We should become socialists. June 17.

[A1 (November 1954)]

On Hans Garbe (Büsching)

1
Garbe with a lawyer, because he has gotten a soldier's wife pregnant (whose husband won't buy her a blouse), with stolen foodstuff as a bribe.

2
Garbe, liberated, continues to work in a private factory. He supports expropriation, tries to expropriate the owner, and is thrown out of the Socialist Unity Party.

3
The ownerless factory is dismantled (the workers rescue the tools).

4
Garbe supports a decrease in the wage rates, harming himself, Garbe as wage shark. (furnace lid)

5
Battle of the furnace.

6
Garbe is against a further decrease in the wage rates, fails.

7
Can the government maintain the new rates? No! Can it cancel them? No! – The government cancels the rates.

8
The June 17 events.

9
The story of his apprentice. Flees to the West.

10
The Russians save the factory. Garbe dies.

11
The apprentice returns. Too late. For now, but not forever.

acts; he is positioned within a situation full of contradictions where right and wrong behaviour is not a given but must be determined. Garbe, from this perspective, cannot be a model hero but functions as a learning object for the socialist collective. His asocial behaviour, both in the past and in the present, raises questions to which the viewers are asked to respond.

A1 This last outline expands the temporal trajectory of Brecht's initial idea for a history play about the events surrounding the furnace repair (December 1949 until February 1950). Now the projected play begins at the end of the war (1944), continues until the workers' uprising in East Berlin on 17 June 1953, which leads to the protagonist's death, and includes a new subplot about his apprentice. As Garbe explained in his conversations with Brecht and Rülicke, he had met and begun an affair with Erika (who later became his second wife) while her husband was stationed on the front, which in the Third Reich was considered a punishable crime for military subversion (hence the lawyer in Scene One). Scene Two alludes to the dominant GDR narrative that the Germans were not defeated in the Second World War but liberated from National Socialism. Scene Three refers to the reparations practice of the Soviet Military Administration in the immediate post-war years, when entire factories and transportation systems were dismantled and shipped to the Soviet Union. The wage rates (*Normen*) mentioned in Scenes Four, Six, and Seven were standards established by the government similar to piece-work wages. Deviations (under- or over-production) would impact individual wages. If the amount of time for any labour process was reduced while maintaining the same expectations of productivity, wages dropped. Garbe's bricklaying innovations increased productivity substantially, leading to over-production and higher wages for his workers' brigade in the short term, but depressing the wages of all bricklayers in the long term unless they adopted his procedures (hence his reputation as a wage shark in Scene Four). A similar conundrum leads once again to the wave of strikes on 17 June 1953 (Scene Eight), elevating the contradictions that arose around the furnace repair to a 'higher level' of public dialogue between the striking workers and 'their' government. Probably Brecht would have introduced choral passages in this scene to reflect on the implications of the intervention of Soviet tanks to quell the uprising. Scenes Nine and Eleven introduce the apprentice (in German 'sein Schüler', or his pupil) who appears in the earliest texts already as Jacob (A6, A19, and B3). These scenes may echo the similar ending of the *Life of Galileo* that Brecht was preparing

> for the Berliner Ensemble staging in 1954 (Galileo's pupil Andrea visits his former mentor in the penultimate Scene Fourteen). In the 1954 outline the apprentice returns after fleeing to the West, suggesting that he has achieved a level of knowledge – having seen the GDR from the outside – that will reinforce lessons learned from his mentor Garbe and inform new actions in the future.

After the events of 17 June 1953, it was clear to Brecht that the material needs of workers in the GDR no longer conformed to the state's expectations. Political conviction, not the material interests of an individual worker, was at stake, and Hans Garbe did not possess this kind of consciousness. Brecht was reflecting on how an audience might develop a historical point of view towards its own contemporary situation, which necessitated a more radical form for the presentation of contradictions. And this is the context in which he was shifting from the concept of epic theatre to what he now called dialectical theatre (*Brecht on Theatre*, 283–4). Unfortunately he never had the time and energy to realize this version of the play. In January 1956, in one of the last public appearances before his death, Brecht spoke about the problems and challenges for young dramatists before the drama section of the GDR Writers' Union: 'what we need to achieve is that a struggle is sparked in the audience, a struggle of the new vs. the old. We have to reach the point where our plays and our productions really divide the audience' (*BFA* 23, 372).[6]

Notes

1 The folios are *BBA* 095, 200, 557, 558; five leaves in *BBA* 557 (07–11a) are copies of leaves in *BBA* 200.
2 The three interviews included the Garbes, Brecht, and Rülicke as well as variously Helene Weigel, Slatan Dudow, and Ruth Berlau. As a birthday gift in February 1952, Rülicke presented Brecht with an album of the material she had collected for the Garbe project; it contained a brief summary of these encounters (*BBA* 1375/08–09) as well as the transcripts of the three interviews. The biographical material was then edited and published under Rülicke's name as *Hans Garbe erzählt* (Berlin: Rütten & Loening, 1952), a thin volume in sixteen chapters.
3 See Rülicke's notes, *BBA* 1375/09, also cited at length in *BFA* 10.2, 1282.
4 For *Theatre Work*, see excerpts in *Brecht on Performance*, 223–47; for *Katzgraben*, see *Brecht on Performance*, 249–75; and for the Stanislavski controversy, see *Brecht on Theatre*, 280–3.
5 Brecht was not the only writer fascinated by the bricklayer Hans Garbe. Eduard Claudius penned a short story ('Vom schweren Anfang: Die Geschichte des Aktivisten Hans Garbe', 1950), then a novel where the worker hero is named Hans Aehre (*Menschen an unserer Seite*, 1951), and finally a film scenario that never went into production; Maximilian Scheer published a biographical portrait ('Der Mann im feurigen Ofen', 1951); in 1952 poems by Paul Wiens ('Hans Garbe spricht') and Uwe Berger ('Siemens-Plania') appeared; and there was extensive press coverage of Garbe's feat as well.
6 In 1956 the young Heiner Müller may well have responded to Brecht's advice when he conceived of the play *The Scab* (*Der Lohndrücker*) in which the protagonist, here named Balke, attempts to rebuild a brick firing furnace against all the odds. It was first staged in Leipzig in 1958, then 'rediscovered' (along with the source material of Brecht's *Garbe/Büsching* fragment) in 1974 in the West Berlin production by the Schaubühne am Halleschen Ufer, and thirty years later Müller himself staged it in a widely acclaimed production at the East Berlin Deutsches Theater in 1988.

www.ingramcontent.com/pod-product-compliance
Lightning Source LLC
Chambersburg PA
CBHW072118290426
44111CB00012B/1700